Free & Fun

Everyone wants to have fun
Whether at home or away
And the beautiful Central Coast
Is a wonderful place to play.

Whether you visit or live here
There's so much to do and see
And the greatest thing about it –
A lot of it is free!

You really can "take it with you"
So buy that souvenir
And take home all the memories
Of the time that you spent here.

~ Joelle Steele

Your Personal Guide
FREE & FUN THINGS TO DO & SEE
MONTEREY COUNTY

Patricia A. Hamilton

PARK PLACE PUBLICATIONS
PACIFIC GROVE, CALIFORNIA

Park Place
Publications

Pacific Grove, CA

www.PersonalGuidetoFreeFun.com

FIRST EDITION
1st Printing

Copyright ©1999
Park Place Publications
1.Monterey Bay Region (Calif.)–
Tours. 2. Monterey Bay National
Marine Sanctuary Region (Calif.)
tours. 3. Pacific coast (Calif.)–
Tours. I. Title

917.9476

Printed in Canada

For information regarding
advertising and bulk purchases,
please contact Patricia Hamilton,
Park Place Publications, P.O. Box
829, Pacific Grove, CA 93950.
831-649-6640

ISBN 1-877809-45-4

ABOUT THE AUTHOR

A 4th generation Californian, Patricia Hamilton loved visiting her grandfather on Park Place in Pacific Grove and moved to the Peninsula in 1990. Her daughter and son-in-law, expecting their first child, reside in Mission Viejo, California.

After a career as a controller with an international restaurant corporation, Hamilton began writing and publishing interior landscape contractor books in 1982, which she continues to market internationally, with several books she publishes by other local authors.

In 1994, she enrolled in UC Santa Cruz and completed her degree in Philosophy at the University of Lancaster, England, then lived in Spain where she taught English in Elche, near Valencia. She wrote and published two books abroad: "Peace Consciousness in Northern Ireland and Findhorn, Scotland," a UCSC President's Fellowship, and "I Can't Be Bothered," about her mates in Lancaster. In 1997 she published "Tell Me More Ancestor Stories, Grandma!," by 9th generation local author, Diana J. Dennett.

"Many of my international friends wanted to visit me here on the famous Monterey Peninsula but had heard it was very expensive. To encourage them to come, I began to collect items of interest that were low cost or free; people here wanted the information too, and the rest, as they say, is history."

Welcome to Monterey County!

The best things in life *are* free! And they're all in Monterey County! Experience the natural wonders of the Monterey Bay National Marine Sanctuary: tidepool, kayak, surf, dive, swim, or just wade in the water. Meander among the succulents and along the sandy beaches to take in the most beautiful sunsets in the world. Walk on Mother Earth in the Ventana Wilderness, along the cliffs of Big Sur, glimpse the Monarchs in their habitat, and sit among the wildflowers at Garland Park. Have a family night out at your library's Storytime, experience the performing arts, tell your story at "Open Mic" night, and take an art walk among the galleries to heighten your sense of the beautiful and the divine. Visit the lighthouse and the museums, walk the Path of History, get a blast from the past at Cherry's Jubilee on Cannery Row, watch the sea lions jump and play off Pt. Joe on the 17-Mile Drive, and cheer marathon runners. Volunteer to be a docent at the State Parks, help the disabled enjoy an outing, meet with friends at the club, surf the Net. Take advantage of the free offers: airplane rides, golf lessons, facials, coffee, maps, tennis lessons, tours, wine-tasting, food samples, and much, much more; support those who are giving. They're all here in ***Your Personal Guide to Free & Fun in Monterey County*** – stress relievers, fitness enhancers, family values and quality of life times.

How to Use This Guide

To make it easy to spot what you're looking for, the following symbols and categories are used throughout the book:

- ■   **ATTRACTIONS**
- ●   **SHOPS, ART GALLERIES, LIBRARIES, BOOKSTORES**
- ▲   **PARKS AND RECREATION**
- ◆   **ENTERTAINMENT**
- ➤   **ADDITIONAL OFFERS & VOLUNTEER FUN**

A simple caveat before you begin: hours and admission policies are subject to change without notice. Please call ahead and be flexible. If you find that an attraction has changed its date or hours, drop me a postcard with the details and I will delete or change the entry in future editions.

I've gathered as many Free & Fun Things to Do and See in Monterey County as I could this year. To make this a complete guide, major for-fee events and attractions are also included – with a listing of any free aspects. I'd like to add new things as they come up. You can help by letting me know what they are. We give free listings to all merchants, clubs, organizations, and individuals who offer free things for any reason; such as a thank-you for patronage, to entice others to try a service or product, to give back to the community, free meetings or lectures, to help others, etc. Use the form for new entries on the last page of this book. If your entry is published in the next ***Your Personal Guide to Free & Fun in Monterey County,*** you'll receive a free autographed copy!

Acknowledgments

I wish to thank my friends and family who encouraged me and supported me throughout the many months I spent doing research and putting this book together: Kathy Slarrow, Shirley Blank, Robert Hamilton, Jane Hammond, Diana J. Dennett, Joelle Steele, Yvette Carroll, Anne and Bob Packard, Sally Higgins and Melanie McCoy. We are all indeed One.

Much appreciation goes to the many kindhearted people in the community who responded to my requests for information, facts, and pictures: All of the Monterey County Chambers of Commerce and Business Associations, the Visitor's Centers, Armanasco Public Relations, the librarians, the art galleries and bookstores, Mike O'Brien at Camera World, Dave Schaechtele at the California State Parks Department, and the many merchants, clubs, and others who sent in their free listings in response to the press releases. There are too many to mention individually, but I remember you all and thank you.

A Special Thanks to Dan Koffman for his help with the cover design.

Photograph Credits

Cover: Rocky Shores, Cannery Row, Fisherman's Wharf, Pt. Piños – Patricia Hamilton; Carmel Walks – Dane Thompson Filmcraft; LONE CYPRESS TREE – Pebble Beach Company, used by permission
Page ii: Garland Park - Carmela Fay
Verso-title page: Kathy Slarrow
Carmel: Artist on beach, Fr. Serra Sarcophagus, Beach with surfers, Street scene with chairs, Carmel Plaza - Randy Wilder
Street scene with leaves - Dane Thompson Filmcraft
Golden Bough - Marv White
Marina: Foundrymen - Chris Gage
Firemen Sculpture - artist Betty Saletta, photo Chris Gage
Artichoke fields, close-up - Sharon Green
Marina Boardwalk - Sharon Fong
Artichoke Festival Parade - Leonardo Rojas 1987
Pacific Grove: Caledonia Park, American Tin Cannery, City Hall, Golf, Lovers Point, Recreation Trail and Hopkins Marine Station - Don Gruber
Back Cover & Pebble Beach: PEBBLE BEACH, the LONE CYPRESS TREE, their respective images are trademarks, service marks, and trade dress of Pebble Beach Company, used by permission
Salinas: Creekbridge Community Park - Duane Meneely Photography
Mariachi Festival - Marv White/Grensted Photography
Page 210: The J. Paul Getty Museum, Los Angeles, Dancers by Frans Van Riel, Print, 1920.
Some photos were supplied without the photographer being identified. I regret this oversight and am very happy to give credit when it is known.

Steps Through Monterey County

Welcome to Monterey County, one of the ecological wonders of the world. We're delighted to have you with us and we'd love to have you back.

Make the most of your stay. Check with your lodging facility for educational materials about the geography, customs, and cultures of Monterey. When you are here make friends with the locals, they are anxious to tell a story or just give directions.

Help us set an example for all. Through our actions toward preserving and protecting the Monterey Bay National Marine Sanctuary, the coastline, the parks, and all our local beauty, we can pass on an important lesson to current and future generations.

Leave only footprints. Take the time to enjoy walking, biking, sightseeing, picnicking, tide pooling, and boating. But as you do, please help us maintain the natural balance of this paradise by refraining from feeding the wildlife, disturbing any living or natural objects, and leaving places you visit as you found them.

Please respect the privacy of others. Inquire before photographing.

Lessen the impact. Walkways, pathways, and boardwalks were built for you. Environmental and forestry staff members work hard to foster growth on dunes, in forests and parks.

Environmental program at work. When possible we sincerely appreciate your help with energy and water conservation, as well as participation in recycling programs.

Getting from here to there. We encourage visitors and residents alike to use environmentally sound methods of transportation. Many walking and biking trails are available, and please ask about Monterey's transit system.

Driving through Monterey County. The beauty can be distracting, so please keep your attention level up and remember to park in designated parking areas. Please turn off your engine if stopped for more than one minute.

Look for establishments that support "Steps through Monterey County." The environmental caravan is gaining steam and you can help.

After you leave, please share your experiences with others. Monterey County is a very special place. We want everyone to come and enjoy what we know as paradise. We're happy to share it with you!

Monterey County Hospitality Association
140 W. Franklin, Monterey, CA 93940
Telephone: 831-649-6544

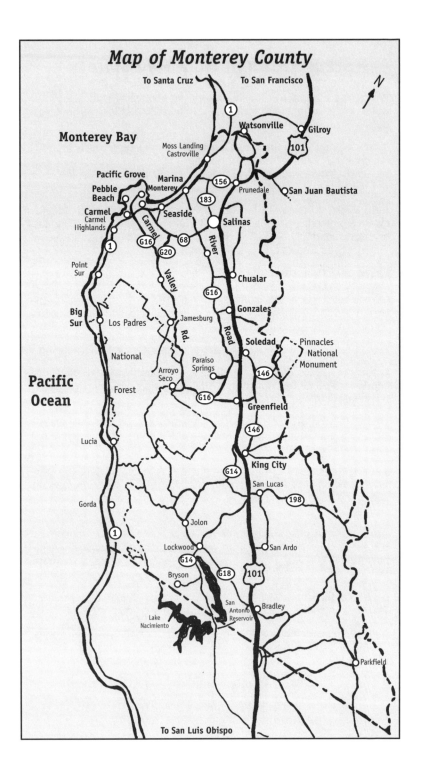

Map of Monterey County

To Santa Cruz   To San Francisco

Monterey Bay

Moss Landing
Castroville

Pacific Grove
Pebble Beach
Marina
Monterey
Carmel
Carmel Highlands
Seaside

Watsonville   Gilroy
① 101

156
183   Prunedale   San Juan Bautista

G16   68
G20   Salinas

Carmel River

Point Sur

Big Sur   Los Padres

National

Forest

Valley   Chualar

Jamesburg
G16   Gonzales

Rd.

Road   Soledad   Pinnacles National Monument
Paraiso Springs   146
Arroyo Seco
G16   Greenfield
146

Lucia

King City
G14
San Lucas
198

Gorda

①   Jolon

Lockwood   San Ardo
G14
Bryson   G18   101

Lake Nacimiento   San Antonio Reservoir   Bradley

Parkfield

Pacific Ocean

To San Luis Obispo

Table of Contents

List of Maps

City maps courtesy of Compass Maps, Inc.©1998

Free & Fun in
Monterey with Kids

Recreation Centers
Pages 51, 57, 117, 156, 178, 198

Playgrounds
Forest Hill Park   51   Carmel Valley Comm. Ctr   57
Dennis the Menace Park   114 Washington Park   153
Caledonia Park   153   Laguna Grande Park   197
More playgrounds: 70, 116, 129, 151, 153, 177, 180-3

Libraries & Storytimes
Libraries: 40, 57, 69, 75, 96, 98, 145, 176, 180-3, 196

At The Beach
Fishing from the Coast Guard Pier   115
Tidepooling   115
Watching the fishermen work at Commercial Wharf #2   90
More beaches: 20, 48, 70, 73, 129, 150, 160, 196

Wildlife Viewing
Carmel State Beach   48   Pt. Lobos State Reserve   49
Cannery Row   123   Monarch Grove Sanctuary   155
Recreation Trail   118, 150   Monterey Bay Aquarium   127

Agricultural Activities
Carmel Valley   54   Salinas Farm Show   173
Castroville artichokes   76   Moss Landing produce stands   72

Sports & Recreation
Recreation Trail   118, 150   Exercise stations   51, 119
Garland Park   56   Golf lessons   71
Sports Museum   128   Horse shows   166
Tennis lesson   53   Gymnastics   75
Martial arts   198   Garrapata Park   20

The Unique & Unusual
Museum of Natural History   136   Dr. Leghorn C. Einstein   124
Cannery Row historic buildings   123   MY Museum   130
Airplane rides at Marina Airport   67   Pt. Piños Lighthouse   151
Maritime Museum Treasure Hunt   84   Custom House & Old Jail   85
National Steinbeck Center   170   Sculpture Center   67
Stargazing   59, 199   *See Index for more listings.*

Helpful Information

Area Code for Monterey County is 831

Police, Fire, Animal Rescue

Emergency Calls Only   911

Non-Emergency Calls:

- Carmel Police, 624-6403, Fire 624-1718.
- Carmel Highlands Fire, 624-2374.
- Mid-Carmel Valley Fire, 624-5907.
- Carmel Valley Fire, 659-2021.
- Cypress District, Carmel/Rio Rd. Fire 624-4511.
- Del Rey Oaks Police, 375-8525, Fire 646-3900.
- Gonzales Police, 675-5010, Fire, 675-5000.
- Greenfield Police, 674-5118.
- King City Police, 385-4848, Fire 385-3430.
- Marina Police, 384-7575, Fire 384-7575.
- Monterey Police, 646-3830, Fire 646-3900.
- Monterey County Sheriff, 755-3950.
- Pacific Grove Police, 648-3149, Fire 648-3110.
- Salinas Police, 758-7236, Fire 758-7261.
- Sand City Police, 394-6811, Fire 646-3900.
- San Lucas Police, 627-2018.
- Seaside Police, 394-6811, Fire 899-6262.
- Soledad Police, 678-1332, Fire 755-5111.
- SPCA Animal Rescue, 373-2631 ext.0, 646-5534.

Officer Shen invites young people into the Monterey Police Station to collect the police sports cards, each with a personal message. Shen's: "As long as you do your best, you will always be a winner!" 351 Madison Street.

Visitor Information Centers

- Big Sur Chamber of Commerce, 667-2100.
- Cannery Row Foundation, on the bay side of 640 Wave, on the Recreation Trail, in the green antique railroad car.
- Carmel Business Association, 624-2522.
- Carmel Tourist Information Center, 624-1711.
- Carmel Valley Chamber of Commerce, 659-4000.
- Castroville Chamber of Commerce, 633-6545.
- Gonzales Chamber of Commerce, 675-9019.
- Greenfield Chamber of Commerce, 674-3222.
- Hispanic Chamber of Commerce, 757-1251.
- King City Chamber of Commerce, 203 Broadway, 385-3814.
- Marina Chamber of Commerce, 384-9155.
- Monterey Chamber of Commerce of the Monterey Peninsula, 649-1770.
- Monterey County Travel & Tourism Alliance, 626-1424.

- Monterey Peninsula Visitors and Convention Bureau, 649-1770.
- Moss Landing Chamber of Commerce, 633-4501.
- Pacific Grove Chamber of Commerce, 373-3304.
- Pájaro Valley Chamber of Commerce, 724-3900.
- Prunedale Chamber of Commerce, 663-0965.
- Salinas Valley Chamber of Commerce, 424-7611.
- Seaside/Sand City Chamber of Commerce, 394-6501.
- Soledad-Mission Chamber of Commerce, 678-2278.

Transportation Information

Monterey-Salinas Transit bus transportation. Monterey 899-2555, Salinas 424-7695. www.mst.org.com.

Waterfront Area Visitor's Express, between Memorial Day and Labor Day weekends, from 9am-6:30pm. $1 ticket good for all day. 899-2555.

Monterey Peninsula Airport: Alaska, American, Canadian, Continental, Hawaiian, Northwest, Reno Air, Skywest/Delta, United and U.S. Airways.

Amtrak Coast Starlight, 800-USA-RAIL. www.amtrak.com.

Monterey County Bicycle Map, call 755-8961.

Local Radio Stations

KAZU 90.3FM	KBOQ 95.5FM	KMBY 104.3FM	KRML 1410AM
KSCO 1080 AM	KUSP 88.9FM	KWAV 97FM	KPIG 107.5 FM
MAGIC 63AM	KLOK 99.5/99.9 Local Spanish language radio station.		
KNRY 1240 AM	Spanish: KCTY 980AM, KRAY 103.5FM, KLXM 97.9FM		

Local Television Stations

"Eye on This Morning," KION-TV CBS46, local news and entertainment program, weekdays 6-9am. www.kiontv.com.

"Central Coast Magazine," TCI Channel 2, every even hour, presents local art, activities, history, people and places. Brad Harlon, producer. 899-7100.

"Classic Arts Showcase" videos to tempt you to visit the arts. "Life in the Arts," interactive classroom. 59 KMST, Monterey County Educational TV. Carried by cable services on channel 26 on the Monterey Peninsula and in Salinas; channel 34 in North Monterey County, channel 5 in the former Ft. Ord area, channel 38 in Greenfield/King City, channel 8 in Soledad/Gonzales and channel 55 in San Ardo/Bradley. MCOE – 755-6424, Arts – 883-1331.

8 KSBW (NBC)	11 KNTV (ABC)	35 KCBA (FOX)	15 KCU (SPANISH)
9 KQED (PBS)	54 KTEH (PBS)	36 KICU (IND)	67 KSMS (SPANISH)
25 KCAH (UHF)			

Tour Operators

- Gael's Monterey Peninsula Tours, 373-2813.
- A-1 Chartered Limo Service, 899-2707.
- Adventure Tours, 375-2409.
- AgVenture Tours, 643-9463.
- Bay Bikes, 646-9090.
- California Heritage Guides, 373-6454.
- California Rail Tours, 443-4277.
- Cannery Row Walking Tours, 373-5727.
- Carmel Valley Trail Rides, 625-2140.
- Carol Robles' Monterey County Tours, 751-3666.
- Elkhorn Slough Safari Nature Tours, 633-5555.
- Eva's Silver Service Picnics & Gourmet Tours, 373-5218.
- Galapagos Travel, 623-2920.
- JLB Tours, 394-3966.
- Joe's Tours, 769-9083.
- Monterey Bay Nature Tours, 375-3226.
- Native Guides, 625-8664.
- Otter-Mobile™ Tours and Charters, 649-4523, fax 333-0832. Owner offers free tours to allied trades. Free hotel pick-up.
- Pacific Host Convention Services, 624-0118.
- Prime Connections, 800-954-8687.
- Reuben W C Limo & Tour Service, 393-2243.
- Steinbeck Country Tours, 659-0333/625-5107.
- Wide World of Golf, 626-2400.

Employment Assistance

ProFile Monterey is a network of proactive professionals who work together toward the common goal of becoming successfuly re-employed. No-fee program which assists members by providing office space, equipment, supplies, job search training, etc. Sandra Stevens 649-2943, fax 649-7174.

CalJOBS, at EDD, will assist you in locating job openings and applying, locally and statewide. Logon to www.caljobs.ca.gov to enroll.

The Marshall Group Personnel Service – www.callmarshall.com

Interim Personnel – www.interim.com

Manpower Staffing Services – www.manpowersj.com

Norrell Staffing Services – www.norrell.com

Universal Staffing Inc. – www.universalstaffing.com

October Statewide Second Chance Week
Re-use • Repair • Re-cycle

The Marina Resale Shop, **Last Chance Mercantile,** *participates in the October statewide Second Chance Week with specials and discounts. You can make a difference by shopping at the Mercantile store and volunteering your time or donating your used items to these local thrift shops:*

- **Alberta's Place**, 1198 Broadway Avenue, Seaside, 393-0479.
- American Cancer Society **Discovery Shops**, 182 Country Club Gate, Pacific Grove, 372-0866. 229 Main St., Salinas, 758-1382.
- **Animal Welfare Benefit Shop**, 206 17th Street, Pacific Grove, 372-1650.
- Carmel Valley **Community Chapel Thrift Shop**, Paso Hondo & Village Dr. upstairs, 659-3030.
- **Church Mouse Thrift Shop**, 204 17th St., Pacific Grove, 375-0838.
- **El Rancho Resale**, 350 Reservation Road, Marina, 883-9349.
- **Fort Ord Thrift Shop**, Lightfighter Drive, Seaside, 899-4975.
- **Goodwill Industries**, 729 Broadway Ave., Seaside, 394-1212.
- **Goodwill Industries**, 571 Lighthouse Ave., Monterey, 649-6056.
- **Goodwill Industries**, 708 E. Alisal St., Salinas, 424-5346.
- **Goodwill Industries**, 1258 N. Main Street, Salinas, 449-6361.
- *(Goodwill free pick-up 800/894-8440)*
- **Mariposa-Go-Round Benefit Shop**, 801 Lighthouse Ave., Monterey, 655-9223.
- **Monterey Peninsula Community Thrift Shop**, 585 Lighthouse Ave., Monterey, 373-3588.
- **Monterey Peninsula Volunteer Svcs Thrift Shop**, 655 Broadway Ave., Seaside, 394-5028.
- **SPCA Benefit Shop**, 216 Forest Ave., Pacific Grove, 373-5822.
- **SPCA Benefit Shop**, 13766 Center St., Carmel Valley, 659-2389.
- **SPCA Benefit Shop**, Lincoln and 6th Ave., Carmel, 624-4211.
- **St. Mary's By-The-Sea Episcopal Church Thrift Shop**, Central Ave. at 12th St., Pacific Grove, 373-4443.
- **St. Vincent de Paul Society**, 1269 Fremont, Seaside, 899-2211.
- **Salvation Army**, 1850 Fremont Blvd., Seaside, 394-6507.
- **Yellow Brick Road Benefit Shop**, 26388 Carmel Rancho Lane, Carmel, 626-8480.

There will also be a 50% off sale at the Last Chance Mercantile, 14201 Del Monte Blvd, Marina, 2 miles north of downtown Marina. Hours: Mon-Sat 8am-4:30pm. 384-5313. Turn in hazardous materials and paint free. "Swap" program: still usable products are free.

Monterey County
1999 Calendar of Events

You will have a lot of fun when you join the festivities in Monterey County. As you will see from this comprehensive calendar, there's a lot going on and something for everybody. You will find all the details for each event on the page referenced, with the free and fun items noted. Most events are free, some are free to seniors or children under a certain age, and many are free to volunteers who help out. While this calendar shows the dates for 1999, most events usually occur on the same weekend of the same month each year. Dates and times are subject to change, so it's best to call ahead to avoid disappointment. "tba" means the date is "to be announced."

ONGOING

			Page
Weekly	FARMERS MARKETS	Monterey	92
Weekly	MARKETFEST	New Mtry	129
Weekly	FARMERS MARKETS	Salinas	171
Monthly	FLEA MARKET	Monterey	92

JANUARY

January/March	WHALE WATCHING	Big Sur	18
January 1	RIO GRILL'S RESOLUTION RUN	Carmel	41
January 13	DINE OUT FOR DAFFODILS	Monterey	99
January 14-17	MONTEREY SWING FEST	Monterey	99
January 15-31	WHALEFEST 1999	Monterey	99
January 18	A VILLAGE AFFAIR	Carmel Vy	60
January 18	MARTIN LUTHER KING JR. PARADE	Seaside	194

FEBRUARY

February	BLACK HISTORY MONTH	Seaside	194
February 1-7	AT&T NATIONAL PRO-AM	Pebble Bch	164
February 7	A TASTE OF PACIFIC GROVE	Pacific Grove	146
February 11	INTERNATIONAL JAZZ PARTY	Monterey	99
February 13	AN EVENING AT THE BUCKEYE	Carmel Vy	60
February 14	A DAY OF ROMANCE	Monterey	99
February 14	A WHALE OF AN ART SHOW	Monterey	99
February 14	TOGETHER WITH LOVE	Pacific Grove	146

			Page
February 16	MARDI GRAS	Cannery Row	130
February 21-27	STEINBECK BIRTHDAY CELEBRATION	Salinas	172
February 23	POST OFFICE CELEBRATION	Monterey	99
February 23-28	MASTERS OF FOOD & WINE	Carmel	41
February 24-28	TALL SHIPS IN THE HARBOR	Monterey	99
February 27	STEINBECK BIRTHDAY PARTY	Monterey	100
February 27	STEINBECK BIRTHDAY PARTY	Cannery Row	130
February 27-28	EAST OF EDEN CAT SHOW	Monterey	100

MARCH

March/Sept	"GRAFFITI NIGHTS AT ROY'S DRIVE-IN"	Salinas	172
March 5-7	ART, CRAFTS, & DIXIELAND JAZZ	Monterey	100
March 5-7	DIXIELAND MONTEREY	Monterey	100
March 8	COLTON HALL BIRTHDAY	Monterey	100
March 13	ANNUAL KITE FESTIVAL	Carmel	41
March 13-14	MINERAL SOCIETY ROCK SHOW	Spreckels	180
March 17-21	SEA OTTER CLASSIC FESTIVAL	Laguna Seca	100
March 20	CA. CHOCOLATE ABALONE DIVE	Monterey	100
March 20-21	CELEBRATION SIDEWALK SALE	Monterey	100
March 27-28	MONTEREY BAY SPRING FAIRE	Monterey	100
March 27-28	SPRING HOME SHOW	Monterey	100
March 31-April 4	SPRING HORSE SHOW	Pebble Bch	164

APRIL

April/Sept	GARDEN TOURS	Carmel	41
April/October	CLASSIC CARS HOT CHILI NITES	Carmel Vy	60
April 1	HARBOR SEAL PANELS	Pebble Bch	164
April 3	EASTER EGG HUNT	Monterey	101
April 3	MARINA 5-MILER	Marina	68
April 9-11	GOOD OLD DAYS	Pacific Grove	146
April 15-17	MONTEREY WINE FESTIVAL	Monterey	101
April 16-18	WILDFLOWER SHOW	Pacific Grove	146
April 17	EARTH DAY/ARBOR DAY '99	Salinas	172
April 17	HOME & GARDEN AFFAIR	Carmel	41
April 17-18	SEAFOOD AND MUSIC FESTIVAL	Monterey	101

			Page
April 18	BOOK FESTIVAL	Monterey	102
April 18	BIG SUR JAZZFEST	Big Sur	18
April 18-19	JUNIOR RODEO	King City	183
April 24	"A SIGNATURE YEAR" ADOBE TOUR	Monterey	101
April 25	BIG SUR INTERNATIONAL MARATHON	Big Sur	18
April 29	A VINTNERS GARDEN GALA	Carmel Vy	185
April 30-May 2	CARMEL GARDEN SHOW	Carmel Vy	60
April 30-May 2	HONDA CHALLENGE	Laguna Seca	101

MAY

May tba	CARMEL ART FESTIVAL	Carmel	42
May 1	INTERNATIONAL DAY	Monterey	101
May 1	ANNUAL WAG 'N WALK	Monterey	101
May 1	HONDA CHALLENGE	Cannery Row	130
May 1-2	CHAMBER MUSIC CONCERTS	Carmel	42
May 1-2	ORCHID MAYFAIRE	Carmel	42
May 2	BRITISH CAR-MEET	Pacific Grove	146
May 7	COOPER-MOLERA TOUR	Monterey	101
May 9	MOTHERS DAY BRUNCH	Carmel Vy	60
May 9, 30	CONCERTS IN THE PARK	Pacific Grove	146
May 13	TASTE OF OLD MONTEREY	Monterey	101
May 13-16	SALINAS VALLEY FAIR	King City	183
May 14	ED RICKETTS BIRTHDAY CELEBRATION	Cannery Row	130
May 15	GARDEN DAY AT COOPER-MOLERA	Monterey	101
May 15-16	ARTICHOKE FESTIVAL	Castroville	77
May 16	RUMMAGE SALE	Carmel Vy	60
May 23	OBSERVATORY TOUR	Carmel Vy	60
May 29-30	GREAT MONTEREY SQUID FESTIVAL	Monterey	102
May 29-30	MEMORIAL DAY REGATTA	Pebble Bch	164
May 29-June 7	TALL SHIPS IN THE HARBOR	Monterey	102
May 31	CONCERTS ON THE LAWN	Monterey	102

JUNE

June tba	MY MUSEUM BIRTHDAY CELEBRATION	Cannery Row	130
June/July	FOREST THEATRE CONCERTS	Carmel	42

			Page
June/July	PARKFEST	Carmel	42
June/July	THEATREFEST	Monterey	102
June-Sept	GARDEN FAIRE	Big Sur	18
June/October	HOT CARS/COOL NIGHTS	Seaside	194
June 5-6	KENNEL CLUB AGILITY TRIAL	Salinas	172
June 5-6	MARINA MOTORSPORTS SWAP MEET	Marina	68
June 6	BONSAI CLUB EXHIBITION	Seaside	194
June 6	MONTEREY SYMPHONY CONCERT	Carmel Vy	60
June 11-13	SIDEWALK FINE ARTS FESTIVAL	Monterey	102
June 12-13	SALINAS VALLEY SALAD DAYS	Salinas	172
June 18-21	TALL SHIPS IN THE HARBOR	Monterey	102
June 19	ANNUAL ART & WINE FESTIVAL	Carmel	42
June 19-20	DOWNTOWN CELEBRATION	Monterey	102
June 21-26	CA STATE AMATEUR GOLF	Pebble Bch	164
June 25-27	MONTEREY BAY BLUES FESTIVAL	Monterey	102
June 26	CACHAGUA COUNTRY FAIR	Carmel Vy	61
June 27	OBSERVATORY TOUR	Carmel Vy	61
June 28	MISSION CHICKEN BBQ FIESTA	Soledad	180

JULY

July/August	BLUES AND ART IN THE PARK	Seaside	194
July 2	CALIFORNIA BREWMASTERS' CLASSIC	Monterey	102
July 4	ANNUAL SALMON DERBY	Monterey	102
July 4	VETERANS' COMMEMORATION	Pacific Grove	146
July 4	FOURTH OF JULY CELEBRATIONS	Monterey	103
July 4	LIBERTYFEST CELEBRATIONS	Salinas	172
July 4	LIVING HISTORY FESTIVAL	Monterey	103
July 4	OLD-FASHIONED FOURTH OF JULY	Soledad	180
July 4	PARADE OF CHAMPIONS	Seaside	194
July 4	SPRECKELS FOURTH OF JULY	Spreckels	180
July 4 weekend	CONCERT ON THE LAWN SERIES	Monterey	103
July 5	MONTEREY BEACH CLEANUP	Monterey	103
July 6-Oct 26	MARKETPLACE SPECIAL	Monterey	103
July 9-11	DOG SHOWS AND OBEDIENCE TRIALS	Carmel	42
July 9-11	MCGRAWSUPERBIKE	Laguna Seca	103
July 10	"GREAT BALLS OF FIRE" DANCE & BBQ	Carmel Vy	61

AUGUST

SEPTEMBER

OCTOBER

DECEMBER

Volunteer To Have Fun

Many volunteer opportunities appear throughout the text of this book as free ways to attend festivals and events, to meet other people and help out around the community, and for the sake of helping others enjoy the free and fun things to see and do. (See index.) If you are a volunteer, I salute you. If you haven't yet tried this form of 'entertainment,' I heartily recommend it. You will profit in ways you never imagined.

In this section you will find more ways to volunteer your time in the service of others. This information is by no means complete and every effort will be made to expand it for the next edition.

Junior Friends of the Pacific Grove Library and librarian Lisa Maddalena

Jefferson Awards Program

Jacqueline Kennedy Onassis and the Honorable Robert Taft Jr. established the Jefferson Awards in 1972 as a way to recognize volunteerism in our local communities. The goal is to honor local volunteers who have made exceptional contributions in their communities. Nomination forms are available at your local Chamber of Commerce or Volunteer Center. Call Julie Ann Lozano at 758-8888 ext. 236 for more information.

Volunteers of Monterey County

- Alliance on Aging: Monterey, 280 Dickman Ave., 646-4636; Salinas, 1188 Padre Dr., Ste. 202D, 758-2811; King City, 415 Queen St., 385-0557.
- Alzheimer's Day Care Resource Center, 200 Coe Ave., Seaside, 899-7178.
- Big Brothers/Big Sisters of Monterey County volunteers provide friendship and mentoring to children from single-parent families. 757-7992.
- Buddy Program of the Monterey Peninsula orientation, 6-7pm. fourth Thursday. Volunteer adult companions for children from single-parent families. Mariposa Hall, 801 Lighthouse Ave., New Monterey. 655-9231.
- City of Marina Volunteer Program, Joy Junsay, 384-3715.
- City of Monterey Volunteer Program, Susan Schiavone, 646-3719.
- City of Salinas Volunteer Program, Kathi Crain, 758-7382.
- City of Seaside Volunteer Program, Rebekka Scullin, 899-6279.
- Community Hospital of the Monterey Peninsula Auxiliary and junior volunteers are needed. For more information, call the Auxiliary office at 625-4555 or visit their Web site at www.chomp.org.
- Docents for Monterey State Historic Park: Be a part of history. Walk and talk where history was made in early California. 647-6204.
- Doris Day, longtime Carmel resident, established the Doris Day Animal League over 10 years ago. Volunteer by writing to Doris Day Animal League, 227 Massachusetts Ave., N.E., Suite 100, Washington, DC 20002.
- *Dorothy's Kitchen, Salinas, 424-1102.
- *Family Resource Center, 394-4622, 757-7915.
- *Genesis Residential Center, Seaside, 899-2436.
- Legal Services for Seniors, 413 Forest Ave., Pacific Grove, 372-3989.
- Meals on Wheels, Salinas, 229 Pajaro St., Ste. #303, 758-6325.
- Ombuddies matches preschool and teenage children with seniors in nursing homes and board and care residences. Call Linda J. Shapero, Coordinator, Monterey, 333-1300, Salinas, 758-4011, fax 333-1323.
- Peninsula Outreach, IHELP , Monterey, 384-3388.
- Red Cross, Monterey County Chapter, 424-4824, 375-5730.
- Salinas Valley Memorial Hospital Service League, Lynn Brooks, 755-0772.
- Salvation Army, 899-4911.
- Service League Informational Meetings held continually. Contact Volunteer Services Office, Salinas Valley Memorial Hospital Service League, for application and meeting dates: Lynn Brooks at 755-0772.
- Volunteer Center of Monterey County, 655-9234. Represents 300 local organizations and 3000 volunteer opportunities. www.yesillhelp.org
- Women's Crisis Center, Salinas, 757-1001.
- *YWCA, 649-0834, 372-6300, or 1-800-YWCA.

*Spanish speaking available

BAYNET

Those people in the blue jackets, with the telescopes trained on sea otters and other interesting bay sights, are volunteering to serve two hours a week after their Bay Net Shoreline Docent Training. They are trained to answer questions about the Marine Sanctuary and other tourist needs.

Bay Net is the first of its kind in the nation to train docents to educate the public about a national marine sanctuary. It was established in 1995 in Monterey and now also serves in Santa Cruz. For more information, visit their website at: www.mbay.net~baynet. To volunteer, call Rachel Saunders or Milos Radakovich at 375-4509.

Community Links Monterey County©

"Getting The Word Out About Monterey County's Community Organizations Via Print, Radio, Television, Telecommunications & the Internet"

Daniel Koffman's comprehensive vehicle for local organizations:

- On The Radio - KXDC 101.7FM, KPIG 107.5FM, CD93.5FM, KBOQ 95.5FM, KMBY 104.3FM

- On Television - KION-TV CBS 46 (6am-9am)

- On the Internet - www.communitylinks.net

- Telecommunications - Toll-Free Hotline 1-888-21-LINKS.

- Pick up Community Links© at the libraries, bookstores, Bagel Bakeries, Borders Books, Meals on Wheels, Visitor Information Center, Bay Bookstore and others. Call for a complete list of distribution points, call 1-888-21-LINKS.

Community of Caring™

Community of Caring Monterey Peninsula is a nonprofit organization dedicated to improving the quality of life for youth and families in our communities. This collaboration sponsors community-based programs and services targeted toward achieving progress on priority issues identified by the TELLUS project and community discussion.

The goals of *Community of Caring Monterey Peninsula* are:

- Promote a healthy set of community norms and values
- Foster a better connection between the community and the education system
- Embrace and promote our rich diversity
- Reduce substance abuse
- Enhance personal safety
- Expand parent education and support mechanisms
- Create additional activities available for youth
- Reduce the incidence of HIV and teen pregnancy

Community of Caring Monterey Peninsula is a coalition of the three Peninsula public school districts, institutions of higher education, the seven Peninsula cities, public and nonprofit agencies, businesses, youth, and the community at large dedicated to teaching and supporting youth and families in everyday life.

We believe in five core values that can empower people to be responsible, caring members of a community:

1. *Caring* for one another
2. *Respect* for one another
3. *Trust* in one another
4. *Responsibility* for one another
5. *Family* loyalty to one another

Get involved by:

- Being part of the community-wide effort
- Making yourself, your business, school or organization a part of Community of Caring Monterey Peninsula
- Practicing the core values
- Getting others involved

To participate in the Community of Caring Monterey Peninsula, call 831/646-3760, or write to P.O. Box 1031, Monterey, CA 93942.

City of Monterey Volunteer Program

The City of Monterey is a special city with a rich and varied history of Native Americans, Spanish and Mexican territories, and as the birthplace of California. You can immerse yourself in a kaleidoscope of historical facts and places. Our beautiful Monterey Bay Marine Sanctuary beckons visitors from all over the world seeking a close up view of sea otters, whales and other aquatic residents or to walk the Path of History and our numerous parks and wonderful recreation trails. Not just visitors, but all of us enjoy this beautiful City and environment.

Be part of this special City! You can volunteer in a variety of programs and services. The City of Monterey is committed to provide opportunities to local citizens for learning about City government through volunteering within various departments and helping with special events.

Current Volunteer Opportunities

Colton Hall Museum: hosts, hostesses

City of Monterey Library: Bookstacks Assistants, Homework Pals Program, Outreach Volunteers, California Collection Volunteers

Public Works: Adopt-A-Park, Beach or Street, Gardening, Information Walkers' Club, Storm Drain Stenciling/Monitoring, Special Events Recycling Team

Fire Department: Neighborhood Emergency Response Team (NERT)

Recreation & Community Services: Preschool Volunteers, After School Activities Volunteer, Recreation Center Receptionist, Special Events, Playground Volunteers

We also encourage "on-call" volunteers

How it works

- Call for complete program information
- Complete an Interest Form
- Meet with the Volunteer Coordinator, Complete Orientation
- Interview with Supervisor
- Start your Assignment!

For a complete information packet with current volunteer opportunities, call 646-3719.

Free & Fun in
Big Sur

The Phoenix Shop

Coast Galleries

Willow Creek Beach

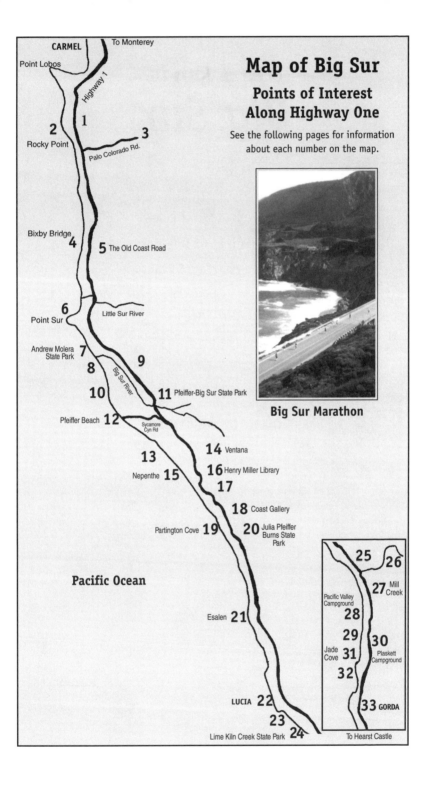

CARMEL
To Monterey

Point Lobos

Highway 1

2
Rocky Point

1

3
Palo Colorado Rd.

Bixby Bridge
4

5 The Old Coast Road

6
Point Sur

Little Sur River

Andrew Molera
State Park
7

8

9
Big Sur River

10

11 Pfeiffer-Big Sur State Park

Pfeiffer Beach 12
Sycamore
Cyn Rd

14 Ventana

13

16 Henry Miller Library

Nepenthe 15

17

18 Coast Gallery

Partington Cove 19

20 Julia Pfeiffer
Burns State
Park

Pacific Ocean

Esalen 21

LUCIA 22

23

Lime Kiln Creek State Park 24

Map of Big Sur
Points of Interest
Along Highway One

See the following pages for information
about each number on the map.

Big Sur Marathon

25 26

27 Mill
Creek

Pacific Valley
Campground
28

29

Jade 31
Cove

30
Plaskett
Campground

32

33 GORDA

To Hearst Castle

Big Sur

The Area Code for Monterey County is 831

Chamber of Commerce, Mon-Wed-Fri, 9:30am-1pm, Big Sur Sta., 667-2100. www.bigsurcalifornia.org.
Road Information, 757-2006.
Big Sur Virtual Tour. www.webtraveler.com/locales/bigsur.
Big Sur Reservations: A variety of services including lodging, weddings and romantic getaways. 667-2929 or www.bigsurreservations.com.

Parks Information

▲ **U.S. Forest Service** often observes National Public Lands Day with open house and free admission to the forest. Call for date: 649-2836, 385-5434. Park reservations call Parknet at 1-800-444-PARK. $4-$6/car day use, 8am-sunset. Camping, summer: River site $23, other $20. Nov-Mar, all sites $16. Free ranger shows around a campfire 8pm nightly (except Fri) June-Aug. When you stay at a campground, adjacent parks are free the next day.

▲ **California State Parks** and **Monterey County Parks** may open some parks free to the public on May 1; with a new administration in Sacramento, no decision has been made at the time of printing. Call 888-588-CAMP, or 755-4899, 667-2315, http://cal-parks.ca.gov. Free parks are noted.

Calendar of Events

Information subject to change. Call to verify.

January/March   WHALE WATCHING   Free
Watch the great gray whales on their annual migration down the California coastline. Vista points: Pt. Lobos, Soberanes Pt., Pt. Sur. Pregnant females lead from the Bering Sea to calving lagoons off Mexico's Baja Peninsula.

April 18   BIG SUR JAZZFEST $$
This year's benefit performance will be at Pfeiffer-Big Sur State Park. Call Erin Gafill for details, 667-2454.

April 25   BIG SUR INTERNATIONAL MARATHON   Spectators free
The Big Sur International Marathon is a spectacular road race set along one of the most breathtaking courses in the world. Benefit for local charities, volunteers always needed. Free training clinics held in Nov. and Dec. Call the Marathon Office, 9-5 Mon-Fri, at 625-6226, fax 625-2119. www.bsim.org.

June-Sept   GARDEN FAIRE   Free
Music, crafts, art, beadwork, herbal works, vintage clothing. Every Saturday, 1 to 6pm, at Loma Vista Cafe Gardens at Big Sur Shell Station. 667-2818.

August 21-22, 28-29   Y'ART SALE   Free
Live music, poetry readings, and drumming, 11am-7pm. Take Highway 1 to Palo Colorado, go 2 miles, look for the dome house. Sofanya, 626-2876.

1 Garrapata State Park, 7 miles south of Carmel, and just past Malpaso Creek. No fee. Park off the highway on either side, approach from the north is shown. 2,879 acres of hiking trails, sandy beaches, rocky shores, dense redwood forests. Rocky Ridge Trail is open. Soberanes Creek Trail is closed (call 624-9423

to help repair El Niño damage). Trail heads along the beach are indicated on numbered gates, or sign posts, at turnouts. Enter gate 13, 15 or 16 to reach Soberanes Point and magnificent views. Rock climbing at south end on the beach. Watch for dangerous surf. Open dawn to dusk.

2 Rocky Point, now the site of Rocky Point Restaurant, with an expansive southern view of the coastline. Open for breakfast, lunch and dinner.

3 Los Padres National Forest, 3 million acres of wilderness covering the Santa Lucia Mountains from Salinas down to the Pacific Ocean along the Big Sur coast. Hundreds of streams flow into the Little and Big Sur Rivers or directly into the ocean. There are hot springs at Tassajara and Esalen. Mountain lions and wild pigs may be seen; streams support fresh trout and steelhead. Rare spottings of the southern bald eagle and American Peregrine falcon. A popular hike begins at the U.S. Forest Service, Bottcher's Gap, public campground at the eastern end of Palo Colorado Road. No fee. Picnics, bring water, restrooms, wildflowers. Other trails lead into the Ventana Wilderness from the Big Sur Station and the Pacific Valley Station. Maps and permits can also be obtained at these stations.

4 Bixby Creek Bridge was the largest single span concrete arch bridge in the world when it was built in 1932. It is 550' long and 260' high. There are more than 20 original concrete bridges along Highway 1 in Big Sur. Many have pull outs nearby where you can get a closer look.

5 The Old Coast Road turns inland from Bixby Creek Bridge on Highway 1, crosses Bixby Creek, climbs Serra Grade, crosses Little Sur River, and rejoins Highway 1 at Andrew Molera State Park. Impassable in wet weather. Views, wildflowers, slow-going but worth it.

6 Point Sur State Historic Park, 19 miles south of Carmel. Adults $5. A century-old lighthouse, dramatically perched on a seaside plateau, with spectacular views, whale watching and guided three-hour tours that explore the light station and surrounding buildings. Participants should be prepared for a one-mile hike that climbs 300 feet and a 65-step staircase.

Tours of the light station and grounds: Saturday 10am and 2pm, Sunday 10am year-round; additional summer tours Wednesday 10am and 2pm. Space is limited; show up early. Volunteer to be a docent. A free video of the lighthouse can be viewed at Big Sur Station, 8 miles south. 625-4419, 624-7195.

7 Andrew Molera State Park. 4800 acres of meadows and woodlands. The Big Sur River winds through the park. Hiking trails, horseback riding, secluded beach, bicycle trails, camping, grasslands, redwood forests, birds, and wildlife. An easy hike is the Bobcat Trail and River Trail Loop, 3 miles. Take the headlands trail from the north end of the parking lot, through the Trail Camp, past historic Cooper Cabin, Big Sur's oldest structure, to the beach. Day use fee, $4 per car. Trail map available at Ranger check-in. Park along Highway 1 and walk in for no fee. 667-2315. **Molera Horseback Tours**, at the park, fees vary, 625-5486.

8 Big Sur River Inn. Music in the summer, Sundays 1-5pm. No cover, full bar, full menu. 625-5255, 800/548-3610.

● **Heartbeat Gift Gallery**, next to the Big Sur River Inn. Jewelry, crafts, gifts, unique drums and musical instruments. 667-2557.

● **Gallery Artemesia**, a collective of Big Sur artists with a working artist on site, 10am-4pm, 667-2027.

● **General Store** has provisions and more, open 7:30am-7pm daily, 667-2700.

● **Big Sur Village Pub**; **Big Sur Towing**, 667-2181.

9 Ripplewood Resort, accommodations, grocery and gas, Sun-Thurs, 8am-8pm, Fri-Sat, 8am-9pm, 667-2242.

10 Fernwood, small settlement with a motel, gas, bar, grill, grocery, gift shop, and private campground.

11 Pfeiffer-Big Sur State Park, 26 miles south of Carmel, turn left off the highway into the park entrance. Fee. 821 acres, nature Center. Call for information about guided nature walks, campfires, and programs for children. Trails include: Pfeiffer Falls and Valley View Trail, 1.3 miles, a one-hour stroll through redwood groves to the 60-foot falls. The 3-mile Oak Grove Trail is an easy hike. Adjacent to the softball field is the "Pioneer Tree," one of Big Sur's largest redwoods, whose top has been severed by lighting. Redwoods may live for 2000 years and grow to 350' tall. 667-2270. For lodge and cabin reservations, call 800/424-4787. **Big Sur Lodge** is at the river crossing, 800/424-4787.

12 Pfeiffer Beach, at the foot of Sycamore Canyon Road, the only paved, ungated road west of Highway 1 between the Big Sur post office and Pfeiffer-Big Sur State Park. Fee. Make a very sharp turn onto the narrow and winding road and follow for 2 miles. Not recommended for RVs or trailers as there are overhanging trees. Large parking area, short, well-marked path to the beach, restrooms. White sands dominated by dramatic large rocks that change colors with the light, and with waves crashing through.

13 Big Sur Center, gifts, gas, video rental, cafe, grocery store.

◆ **Loma Vista Cafe Gardens**, just south of the Big Sur Center, has music Saturdays, 2-5pm, during the summer. No cover. 667-2818.

14 Store and Gallery at Ventana. Local artists, jewelry, pottery, gifts and more. 9am-10pm daily. 667-2787. On the west side of Highway 1 is the **Post Ranch Inn**, shop at the **Polaris** for fine gifts; call for dinner reservations at the elegant **Sierra Mar** restaurant, 667-2200.

15 The Phoenix Shop at Nepenthe. Impressive wooden phoenix sculpture in the garden is pictured at right. Gifts, books, jewelry, toys, and clothing. Restaurant, bar, fabulous views, al fresco dining. 10:30am-7pm summer, 10:30am-6pm winter. 667-2347.

• **Hawthorne Gallery**, 48485 Highway 1, across from Nepenthe. Contemporary painting, indoor/outdoor sculpture, blown glass, ceramics. Representing five Hawthornes, Albert Paley, and selected guests. 667-3200.

16 Henry Miller Library with rare books and artwork of Henry Miller, the great American writer and artist who lived in Big Sur from 1944-1962. Just south of the quiet village of Big Sur, about 30 miles south of Carmel. Tues-Sun, 11am-5pm, Thurs-Sun during winter. Literary, music, and art events, exhibits, workshops and more! Picnicking encouraged. www.henrymiller.org, hmlib@henrymiller.org, 667-2574.

17 Deetjen's Big Sur Inn, bed and breakfast inn, serves non-guests breakfast and dinner by reservation. A rustic Norwegian-style inn built in the 1930s. 667-2377.

18 Coast Gallery Of Big Sur, 3 miles south of Nepenthe. Historic showplace for local artists and craftsmen. Henry Miller watercolors. Gallery, gift shop, cafe, candle studio, and boutique. One of the world's largest collections of American crafts. 9-5 daily. 667-2301. www.coastgalleries.com.

19 Partington Cove is a secluded beach at the end of an old dirt road, once a shipping point for tanbark oak by early pioneers. No fee. A picturesque hike takes you from the point where Highway 1 curves across Partington Canyon. Enter at the gate for a steep walk down, past an interesting sign about the undersea forest, branch to the left across a narrow wooden bridge and through a tunnel and onto the beach. Branch to the right leads to Partington Cove with dangerous surf on the rocks. Another trail, on the east side of Highway 1, leads upstream into Partington Canyon, through a beautiful redwood canyon and to the remains of an old tanbark cabin, eventually reaching the Tin House with beautiful coastal views. 4-5 miles.

20 Julia Pfeiffer Burns State Park, 3500 acres. Fee. Large underwater park with canyons and caves for experienced divers. Ten-minute hike on a cliffside trail leads to an 80-foot waterfall into the Pacific Ocean, giant redwoods, ocean views. A popular, six-mile trail leads hikers on a tour through the park. Two primitive hike-in campsites are available. Trail brochures available, restrooms, pay phone, no dogs. 667-2315.

21 Esalen, 45 miles south of Monterey. A center to encourage work in the humanities and sciences with public seminars, work-study, conferences, research. Nightly hot springs: 1-3:30am, $10, reservations, 667-3047. To request a catalog: 667-3000. www.esalen.org.

22 Lucia, overnight accommodations in a comfortable atmosphere. Fine restaurant featuring al fresco dining overlooking the South Coast. Provisions also available. 667-2391.

23 **Immaculate Heart Hermitage, New Camaldoli,** the self-sufficient community of Camaldolese Monks, offers retreats to men and women. Gift shop sells their famous Hermitage fruitcake, religious artifacts, and books. For retreats, write to Guestmaster, Immaculate Heart Hermitage, New Camaldoli, Big Sur, CA 93920, or call 667-2456.

24 **Lime Kiln Creek State Park**, offers hikes to historic kilns and coastal access with campsites for a fee, 667-2403.

25 **Kirk Creek and Campground**, has fee campsites on an open bluff above the ocean. Follow Kirk Creek trail on the east side for ocean views.

26 **Nacimiento-Fergusson Road** off Highway 1 is very steep (to 4000'), windy and narrow as it cuts through the Ventana Wilderness. Ocean views, wildflowers, redwoods, oaks. At the summit is the **Los Padres National Forest Ranger's Station** with information, maps, water, and camping permits. Past Ft. Hunter Liggett Military Base at Jolon, Mission San Antonio de Padua (see Dutton Hotel ruins and the Hacienda designed as a hunting lodge for W.R. Hearst by Julia Morgan in 1935), to Mission San Antonio.

27 **Mill Creek** picnic area and a small beach. No fee.

28 **Pacific Valley Center** will reopen with a big millennium party, December 31, 1999. Call owner Harry Harris at 805/927-8655 for details. His plans for the Center include a restaurant, bar, gift shop, mini-market, campground, and 6 luxury units next year. **The Big Sur Jade Co. and Museum** will reopen with new jewelry at the same location, with free admission.

29 **Sand Dollar Beach**, 1 mile south of U.S. Forest Service station in Pacific Valley and 14 miles north of San Luis Obispo County line, across from **Plaskett Creek Campground**. No fee. Widest expanse of sand and mildest weather on the coast.

30 **Plaskett Campground**, a beautiful spot on the east side with big trees and ocean views, fire pits. Fee. U.S. Forest Service.

31 **Jade Cove**, 2 miles south of Sand Dollar Beach, is famous for its jade reserves and popular with beachcombers and rockhounds. No fee.

32 **Willow Creek picnic area**, pictured below, is a good place to look for jade pieces among the rocks on the beach. No fee. *Remember: Never turn your back to the surf on any Big Sur beach, to avoid being swept away.*

33 **Gorda**, the southernmost town in Monterey County on the Big Sur Coast, 66 miles from Carmel, with gas, cabins, grocery store, espresso, info. See the llamas grazing behind a fence on an adjacent lot.

➤ **Hearst Castle** at San Simeon is 26 miles south of Gorda. Call for tour reservations, 800-444-4445.

Free & Fun in

Carmel-by-the-Sea

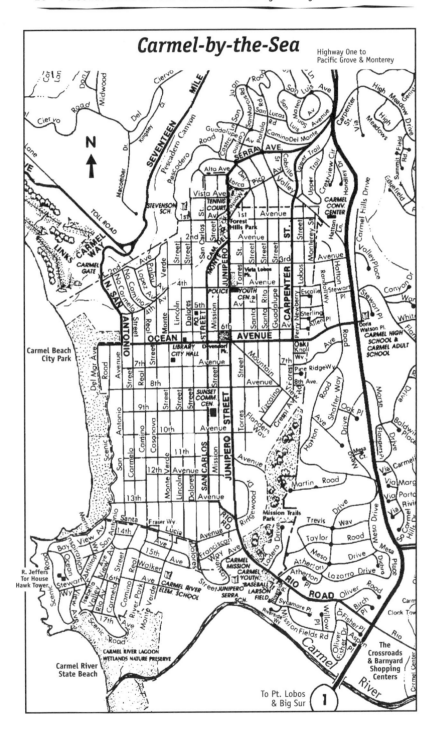

Carmel-by-the-Sea

Downtown Walking Tours
Charming Shops & Courtyards

Start on Monte Verde, half a block south of Ocean Avenue, in front of City Hall. Although Clint Eastwood is no longer Mayor, he is still active in local politics. You might see our current mayor, Ken White, arriving at the office. As you face City Hall, you will see a pathway passing next to one of Carmel's Inns. Go up this path, and you will be in the Court of the Golden Bough.

A small stationery shop with its warm cottage atmosphere and stone fireplace will be on your right as you enter the court. Walk through, under an arcade, and up the stone-flagged path onto Ocean Avenue. Turn right, and up half a block to Lincoln Street.

Turn right again and on the west, or right side, halfway along the block is the La Rambla building, a Spanish style building with wrought iron balconies, built in 1929. Through the center of this building is an arcade leading to a garden shop with fountains and sculptures.

Returning on to Lincoln, turn left to Ocean and turn east, or right, up Ocean, halfway along the block and on the right-hand side, is a tiny arched entrance way to Der Ling Lane. A shop runs along one side of this quaint lane. Paved in Carmel stone, with an arched roof of creepers and flowers, this attractive little lane leads to another garden area, a peaceful and quiet spot, and a gallery in the back.

Return to Ocean, continue up again to the next cross street, Dolores. Turn right, or south on Dolores, and halfway along the block on the west side, is Piccadilly Park. Benches, placed outside at the entrance and inside in shady spots, are ideal places to sit for a snack or rest break.

Back on Dolores, cross the street toward a quaint little English tea room, Tuck Box Restaurant in the Hansel & Gretel design, and on that side of the street, still walking south, you will come to El Paseo Building, almost on the corner. Walk into this little courtyard with its brick flagstone, and see the two Spanish figures that were sculptured by Jo Mora in 1928. Real estate offices and shops here, and in other locations, often have fireplaces; the light from the flickering fires adds a further attraction. Walk out of this courtyard, by the other exit, onto 7th Street and turn left, or east, towards San Carlos.

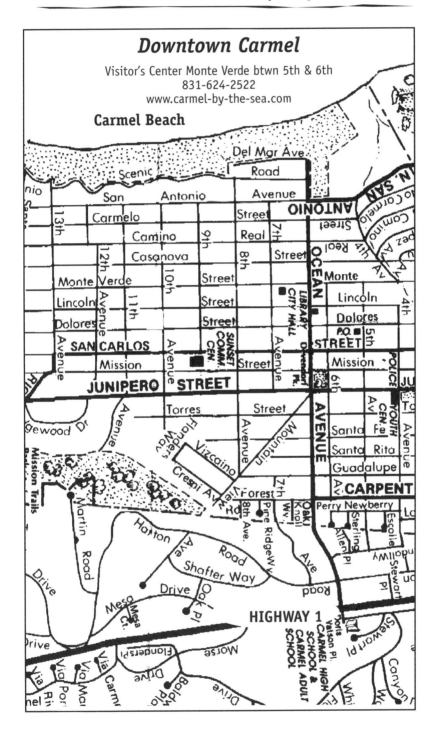

Downtown Carmel

Visitor's Center Monte Verde btwn 5th & 6th
831-624-2522
www.carmel-by-the-sea.com

Carmel Beach

Cross San Carlos continuing on 7th and just past the old-fashioned grocery store, on the left you will see steps leading up into the Court of the Fountains. Walk into the courtyard. Pass the pool and fountain, pass two attractive gazebos, and turn right, out of the court and onto Mission Street.

Cross Mission Street, turn up (left) toward Ocean, and right, down the steps into the Carmel Plaza. Fifty-seven stores and restaurants, two hours free parking with validations at covered parking garage at Mission and 7th. There are benches and comfortable resting places among flowers, trees and a fountain. Restrooms are on the 3rd level at the top of the escalator.

When you leave the Carmel Plaza, coming back onto Mission Street, turn up to the right toward Ocean Avenue. You can cross Ocean and enter Devendorf Park to stroll or rest. In the northwest corner of the park is a statue of Fr. Junipero Serra and memorials dedicated to Carmel residents who served in W.W.II. There are public restrooms located in the far corner of the park.

You can continue exploring the Courtyards of Carmel crossing through the park to 6th Avenue. At the corner of 6th & Mission, turn to the north, or right, and walk up the west side of Mission to the Jordan Center which contains an art gallery, coffee house/restaurant, and shops.

The next pathway is the May Court, a little further to the north you'll come to the Mission Patio which is occupied by a variety of artisans – a furniture maker, jeweler, designer, sculptor, and even a Christmas shop. In the back of the Mission Patio on the left, you will see steps leading to The Mall, the next courtyard on your tour. The Mall connects Mission Street to San Carlos and is filled with art galleries, shops, jewelers and a small pub. Stroll through The Mall to San Carlos. Immediately across San Carlos are two pathways that will lead you through to Dolores Street.

Cross to the corner of San Carlos & 6th, you'll see "Cottage Row," a corner of Carmel cottage-like shops. Go north up San Carlos on the west side and you will see a small sign indicating passage to Dolores Street. If you choose to take this route you will be lead through one of Carmel's hidden treasures, the Secret Garden. If you continue north on San Carlos, you will pass the office of the Carmel Business Association/Carmel Visitors Information Center. This would be a good time to stop in for information on inns, dining, points of interest, etc.

Just past the Visitor Information Center is a pathway leading to the Hog's Breath Restaurant and the second passageway to Dolores Street. Walk down the path, through the patio (notice the mural of Carmel Valley by local artist, G.H. Rothe) and down the pathway to Dolores Street. Carmel's post office is located on the corner of Dolores & 5th – Carmel does not have street addresses, everyone goes to the post office to receive mail....it is a wonderful place to greet locals!

On the northwest corners of 5th & Dolores are benches where you can rest or enjoy a snack. Walk south on Dolores on the west side to Su Vecino Court/San Remo Cortiles. This is yet another courtyard filled with artisans, restaurants, and shops that will lead you through to the next street, Lincoln.

On the northwest corner of Lincoln & 6th, you will find Carmel's First Murphy House Park. **The First Murphy House**, the oldest in Carmel, was built at the turn of the century. The park adjacent offers a lovely deck with a spectacular view of Carmel Bay. Public restrooms <u>Free admission</u>, Wed-Sun, 1-4pm. Carmel Heritage Society, 624-4447. www.carmelnet.com/heritage.

Crossing 6th to the south, you will see the Pine Inn courtyard. The Pine Inn is Carmel's oldest hotel, and the brick-paved, flower-filled courtyard is charming. Walk through the courtyard and exit on Ocean Avenue. To the west, or the right, is Monte Verde. By crossing to the south, you will find yourself at the beginning of your tour. *Text courtesy Carmel Business Assn.*

Free Coffee, Tea, Chocolate, and more...

➤ Between walks, show your *Free & Fun Guide* to receive a <u>free cup of coffee or tea</u> at **Coffee Beans & Tea Leaves,** in the Court of the Golden Bough. Open 10:30am-5:30pm daily. 624-4504.

➤ **Stefan Mann Luggage,** Dolores, between 5th & 6th, will give you a <u>free packing demonstration tailored to your needs</u>. 9am-7pm. 625-2998.

➤ **Carmel Candy**, in the Carmel Plaza, will give you a <u>free taste of their homemade fudge</u>. Open 10am-6pm daily, 625-3559.

➤ **Carmel Walks**, Sat 10am & 2pm, Tues-Fri, 10am. $15 per person. 2 hour guided walk through Carmel courtyards. Meet in the outdoor courtyard of The Pine Inn on Lincoln St. at Ocean Ave. Reservations: 642-2700.

➤ **Historic walking tour** with Kay Prine, first Saturdays. Meet at the Murphy House, Lincoln & 6th. $7. Call 624-4447 for times.

Interesting Architecture Walks
Most are private homes, please do not disturb.

Frank Lloyd Wright House
Overlooking the ocean, on west side of Scenic Road, east of Martin Way.

Robert Stanton Buildings
Robert Stanton was a prominent architect and civic leader who designed Monterey Peninsula College, the Monterey County Courthouse in Salinas and numerous buildings with an old world quality in Carmel.

Fisher Cottage	1926	West side Carmel btwn 11th & 12th
Young Cottage	1926	Southwest corner Carmelo & 11th
Church of the Wayfarer	1923-40	Northwest corner Lincoln & 7th
Normandy Inn	1927-50	Southwest corner Casanova & Ocean
N.B. Flower Shop	1942	Southwest corner Ocean & Monte Verde

Hugh Comstock Houses
Hugh Comstock started building 'doll houses' in 1924 for his wife, Mayotta Brown's, 'otsey-totsey' dolls. He used only native and natural materials, and fashioned each house with his own hands, although he was not trained as an architect or builder. You will enjoy a walking tour to view these lovely and unique houses, listed here in the order in which they were built.

HOUSE	DATE	LOCATION
Hansel & Gretel	1924-25	East side Torres btwn 5th & 6th
Ober Cottage	1925	Northeast corner Torres & 6th
Snow White's	1926	West side of Lincoln btwn 12th & 13th
Comstock Studio	1926-40	Northwest corner Santa Fe & 6th
The Woods	1927	Northeast corner Ocean & Torres
Our House	1928	West side Santa Fe btwn 5th & 6th
"Maples"	1928	West side Santa Rita btwn 6th & Ocean
Yellow Bird	1928	South side 6th btwn Santa Fe & Santa Rita
Comstock Cottage	1928	North side Ocean btwn Santa Fe & Santa Rita
The Doll's House	1928	Northwest corner Santa Rita & Ocean
Birthday House	1928	Southwest corner 6th & Santa Rita
Twin on Palou	1929	West side N. Casanova & East side Palou
Curtain Calls	1929	West side Junipero btwn 2nd & 3rd
Jordan House	1929	Southwest corner Vista & Mission
Angel	1929	West side San Antonio btwn 10th & 11th
Los Arboles	1934	East side Santa Fe btwn 8th & 9th
Welsh Cottage	1937	South side 8th btwn Santa Fe & Mt. View
Post Adobe	1937	South side 8th btwn Santa Fe & Mt. View
Slaughter House	1941	Northeast end of 6th near Perry Newberry
Windhorst	1942	West side Santa Fe btwn 2nd & 3rd
Village Inn	1954	Northwest corner Ocean & Junipero

SKETCH BY GRANT WALLACE.

A Self-Guided Walking Tour of the Heritage Trees of Carmel-by-the-Sea

*Provided by the Carmel-by-the-Sea 75th Anniversary
Celebration Committee & Friends of Carmel Forest*

Choosing the Heritage Trees

Carmel-by-the-Sea from its beginning has been known as "a village in a forest." As part of the celebration of the 75th anniversary of Carmel's incorporation (1991), the public was invited to nominate candidates for Heritage Tree designation. Final selection was made by the Celebration Committee: Barbara Livingston, Dr. Roy L. Thomas, Roger Newell, Gary Kelly, and Howard Skidmore.

The Heritage Trees are a Legacy

Lift up your eyes! In every part of Carmel you will see the lofty crowns of magnificent trees. The trees are a legacy to us from the past. Men and women in years gone by planted and nurtured many of the big trees we see today. Now it is for us not only to enjoy this heritage, but to preserve and protect it. The trees of choice for many, today seen all over town, were the native Monterey Pine and Coast Live Oak. The pine is native only to the Monterey Peninsula and to four small areas along the Pacific Coast. The Monterey Cypress is also seen and is native to Cypress Pt. and Point Lobos. Also seen today are immense Coast Redwoods and the Blue Gum Eucalyptus, said to have been imported from Australia to California in 1856.

Blue Gum Eucalyptus the Largest Tree

Standing by itself on the northwest corner at Ocean and San Antonio Avenues is the largest tree in the village, a Blue Gum Eucalyptus, at 22 feet 8 inches around the trunk. How did this immense tree, presumably predating

any real-estate development in Carmel, come to be planted where it is? Possibly it marked a boundary around the grounds of the original rancho. A house said to have been built in 1846, making it the oldest in the village, is located in a windbreak grove of eucalyptuses a few hundred yards to the north. One theory is that the Spanish padres brought the Australian eucalyptus to California even before 1856. A possible support for this idea is the size of the two trees of the species just a few steps from the 1771 Carmel Mission. One tree is 34 feet in girth, the other 26 feet. They are by the so-called bunk house at the historic Mission Ranch, just outside the boundaries of Carmel-by-the-Sea. *(Text by Howard Skidmore)*

Locating the Heritage Trees

In tree locations, the abbreviations "we," "es," etc., refer to "west side of street," "east side of street," etc.; 3 so. of 4th" refers to 3rd house south of 4th Ave." Tree measurements are in feet and inches of circumference, taken $4^1/_2$ feet above natural ground level. For multi-trunked trees, such as Coast Live Oaks, when a figure is given it is for the compounded circumference (not the total circumference) for all trunks. "Sea-shaped" refers to the seaside effects of wind, fog, and salt air. *(A complete list of heritage trees and a map is available at City Hall, Monte Verde between Ocean and 7th, and the Park Branch, Mission at 6th.)*

Ocean Avenue between Junipero and Monte Verde:

- "The Patriarch," sw corner of Devendorf Park, a Coast Live Oak, 12+ft, may be the largest oak in the village.

- Center Island at San Carlos, ws, Monterey Pine, 9ft.

- Center Island between Lincoln and Monte Verde, "The Contortionist," Toyon, sea-shaped.

North of Ocean, West of San Carlos:

- Lincoln, es, between 5th & 6th, Blue Gum Eucalyptus, 14+ft, largest of species downtown.

- Lincoln and 2nd, sw corner in street, Monterey Pine, 15+ft, largest pine on city property.

- Monte Verde and 4th, 30 Blue gum Eucalyptuses along so. side 4th to San Antonio. Trees line what was early road leading to rancho on west side of San Antonio.

North of Ocean, East of San Carlos:

- San Carlos and 5th ne corner, in lodge courtyard, Coast Redwood 16+ft. Largest tree in downtown.

South of Ocean, West of San Carlos:

- San Carlos and Santa Lucia, nw corner, in courtyard, Monterey Pine, 17ft, largest pine in Carmel, said to be largest in county. Private property.

- Monte Verde es so. of Ocean, City Hall, in front, Coast Redwood, 11+ft.

- Camino Real and 8th se corner, Monterey Pine 13+ft, to left of entrance to historic La Playa Hotel (built in 1904 and restored in 1984).

- San Antonio between 10th and 12th, "The Arcade," large Monterey Cypresses meet overhead. Planted in early 1900s.

- Scenic & Ocean, 2 w on Ocean, ns, "Contortionist II," Acacia, sea-shaped.

Friends of Carmel Forest

To become a member, write to P.O. Box 344, Carmel, CA 93921

Other Places of Interest

■ **Robinson Jeffers' Tor House and Hawk Tower**, 26304 Ocean View Ave. near Stewart Way. The former home of poet Robinson Jeffers, whose poetry was inspired by the rugged Big Sur coast. Tor House contains original furnishings and Jeffers' memorabilia. Drive by Hawk Tower on Stewart Way. Jeffers gathered the stones from nearby Carmel Beach and the outside retaining wall contains rock from the Temple of Peking, lava from Hawaii, and a piece of the Great Wall of China. He built Hawk Tower as a symbol of his love for his wife. Tours of the gardens, house, and Tower, Fri-Sat, every
hour, on the hour, 10am-3pm. Only 6 people can be accommodated on each tour, so reservations must be made ahead. $7 adults, $4 college, $2 high school, no children under 12. Robinson Jeffers Festival, in October, affords a free walk with poets. 624-1813.

■ **The Basilica of Mission San Carlos Borromeo del Rio Carmelo** (Carmel Mission Basilica), 3080 Rio Road and Lausen Drive (831) 624-1271, 624-3600. Originally founded by Father Junipero Serra, June 3, 1770, in Monterey (now the Royal Presidio Chapel), the church was moved to this site in 1771. The present stone church was dedicated in 1797. Father Junipero Serra is bur-
ied in the Basilica. A donation of $2 for adults and $1 for children 5 and older is requested to continue the restoration which is privately funded. The Mission is considered the most authentically restored Franciscan mission. Open Mon-Sat, 9:30am-4:15pm, Sunday, 10:30am-4:15pm. Open until 7:15pm, June through August. This is a fabulous place to connect with the history of the Monterey Peninsula, and a sight not to be missed. The rooms are filled with utensils, clothing, tools, baskets, church vestments and more. The courtyard and gardens have several benches for resting and meditating, lots of old statues, and a good collection of specimen plants, native shrubs, and flowers.

Masses: Sat 5:30pm; Sun 7, 8, 9:30, 11, 12:30 and 5:30pm; weekdays: 7am, 12noon and 5:30pm (in Blessed Sacrament Chapel); Eve of Holy Days, 5:30pm; Holy Days: 7, 9:30, 11am, 12:30 and 5:30pm. Mission: St. Francis of the Redwoods Mass Sunday 10:30am.

Gift Shop is open 9:30am-4:30pm, 624-3600.

Mission San Carlos Borromeo del Rio Carmelo
Joelle Steele, 11x17 watercolor, 1996.

Art Gallery Walk

Carmel is known for its artists and its art galleries. There's the whimsy of Will Bullas, the poignancy of Rodrique's Blue Dog, sculpture by MacDonald, New Renaissance Masters, and everything in-between. You can spend an entire lifetime soaking up the art treasures found on these streets. Be prepared to add to your own art collection. Not all galleries are listed here.

Mission Street

● **Dyansen Gallery**, in the Carmel Plaza. Contemporary art, graphics, and sculpture. Sun-Thur 10-6, Fri-Sat 10-9. 625-6903.

● **It's Cactus**, between Ocean and 7th. Imported handmade folk art of all things rare and unusual. 626-4213.

● **Edward Montgomery**, between Ocean & 7th. Contemporary paintings, prints, and sculpture. Daily 10-6, Sun 12-5. 622-9292.

● **Cottage Gallery**, near 6th. Traditional art: landscape, seascape, still life. Daily 10-5. 624-7888.

● **Alexander of Florence**, between 5th & 6th. Original contemporary Italian art. 620-0732.

San Carlos Street

● **Jones & Terwilliger**, between 5th & 6th. 30 artists. Daily 10-6. Fri-Sat 10-10. 626-9100.

● **European Galleries**, between 5th & 6th. Contemporary originals. Daily 10-6, Fri-Sat 10-10. 624-2010.

● **Andrew T. Jackson Studio**, at 6th. 626-8354.

● **Mudzimu Gallery**, San Carlos Mall btwn 5th & 6th. Contemporary African stone sculpture. Daily 11-6, closed Tues. 626-2946.

● **Silver Light Gallery**, at Ocean. Fine art photographers. Daily 10-5. 624-4589.

● **Will Bullas Fun Art**, between Ocean & 7th. Humorous, appealing work
● Will Bullas in Carmel Square. 11am-3pm daily. 625-4112.

● **Canapo Gallery**. 624-7462.

● **Trotter Galleries**, at 7th. Early California. 625-3246.

● **Winters Fine Art Galleries**, Doud Arcade and Plaza San Carlos. Wide selection. Daily 10-5, closed Sun. 626-5452, 626-5535.

● **Richard MacDonald**, near 6th. Figurative sculpture by MacDonald. Daily 10-6, Fri-Sat 10-9. 624-8200.

● **New Renaissance Masters**, between 5th & 6th. Limited edition Serigraphs, Lithographs. Contemporary and Old Masters. Sun-Thur 10-6, Fri-Sat 10-10. 622-5255.

- **Simic New Renaissance**, between 5th & 6th. Original Impressionism and Realism. Mon-Wed 10-6, Thur-Sat 10-10, Sun 10-8. 624-7522.
- **Center for Photographic Art**, Sunset Cultural Center, San Carlos and 9th. Fine art photographs and exhibitions. Tues-Sun, 1-5pm. 625-5181.

Dolores Street

- **Joie De Vivre Gallery**, between 5th & 6th. Contemporary Masters from Italy, Spain, France, China, and the United States. Sun-Thurs 10-6, Fri-Sat 9-9. 620-0156.
- **Richard Thomas Galleries**, between 5th & 6th. Contemporary masters and traditional. 625-5636.
- **Gallerie Amsterdam**, between 5th & 6th. European paintings. Sun-Wed 10-6, Fri-Sat 10-10.
- **Golf Art & Imports**, between 5th & 6th. Golf-themed art, collectibles, and antiquities of all kinds. Mon-Sat 10-5, Sun 11-5. 625-4488.
- **Pitzer's of Carmel**, on 6th. Original paintings, sculpture, prints, and porcelain. Mon-Sat 10-6, Sun 10-5. 625-2288, 800/843-6467.
- **Photography West Gallery**, S.E. corner of Ocean. Classical and contemporary photography. Fri-Mon 10-6. 625-1587.
- **Bleich Gallery West**, south of Ocean. George J. Bleich, a renowned plein-air painter. Daily 10:30-5:30. 624-9447, 372-2717.
- **China Art Center**, between 7th & Ocean. Impressive collection of museum-quality paintings from the Sung and Ming Dynasties to modern times, silk, screens, furniture, jewelry. Mon-Sat 10-6. 624-5868.
- **Gallery 21**, between Ocean & 7th. Collection of Eyvind Earle, a former Disney animation artist. Daily from 10am. 626-2700.
- **Zimmerman Gallery**, between Ocean & 7th. Marc Zimmerman combines classical Renaissance with contemporary. Daily 10:30-5. 622-9100.
- **David Lee Galleries**, at 7th.
- **New Masters Gallery**, between Ocean & 7th. Contemporary paintings and sculpture. 625-1511.
- **Gallery 1000**, between Ocean & 7th. Original oils and watercolors. Daily 10-6. 624-9094.
- **Carmel Art Association Galleries**, between 5th & 6th. Oldest gallery (1928) with over 120 artists. There are some interesting sculptures in the front garden. Daily 10am-5pm. 624-6176.
- **47 Gallery Sur, Inc.**, at 6th. Nature photography. Daily 10-6. 626-2615.

- **Josephus Daniels Gallery**, 6th, Su Vecino Ct., upstairs. Prints and photographs. Tue-Sat 1-5, Sun 1-4. www.danielsgallery.com. 625-3316.
- **Savage Contemporary Fine Art**, between 5th & 6th. Contemporary figurative and abstract. Daily 10-6. 626-0800, 888/626-0808.
- **James J. Rieser Fine Art**, between 5th & 6th. Early California paintings and local artists. Daily 11-5. 620-0530.
- **Highlands Sculpture Gallery**, between 5th & 6th. Innovative gallery of sculpture, monotypes, paintings. 624-0535.
- **S.R. Brennen Galleries**. Corner of 5th. Eclectic collection. 10-6 daily. 625-2233.
- **Harrison Gallery**, at 5th. Plein-air, still life, landscape art; virtually every medium. Daily 10-6. 622-7772, 622-0828.
- **William A. Karges Fine Art**, at 5th. Early California impressionists. Daily 10-5. 625-4266.
- **Atelier Carmel**, at 5th. Classic fine art. Daily 10-6. 625-3168.

Sixth Avenue

- **Classic Art Gallery**, at San Carlos. Traditional fine art. Daily 10-6, Fri-Sat 10-9. 625-0464.
- **Regal Art Galleries**, between San Carlos & Dolores. Original paintings and sculptures. Sun-Thurs 10-6, Fri-Sat 10-10. 624-8155.
- **Howard Portnoy Gallerie**, between Dolores & San Carlos. Original art including French impressionists; figurative bronze sculpture. Daily 1-5. 624-1155.
- **The Decoy**, between Dolores and Lincoln. Wildlife, waterfowl, and sporting dog themes. 625-1881.
- **Martin LaBorde Gallery**, between Lincoln & Dolores. LaBorde's paintings, serigraphs, and drawings. 10-6 daily. 620-1150.
- **Weston Gallery**, between Dolores & Lincoln. Photography of the 19th and 20th centuries. Wed-Mon 10:30-5:30, closed Tues. 624-4453.
- **D.E. Craghead/Fine Art Gallery**, between Dolores & Lincoln. Diverse paintings and sculpture. Daily 10-5:30. 624-5054.
- **Phillips Gallery of Fine Art**, between Dolores & Lincoln. Original paintings, stone sculptures. Sat-Thurs 10-6, Fri 10-8.
- **Gallery Americana**, corner of Lincoln. Contemporary paintings and sculpture. Mon-Sat 10-5:30, Sun 10-5. 624-5071.
- **Lynn Lupetti Gallery**, between Dolores & Lincoln. Luminous paintings by Lupetti, other fine artists. Daily 10-5. 624-0622.
- **Rodrigue Studio**, between Lincoln & Dolores. "Blue Dog" series. Daily 10-6. 626-4444.

- **Loran Speck Art Gallery**, near Dolores. Speck retrospective on Dutch and Italian painters of the Renaissance. Daily 10:30-5pm. 624-3707.

- **Lilliana Braico Gallery**, near Dolores. Mediterranean scenes, abstracts, portraits, and florals. Fri-Tues 11-5, Wed-Thurs by appt.

- **Winfield Gallery**, 6th Ave. Contemporary fine art and crafts. 624-3369.

- **Garcia Gallery**, between Dolores & San Carlos, upstairs. Danny Garcia impressionism, realism, and abstraction. Daily 10-5. 624-8338.

- **Zantman Art Galleries, Inc.**, at Mission. Paintings and sculpture of living American, European and Asian artists. Daily 10-5. 624-8314.

Lincoln Street

- **Avalon Gallery**, between Ocean & 7th in Morgan Court. Contemporary handmade works on paper, fine woodworking, and nudes. Wed-Mon 11-5 and by appt. 622-0830.

- **G.H. Rothe Gallery I & II**, between Ocean & 7th in Morgan Court. Original mezzotints, oils, pastels, mixed media, pencil, and watercolors. Daily 10-6. 626-1338, 624-9377.

Seventh Avenue

- **Nancy Dodds Gallery**, between San Carlos & Dolores. Contemporary works on paper: watercolors, etchings, oil, lithographs and monotypes. Mon-Sat 10:30-5:30, Sun 12-5. 624-0346.

- **Chapman Gallery**, between San Carlos & Mission. Works by past and present masters, including Hank Ketcham, S.C. Yuan, and Gail Reeves. Tue-Sun 10-4:30. 625-2018.

1995 Carmel Art Festival Poster
Carmel beach. S.C. Yuan (1911-1974)

Public Libraries & Bookstores

● **Harrison Memorial Public Library**, Ocean Ave. and Lincoln, 624-4629. Reference: 624-7323. Hours: Mon-Wed, 10am-8pm, Thurs-Fri, 10am-6pm, Sat-Sun, 1-5pm. 7 internet stations. Outreach Program: For people unable to come to the library. Delivery of books and books-on-tape, loan equipment which helps physically challenged people use library materials, braille and talking books. 624-7323. Audiovisual collection of local history includes tapes which can be viewed from 1-5pm, Tues-Fri.: "Big Sur, The Way It Was," "Don't Pave Main Street," "Ford Ord, A Place in History," "Longtimers" Part I and II," "Remembering Carmel" Part I, II and III. Become a Friend and help at the annual tea and book sale. www.hm-lib.org.

● **Library Park Branch**, 6th Ave. and Mission St. 624-1366. Hours: Tue, 10am-8pm, Wed-Fri, 10am-6pm, Sat, 1pm-5pm. Local History Department with hundreds of books on California and Carmel history, biography and art. Works by local authors and artists, historical photographs, and Carmel newspapers on microfilm. 624-1615. The Youth Services Department has library materials for infants through young adults and a collection of books about parenting with a browsing area for parents to use and enjoy. Programs: Tues, 10:30am, preschool, 7pm, families; Wed, 10:30am, preschool; Fri, 10:30am, babies and toddlers, 11:15am, toddlers and preschool. Youth services librarian: 624-4664.

● **Kingdom Come Books and Gifts**. Christian Bookstore. Protestant, Catholic, Jewish books, gifts, music, jewelry, greeting cards, Hermitage fruitcakes. Mon-Sat 10am-5:30pm. 26386 Carmel Rancho Lane. 624-1290.

● **Pilgrims' Way Bookstore**. Metaphysical books and music, astrology reports, incense, gifts. Lectures & book signings. Mon-Sat 10am-6pm, Sun 11am-5pm. Dolores & 6th Ave. www.pilgrimsway.com. 624-4955.

● **Sierra Club–Ventana Chapter**. Nature books and trail guides. Ocean between Dolores & San Carlos, upstairs. 624-8032.

● **Thunderbird Bookshop and Cafe**. Book signings and weekly lectures. Local art on the walls, cozy cafe with fireplace, solarium patio. *Evening Book Club* meets 7pm, third Wednesdays. *Morning Book Club* meets 10am, 2nd Tues. Call for information: Books & Dinner on 3rd Thurs, Writing & Poetry classes. In The Barnyard, Highway 1 and Carmel Valley Rd. 624-1803. http://internet-books.com.

Poets & Writers Invited

➤ **Poetry on the Beach**, in the Bohemian tradition, at sunset on last Saturdays with Tad Wojnicki at Carmel Beach, foot of 13th Avenue. Bring a potluck dish, flashlight, poem/story, or a fire log. 770-0107.

➤ **Creative With Words** publications for poets/writers. Submit entries to *The Eclectics*, writers age 20 and up, and *We Are Writers, Too!*, age 19 and under. Write or fax for details and entry forms: PO Box 223226, Carmel 93922. Fax 655-8627.

1999 Calendar of Events

Information subject to change. Please call in advance to verify.

January 1   **RIO GRILL'S RESOLUTION RUN**   **Spectators free**
New Year's Day 10K race to benefit the Suicide Prevention Center. 6.8 mile foot race over roads, trails and scenic beaches. 3 mile Family Fun Run is ideal for all ages and capabilities. From The Crossroads, through Carmel, and ending at the Carmel Mission. If you want to participate, fee is $21 for adults, $16 for ages 12 and younger. Registration includes a long sleeve T-shirt, scrumptious brunch, and entry for great prize drawings. Crossroads Shopping Center, Highway 1 at Rio Road. Info 644-2427; to volunteer 375-6966.

FEBRUARY

February 23-28   **MASTERS OF FOOD & WINE** $$
13th Annual at the Highlands Inn, various times. Exceptional gastronomic event with internationally famous chefs and winemakers. Lunches, dinners, winery tours, wine tastings. Free cooking demonstrations. http://www.1bookstreet.com/foodandwine.asp 624-3801.

MARCH

March 13   **ANNUAL KITE FESTIVAL**   **Spectators free**
Kites must be homemade except for the kids-only commercial category. Noon registration, judging begins at 12:30. Carmel Beach at the end of 13th Avenue. For more information about categories, prizes and rules, contact Carmel Community Activities, 626-1255.

APRIL

April-Sept   **GARDEN TOURS**   **Free**
Guided tours of The Barnyard gardens every Sunday at noon. 624-8886.

April 17   **HOME & GARDEN AFFAIR** $$
Garden tour and festival with gardening demonstrations, music, entertainment, and refreshments. 1-5pm. The Barnyard Shopping Village, Highway 1. 624-8886.

April 25   **BIG SUR INTERNATIONAL MARATHON**   **Spectators free**
13th Annual. Includes the 26.2 mile footrace, the marathon Relay Teams, the 21 mile Power Walk, 5K footrace, and the 10.6 mile noncompetitive walk – all to raise money for charities. Classical musicians play along the course. Volunteers always needed. Free training clinics held in November and December for next year's race. Sign up to run/walk on-line: www.bsim.org or call the Marathon Office at 625-6226, fax 625-2119.

MAY

May tba   **CARMEL ART FESTIVAL**   **Free**
Local art, youth art, sculpture-in-the-park exhibit, and demonstrations. Devendorf Park on Mission Street between Ocean and 6th avenues. 624-5588.

May 1-2   **ORCHID MAYFAIRE**   **Free**
Spectacular orchid show presented by the Carmel Orchid Society. Crossroads Shopping Center, Rio Road and Highway 1. Contact Sheila Bowman, 622-0292.

May 1-2   **CHAMBER MUSIC CONCERTS**   **Free**
Saturday at 1pm, an afternoon of performances by chamber ensembles from the nation's top university music departments and conservatories, judged by a panel of renowned chamber musicians. Sunday at 3pm, competition Finalists Concert. Sunset Center. Chamber Music Monterey Bay. 625-2212.

JUNE

June/July   **FOREST THEATRE CONCERTS**   **Free**
Sundays, free concerts at 2pm at the Outdoor Forest Theater, Mountain View and Santa Rita. Presented by The Sunset Center with funding provided by the Mayor's Youth Fund. 626-1255.

June/July   **PARKFEST**   **Free**
Musicians and performers, free hot dogs for the kids. Noon on Fridays at Devendorf Park, Ocean and Junipero. 626-1255.

June 19   **ANNUAL ART & WINE FESTIVAL**   **Free+$$**
Enjoy art throughout the gardens, with live music. Wine tasting and food. Fifteen local vintners, food samplings from Barnyard restaurants. To benefit MCAP. 1-5pm at The Barnyard, Highway 1 to Carmel Valley Rd. 624-8886.

JULY

July 9-11   **DOG SHOWS AND OBEDIENCE TRIALS**   **Free**
Del Monte Kennel Club All-Breed, Santa Clara Valley Kennel Club All-Breed Dog Shows & Obedience Trials. Free admission daily, parking $3 daily. Food available from Carmel Kiwanis. 8am-5pm at Carmel Middle School. Ruth 649-4280.

July 17-Aug 8   **CARMEL BACH FESTIVAL**   **Free+$$**
A lively celebration of baroque music. Enjoy their "Discovery Series" of free events including open rehearsals, concerts for kids and families, lectures, brass concerts, and free ice cream. Volunteer to be a hostess or an usher to enjoy the concerts. Festival office at Sunset Center. Information: 624-2046, 624-1521, fax 624-2788, www.bachfestival.org.

July 30-Oct 10   **SHAKE-SPEARE FESTIVAL**   **$$**
Take-off on the Bard's tales - lots of fun. 622-0100.

AUGUST

August 12   **PORSCHE RALLY**   **Free+$$**
Cars gather at 11am in the south parking lot to have pictures taken and begin the rally, returning to The Barnyard around 4:30pm. 624-8886.

SEPTEMBER

Sept or Oct   **GREAT SAND CASTLE CONTEST**   **Free**
No entry fee for this theme-based contest within the boundaries of 10th and 12th avenues. Anyone and everyone is invited to participate. Top prize is the Golden Shovel Award with almost 30 lesser prizes awarded, including Advanced Soapbox and the Sour Grapes Award (given to the best–or worst–whiners). Carmel Beach, end of Ocean Ave. 626-1255.

September 4-5   **CARMEL OUTDOOR ART FESTIVAL**   **Free+$$**
Enjoy fine-art exhibits and live music. Benefit for the Carmel Cultural Commission. Sunset Center, San Carlos & 9th. 624-3996.

September 26   **CARMEL MISSION FIESTA**   Free
Mariachi dancers and singers, bagpipers, Irish dancers, strolling musicians, flamenco dancers, country line dancing, children's games, arts and crafts, farmers market, food vendors. 11am-5pm at the Mission, on Rio Road west of Highway 1. Info: 624-1271. Advance barbecue tickets: 626-4567.

September 26   **Fine Arts 5K Run/Walk**   Spectators Free
Meet at 7am at Carmel Beach, Scenic Drive and Ocean Ave. 758-8406.

OCTOBER

October tba   **CARMEL FINE ARTS 5K RUN/WALK**   Spectators free
After the race, a feast on the beach with light jazz. $14-$30 includes race, brunch, T-shirt. Auction. Proceeds benefit Carmel Open Space Task Force. 9am Sunday. 624-2471.

October tba   **THE ROBINSON JEFFERS' FESTIVAL**   Free+$$
Presented by the Tor House Foundation, beginning with a reception at Jeffers' home, Tor House, on Friday night, to honor festival speakers. This event is $5, or free to those with advance reservation for the Saturday seminars and banquet. Free Jeffers Poetry Walk on Sunday morning. Meet in room 14-B at Sunset Cultural Center at 8:30am for coffee and the walk ends with a brown bag lunch at noon on Carmel beach. 624-1813, 624-1840. www.torhouse.org.

October 1-17   **CARMEL PERFORMING ARTS FESTIVAL**   Free+$$
The finest regional and national theatre, dance and music…and a few surprises… in the intimate and historic theatres of charming Carmel. Free dancing, music, and receptions at galleries, parks, and shopping centers in Carmel during the festival. Call for places and times. Tickets $3-$40. 644-8383, 624-7675, fax 622-7631. www.carmelfest.org.

October 31   **ANNUAL HARVEST FESTIVAL**   Free
Enjoy a fun, safe, family-oriented Halloween at The Barnyard. Trick-or-treat, pony rides, the lion, tinman, and scarecrow from the Wizard of Oz, inflatable fun houses, costume contest with prizes, hayrides, and entertainment. 1-4pm at The Barnyard, Highway 1 and Carmel Valley Road. 624-8886. Spirits of Halloween readings, 3pm, Thunderbird Bookshop, The Barnyard. Free. 624-1803.

October 31   **HALLOWEEN PARADE & BARBECUE**   Free+$$
83rd annual. Costumed children parade from Junipero down Ocean to Monte Verde and back. Free parade 11am at Devendorf Park, barbecue at noon, adults $10, children $3. Free ice cream for the children. Entertainment by local band. Benefit for the Mayor's Youth Fund. Tickets at City Hall or call 625-0450, 624-2781.

October 31   **SUNDOWN BEACH FIRE**   Free
On Carmel Beach, 13th and Scenic Drive, at sundown with Taelan Thomas. For twenty years, local bohemians meet to share ghost stories, poems, readings and mythic tales. Bring log, soulful story, poem, or music to share. 659-3947.

NOVEMBER

November tba   **ANNUAL HOLIDAY FESTIVAL**   Free
Based on the beginning of the advent season, balladeers, carolers, minstrels, entertainers, and booths in a magical outdoor marketplace. St. Nick rides in on his white horse and offers a surprise. 1-4pm at The Barnyard, Highway 1 and Carmel Valley Road. 624-8886.

DECEMBER

December   **KINDERGARTEN ART SHOW**   **Free**
Pat Spencer's kindergarten class artwork show in the cafe area of The Thunderbird Bookshop in The Barnyard Shopping Village. 624-1803.

December 3   **CARMEL LIGHTS UP THE SEASON**   **Free**
An open house at Carmel Plaza. Complimentary photos with Santa follows the tree lighting ceremony. 5pm at Devendorf Park, on Ocean Ave. between Junipero and Mission Streets. 624-0137.

December 4-5   **CHRISTMAS FESTIVAL**   **Free+$$**
1-4pm each day. Music, carolling, entertainment, food and more. Benefit High School Padres. The Barnyard. 624-8886.

Support The Performing Arts in Monterey County

Some of these organizations offer free performances, and all are run with the generous help of volunteers. Call for more information.

Monterey County Theatre Alliance

- California's First Theatre
  Scott & Pacific Streets, Monterey, CA 93940. 375-4916
- Carmel Ballet Academy & Dance Kids, Inc.
  P.O. Box 2586, Carmel, CA 93921. 624-3729
- Forest Theater Guild - also CCMC member.
  P.O. Box 2325, Carmel-by-the-Sea, CA 93921. 626-1681
- Magic Circle Theatre
  15475 Via Los Tulares, Carmel Valley, CA 93924. 659-8244
- Monterey Peninsula College Theatre
  980 Fremont St., Monterey, CA 93940. 646-4213
- Pacific Repertory Theatre - also CCMC member.
  P.O. Box 222035, Carmel, CA 93922. 622-0100
- Practically Perfect Productions
  P.O. Box 222846, Carmel, CA 93922. 649-1531
- Third Studio
  602 Larkin St., Monterey, CA 93940. 373-4389
- Unicorn Theatre
  320 Hoffman Ave., Monterey, CA 93940. 649-0259
- The Western Stage - also CCMC member.
  156 Homestead Ave., Salinas, CA 93901. 755-6816 or 375-2111.

Cultural Council for Monterey County

- Carmel Bach Festival, 624-2046
  Concerts at Sunset Center and Mission; Chapel in the Forest, P.B.
- Carmel Music Society, 625-9938.
  All concerts at Sunset Center, Carmel.
- Chamber Music Society of the Monterey Peninsula, 625-2212
  All concerts at Sunset Center, Carmel.
- Great Performances, 977-1690
  Performances at Sherwood Hall, Salinas.
- Keyboard Artist Series, 624-7971
  All concerts at Sunset Center, Carmel.
- Monterey Blues Festival, 394-2652
  All concerts at Monterey Fairgrounds.
- Monterey County Symphony, 624-8511
  Concerts at Sunset Center, Carmel, and Sherwood Hall, Salinas.
- Monterey Jazz Festival, 373-3366
  All concerts at Monterey Fairgrounds.
- Mozart Society of California, 625-3637
  All concerts at Church of Religious Science, Monterey.
- Performance Carmel, 624-3996
  Concerts at Hartnell College Main Stage, Salinas.
- Portofino Presents, 373-7379
  Performances at P.G. Art Center, and Church of Religious Science.

Entertainment
Music & Dancing

◆ **Mission Ranch**. Dinner music, then sing-along/Open Mic at piano bar. Tue-Thurs, 6-9pm, piano music, 9-midnight. Sunday brunch jazz, 10am-2:30pm. No cover. 26270 Dolores (behind Carmel Mission) off Rio Road. Wonderful pastoral views from the dining room. 1850 Farmhouse at the Ranch, opposite. 625-9040.

◆ **Highlands Inn**. Dancing 9-midnight Fri-Sat; piano jazz Mon/Wed, 6-9pm. No cover. Unbeatable ocean views. Carmel Highlands, Highway 1, four miles south of Carmel, 624-3801.

◆ **Cypress Inn**. Afternoon Tea, 2-4pm, reservations required. A Carmel tradition. Fee. Happy Hour, 5-7pm. Lincoln & 7th. 624-3871, 800-443-7443.

◆ **Robata Grill & Sake Bar**. Happy Hour, Thurs 5:30-7:30pm. Live music on the patio. No cover. 3658 The Barnyard, 624-2643.

◆ **La Gondola**. Live music every Fri-Sat 7:30-11pm; piano bar until 2am; Happy Hour, Wed-Fri 4-7pm. Dine 'til midnight 7 days a week. 3690 The Barnyard, Highway 1 and Carmel Valley Road. No cover. 626-0430.

◆ **Lugano Swiss Bistro**. Dancing Fridays 7-11pm. No cover. Under the windmill in The Barnyard, Highway 1 and Carmel Valley Road. 626-3779.

◆ **Caffé Cardinale Coffee Roasting Company**. Live music on Friday nights during the summer. No cover. Ocean Avenue and Dolores Street. 626-2095.

◆ **The Jazz Store**. The World's First All-Jazz Store. Official Monterey Jazz Festival off-site merchandise headquarters. Watch DJs at work playing your jazz favorites live on-air while you shop. 236 Crossroads Blvd. Call for entertainment dates and prices, 624-6432.

Music & Dancing Groups

◆ **Big Band Swing & Latin lessons** Sun 6 and 7pm, Carmel American Legion. Pre-registered intro, $5; ongoing, $8; drop-ins $10. 800/368-0415.

◆ **Greek Folk Dancing** with Greek Dancers of the Monterey Peninsula at Sunset Center, Rm. 10, 9th and San Carlos. Beginners, Tues, 6:30pm, Intermediate and advanced, 7:30-9pm. No partner needed; all ages welcome. Darold Skerritt, Judy Lind, 375-2549. $4 night. September through June. http://members.xoom.com/xoros/. The Greek Village Dancers provide free entertainment monthly at various Monterey Peninsula convalescent homes and hospitals and perform at the Greek Orthodox Church in Monterey, the Feast of Lanterns in Pacific Grove, and First Night® Monterey.

◆ **Music Together**, cutting-edge music enrichment program for infants, toddlers, preschoolers and their parents & caregivers. Songs, chants, movement, instrument play, free demonstration classes. 642-2424.

Theatre & Dance

◆ **'Dances of Universal Peace'** held 7-9pm, second Saturdays at the Community Church of the Monterey Peninsula on Carmel Valley Road, one mile from Highway 1. Participants will learn how to dance and chant in unison with guitar, drum, and flute music. No experience or partner is required; a $5 donation. Margot Edwards, 375-1974 or Pat Dally, 625-1136.

◆ **Carmel Music Society.** All concerts at 8pm at Sunset Center. Students in grades 6-12 can attend free concerts through the student ticket program which is funded by grants through local schools. 625-9938.

◆ **Pacific Repertory Theatre.** Presents free performances at TheatreFest during the summer. Live theatre at Golden Bough Theatre, Monte Verde btwn 8th & 9th; Circle Theatre, Casanova btwn 8th & 9th; Forest Theater, Santa Rita and Mountain View. Presents Spring Festival in March/April, Summer Festival May-July, and Carmel Shake-speare Festival, July-October. For details, contact Marcia Hardy at 622-0700.

◆ **Santa Catalina School** Drama Department, puts on some free performances. Call 655-9341 for dates and times.

◆ **Children's Experimental Theatre.** 624-1531.

Movie Theater

◆ **Crossroads Cinemas**, free refill on large popcorn and large drinks. Highway 1 at Rio Road. Seniors and matinees before 6pm, $4.50. 624-8682 (call 777-FILM #118). www.cinemacal.com

Yoga Classes

◆ **Kundalini Yoga** class is ongoing, meets 7:30-9pm Wednesdays. Bring mat, wear loose clothes, eat lightly. Unitarian Universalist Church, 490 Aguajito Road, Carmel. Donations accepted. 659-2969.

◆ **Yoga Center** in Carmel offers free yoga classes in July for kids 10-17. Ongoing Hatha Yoga classes, variety of styles. Yoga Center, Cottage 17, Sunset Center, San Carlos Street between 8th and 9th Avenues. 624-4949.

Parks & Recreation
Waterfront Activities

▲ **Carmel Beach**, west end of Ocean Ave., is a favorite beach for locals and visitors alike. White sand, beautiful sunsets, native cypress trees, walks, surfing, kites, sunbathing, and picnics. Fires allowed on the beach only south of 10th Avenue. No leash law for dogs on this beach or in city parks. Site of several city and private celebrations. 6am-10pm. 620-2000, 624-3543.

➤ **Monthly beach cleanup** by the Carmel Residents Association, from 10am-noon. Volunteers should bring their own gloves. 624-3208.

▲ **Carmel River State Beach**, Carmelo Road. Take Rio Road off Highway 1, turn left on Santa Lucia St., then left on Carmelo Road and into parking lot. Also called "Carmel River Lagoon and Wetlands Natural Preserve." Trails,

shallow lagoon for children, wildlife viewing, restrooms. Dogs on leash. Dangerous surf. California Sea Otter Game Refuge continues from the Carmel River south to San Luis Obispo County. Stewart's Cove is at the north end. To the south is a wonderful view of Pt. Lobos, and you can follow a small land trail to Monastery Beach. 624-4909.

The east side of the marsh is a protected bird sanctuary. Species: willett, heron, gull, Canadian Goose, kite, harrier, swallow, hawk, teal, mallard, tern, egret and killdeer. South of the river there is access from Ribera Road, near the white wooden cross. Portolá Cross, on the hill, marks the approximate spot where Gaspar de Portolá erected a cross in 1769 to signal passing ships. Open 7am-10pm.

■ **Carmelite Monastery Chapel** and gardens are open free to visitors 7:30am-4:30pm daily. Mass is 8am daily, except Thursday, and 9am on Sunday. 624-3043.

▲ **Monastery Beach**, across from the Carmelite Monastery, about 1.5 miles south of Ocean Avenue. No fee. Experienced scuba divers only. Unsafe for swimming or wading; wear shoes for walking on rocky sand. Open 7am-10pm; parking lot closes at sunset. 624-4909.

▲ **Point Lobos State Reserve**, 3 miles south of Carmel on Highway 1. You may park along Highway 1 and walk in free. Open 9am-5pm daily, with extended hours during summer. 624-4909. The crown jewel of California's state park system, called "the greatest meeting of land and water in the world" by landscape artist Francis McComas. R.L. Stevenson visited here in the 1840's and his *Treasure Island* is believed based on Pt. Lobos. Photography, painting, nature study, picnicking, diving and hiking, and spiritual contemplation are popular activities. 750 acres of underwater and 550 acres of ecological reserve filled with scenic trails, abundant wildlife and marine and terrestrial points of interest. Admission is $7 per car, $1 discount for seniors, and includes a trail map. Picnic tables, restrooms, telephone at main entrance. Docent talks and slide programs by previous arrangement.

Trails include: Lace Lichen Trail and Sea Lion Rocks, 3 miles, easy; Whaler's Cove & North Shore, 2.5 miles, moderate; Lace Lichen & Cypress Grove Trail, 3 miles, easy; South Plateau Trail & Bird Rock, 3 miles, moderate.

Diving is permitted only in Bluefish and Whalers Coves, swimming at China Cove. Underwater Reserve, the only underwater trail in the U.S., is accessed off Bluefish and Whalers Cove. Reservations for divers: ptlobos@mbay.net or 624-8413.

More Free Recreation Fun

➤ **Tennis Courts.** In addition to the one court at Forest Hill Park, Del Monte and Junipero, several free tennis courts are available at Carmel High School and Carmel Middle School, after school and on weekends. 624-3543.

➤ **Labyrinth Walk:** This ancient ritual for meditation and creative insight is available free to the public on the fourth Sunday of every month in Woodhull Hall at the Community Church of the Monterey Peninsula, one mile east of Highway 1 on Carmel Valley Road. A 40' diameter permanent labyrinth will be built on church grounds patterned after the one located in Chartres Cathedral, France (1220) and Grace Cathedral, San Francisco (1997). A 36' portable labyrinth is available now. Walks begin between 3 to 5 pm. Donald Mathews, 373-7809. To find more labyrinths: www.gracecathedral.org, click on "Veriditas."

➤ **Sierra Club, Ventana Chapter.** Free outings, call 624-1467. Meetings last Thursday of the month; call for meeting place and time. P.O. Box 5667, Carmel 93921 624-8032, fax 624-3371. http://ventana.org. Chapter Office and Sierra Club Book Store, Las Tiendas Building, Ocean Avenue between Dolores and San Carlos.

➤ **Peninsula Walk Walk Walk Club** meets at 8am, Mon-Fri, at the Carmel Mission; free and open to all. All levels welcome. Learn race walking on Thursdays. Call 372-2592 to arrange time.

➤ **On the Beach Surf Shop**, Ocean & Mission St. offers free wax and stickers with any purchase. Their walls are covered by surfboards dating back to the 1930s. 10-6 daily. 624-7282.

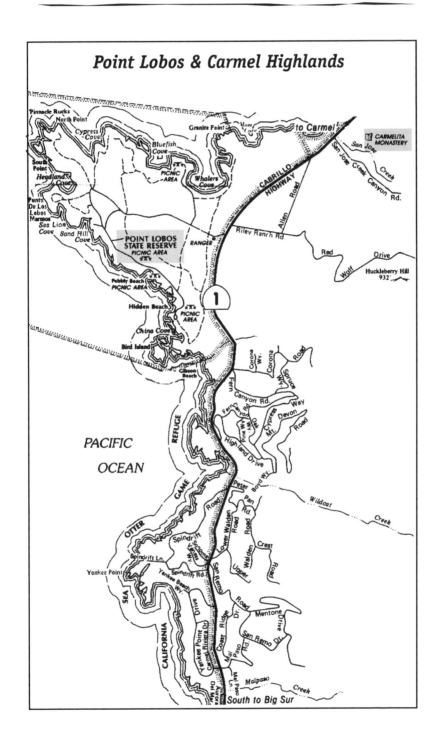

Point Lobos & Carmel Highlands

City Parks

▲ **Devendorf Park**, corner of Junipero and Ocean Ave., across from Carmel Plaza. A large open grassy area surrounded with benches and shade trees. WWII memorial, fish pond, restrooms, and a bus stop adjacent. Site of community events.

▲ **Piccadilly Park**, Dolores St., between Ocean and 7th Ave. 6am-11pm. Another downtown park, small and quaint and the perfect place to sit on benches, read, or relax under the giant shade tree. Granite fountain, restrooms. Designated open space through the efforts of the Carmel-by-the-Sea Garden Club.

▲ **Vista Lobos**, on 3rd between Torres and Junipero. A small park with vistas of Point Lobos. A recreational facility is housed and managed by City staff. Outdoor tables, barbecue, benches. Free parking. 624-3543.

▲ **Forest Theater**, Mountain View Ave., is a 2-acre park that houses the first outdoor theater west of the Rocky Mountains. Where the Mission Trail Nature Preserve ends.

▲ **Forest Hill Park**, Scenic Rd. and Camino del Monte. 5$^1/_2$ acres. Children's play area, volleyball and basketball court, grills, trails, tennis court, picnic tables, a horseshoe pit, shuffleboard, restrooms. No close parking. There are World Exercise stations along the road, for a good workout. 624-3543.

▲ **Mission Trail Nature Preserve**, Rio Road across from the Carmel Mission Basilica and Museum. Other access: Mt. View and Crespi, 11th, Hatton Road. 35 acres. Trails, benches, playground, trees, and wildflowers, spring and winter. **Rowntree Arboretum**, a native garden, dominates. **Flanders Mansion**, 1924, owned by the City of Carmel, is next to the garden. Dogs are welcome except in  the Arboretum, which has hitching posts at each entrance. Open dawn to dusk. Brochures for self-guided tours are available at all park entrances and at the Visitor Center, Eastwood Bldg., San Carlos near 5th. 624-3543.

Recreation Departments

▲ **Carmel Recreation Department**, San Carlos between 8th and 9th. The City provides programs and coordinates community activities through their offices at Sunset Community and Cultural Center. 626-1255.

▲ **Carmel Adult School**, 624-1714.

▲ **Carmel Youth Center** at 4th Ave. and Torres St., open 2-6pm Mon-Thurs; 2-11pm Fri; 3-10pm Sat, for middle and high school students. Ping-pong, billiards, video games, music, snack bar, weight room. 624-3285.

At the Mouth of the Valley

Carmel Rancho Shopping Center

Shop 'til you drop! Albertson's Food & Drug, Yellow Brick Road Thrift Store, Bagel Bakery, Rite Aid Drug Store, Cornucopia Health Foods, Brinton's House and Garden Shop, and more. Center office, 624-4670.

The Barnyard Shopping Village

A village of fifty shops, international restaurants and fine galleries situated in rustic barns amid lush gardens. Over an acre of gardens, brick walkways and authentic California architecture. Shops for apparel, fine art, gifts, home accessories, books, records and jewelry. Free events include tours of the gardens every Sunday at noon in the summer with horticulturist Margot Grych. Meet in front of the Thunderbird Bookshop/Cafe. www.thebarnyard.com. Free parking. Village office, 624-8886.

The Crossroads Shopping Center

In the summer, free music and dancing, Saturdays 1-3pm in the gardens. More than 90 boutiques and shops with apparel and shoes, jewelry and accessories, home accents, personal services, gifts and cards, specialty foods, entertainment, health and fitness. Open 10am-6pm daily. Tourist information, restrooms. Free parking. www.carmelcrossroads.com. 625-4106.

➤ **Cornucopia Community Market**, 26135 Carmel Rancho Blvd. 625-1454. Occasional free events.

➤ **Bountiful Basket**, in The Crossroads, offers free International Olive Oil & Vinegar Tastings, with a detailed history, 11am-5pm daily. 625-4457.

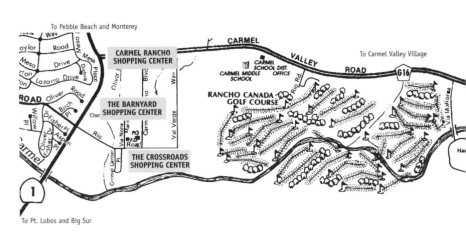

Free & Fun in
Carmel Valley

For a delightful day trip into the countryside, explore Carmel Valley with its rolling ranchland, expansive parklands, wine-tasting rooms, and a variety of shopping and entertainment opportunities. Carmel Valley Road intersects with Highway 1 just south of the Ocean Avenue exit to Carmel by-the-Sea. Follow Carmel Valley Road twelve miles east to Carmel Valley Village, a true country town with 283 days of sunshine a year, friendly inhabitants, and lots to see and do. Follow the numbers on the maps.

1 Encino de Descanso. Stone commemorating site where Indian carriers rested with their dead on the way to burial grounds deep in the valley.

2 Covey Restaurant. Live music, Fri-Sat, 6:30-9:30pm. <u>No cover.</u> Panoramic view of the valley. Quail Lodge Resort & Golf Club, Valley Greens Dr. 624-1581.

3 <u>Free outdoor community concert</u> by **The Monterey Symphony** at Quail Meadows adjacent to Quail Lodge, June 6, 1999. For info, call 624-8511.

4 Carmel Valley Racquet & Health Club. <u>First tennis lesson free</u>. 4 lessons for $40, plus free class. 27300 Rancho San Carlos Rd., 624-2737.

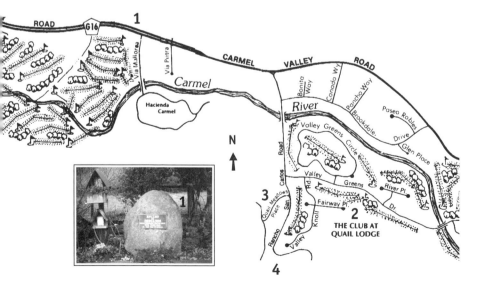

5 Valley Hills Shopping Center

An opportunity to stretch your legs and browse the shops: Baja Cantina Restaurant, Carmel Floral Company, Carmel Valley Antiques, Tancredi & Morgen Country Store, Hacienda Hay & Feed, Wagon Wheel Restaurant, Barbara's Bakery and Deli. More shops at Mid-Valley (see next page).

◆ **Baja Cantina.** Bands on Friday, 7:30-10:30pm; jazz guitar on Sundays, 1-4pm. No cover. Other special events, such as Super Bowl Sunday, Hot Chili Nites. Call for dates and information, 625-2252.

● **Hacienda Hay & Feed**, flowers and a good selection of decorative stone and ceramic pots at near wholesale prices. 624-5119.

6 Earthbound Farm – Organic farming at its best. Produce stand open to the public during the growing season, ending with a pumpkin patch at Halloween. Pick your own bouquet in their flower fields. 625-6219.

7 Farmer Joe's. Fruit, vegetable, and flower stand open daily during the summer months with a delectible variety of locally grown produce.

8 Carmel Valley Manor invites you in to see the local art on display. 8545 Carmel Valley Road. Daily 9am-5pm. 626-4711.

9 Chateau Julien – Free wine tasting, Mon-Fri, 8:30am-5pm. Sat-Sun, 11am-5pm. Free tours by reservation, Mon-Fri, 10:30 & 2:30, Sat-Sun, 12:30 & 2:30. 8940 Carmel Valley Rd. www.chateaujulien.com. 624-2600.

10 Griggs Nursery – Large nursery with shrubs, trees and flowers. Open Mon-Sat, 8am-5pm, Sun,10am-4pm. 9220 Carmel Valley Road. 626-0680.

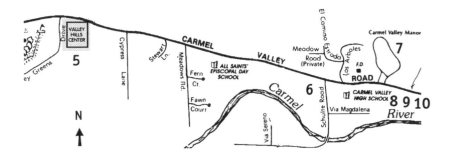

11 Mid-Valley Shopping Center

● **Micro Fudge**, offers <u>free samples</u>, 50¢ off when you buy ¼ lb. or more, and ¼ lb. FREE when you buy 1 lb. of their freshly-made cream and butter fudge. Mon-Sat, 10am-5pm. 620-1468.

● **Robin's Jewelry**, designs by Robin Mahoney. Robin will give you a <u>free magic wand</u> with any purchase. 11[ish]am-5pm, Tues-Sat, 626-4119.

● **Mid-Valley Antiques and Collectibles** has furniture, art, jewelry, toys, etc. Mon-Sat, 10:30am-5pm. 624-0261.

● **Deli Treasures**, deli, wine, catering, gift baskets. Mon-Fri, 7am-6:30pm, Sat 8am-5pm, Sun 9am-4pm. 624-9140.

● **Carmel Valley Coffee Roasting Co.**, espresso, latte, whole beans, etc. Mon-Fri, 7am-5pm, Sat-Sun, 7:30am-3:30pm. 624-5934.

12 **Trade Bead Museum & African Art Gallery**, <u>free</u>, upstairs, 27885 Berwick Dr. Collection of beads and original African Art. 624-4138.

13 **Paul Wilson Sculpture**, 27881 Robinson Cyn Rd. Unusual wood, stone, and concrete fountains and sculptures in the yard. 625-3112.

14 **Korean Buddhist Temple Sambosa**, 28110 Robinson Cyn Rd. You are invited to attend their Sunday services at 10am; see the beautiful altar. 624-3686.

15 **Oaks Lounge**. Jazz, Fri-Sat, 7-10pm. <u>No cover</u>. Carmel Valley Ranch Resort, 1 Old Ranch Road, 6 miles from Carmel, off CV Rd. 626-2533.

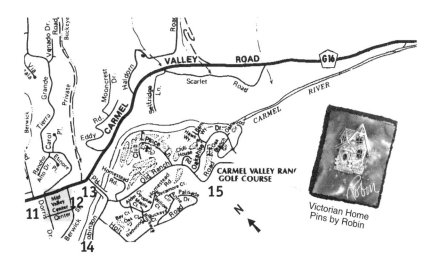

Victorian Home Pins by Robin

16 Garland Regional Park, 700 W. Carmel Valley Rd., 8.6 miles from Highway 1. Free admission; dogs are welcome. 4462 acres. Open year-round from sunrise to sunset. Carmel River flows at the entrance, near a visitor's center complete with maps and informative literature, docents and plant and wildlife exhibits. Day use activities include hiking, photography, horseback riding, nature study and educational field trips, landscape painting, walking & jogging, solitude, and limited mountain bike riding at the Cooper Ranch only. Picnic areas, restrooms. 659-4488.

▲ **Trails include:** Redwood Canyon River Trail, 3.5 miles, moderate; Lupine Loop with stone cliff and waterfall, 2.4 miles, easy. Call ahead for naturalist-led hikes, classroom programs and lectures: 659-6062.

▲ **Junior Rangers** meet every Wednesday afternoon 1-4 p.m. at Garland Park Visitor Center, 659-6062.

▲ **MIRA**, The Monterey Institute for Research in Astronomy, hosts a Star Party here, with telescopes available for public viewing plus Native American folk tales by the campfire. Call for dates, 659-2809.

17 Boronda Adobe, Boronda Rd., built in 1840 by Don José Manual and María Juana Boronda, maker of the original Monterey Jack Cheese. Now a private residence; drive-by only please.

18 Los Laureles Country Inn. Restaurant to reopen mid-1999 with new owners. Call for information about free entertainment, 659-2233.

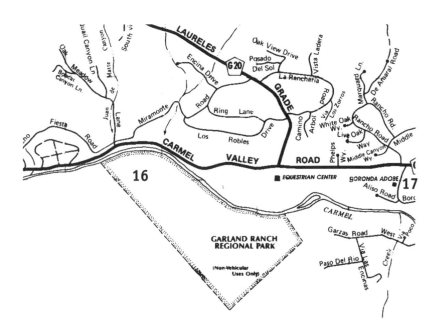

Carmel Valley Village #19

- **Carmel Valley Chamber of Commerce**, in the Village, 13 W. Carmel Valley Rd., Wed-Thurs-Fri, 11-5pm, Sat, 11am-3pm. 659-4000.

- **Durney Vineyards** has a new tasting room in the Village, 69 W. Carmel Valley Rd. $3 wine tasting cost applied to any purchase. Open Mon-Fri, 11am-5pm, Sat-Sun, 10am-5pm. 659-6220.

- **Robert Talbott Vineyards** has a new tasting room in the Village, open Sun-Thurs, 11-5pm; free glass with tasting price. Karen, 675-3000.

- **Georis Winery.** Minimum half-bottle purchase. Thurs-Sun, 12-4pm. Call for information about special events. 4 Pilot Road. 659-1050.

- **Bernardus Winery,** Free white wine tasting, red $3. Daily 11am-5pm. 5 W. Carmel Valley Road, in the Village. 659-1900.

- ◆ **Plaza Linda Mexican Restaurant.** Wed, Mexican music, 6-8pm, Thurs, blues music, 6-8pm, Fri, flamenco music, 6-8pm, Sat, jazz, 6-9pm. No cover. Authentic Mexican food. 9 Delfino Place. 659-4229.

- **White Oak Grill** displays local art. Thurs-Mon, 11:30-2:30 for lunch, 6-8:30pm for dinner. 9 Carmel Valley Road, in the Village. 659-1525.

- **Carmel Valley Library**, 65 W. Carmel Valley Road. Tues-Thurs, 10am-8pm, Fri-Sat, 10am-6pm. Storytime Theater Fri at 10:30am, Homework Center, Tues-Thurs, 3-5pm for all students. Great Books Reading Group every Fri, 2:30-4pm, adults. Figero Investment, 1st Tues, call 659-2377.

- ▲ **Carmel Valley Branch of the Boys & Girls Club** of the Monterey Peninsula, Community Hall, 25 Ford Road. Mon-Fri, 9am-6pm. Sports, arts & crafts, computer club, movies. Contact Jeff Magallanes, 659-2308.

- ▲ **Carmel Valley Community Park and Youth Center** facilities include activity hall, swimming pool, horseshoes, volleyball court, gazebo stage, play area, barbecue pits, and open space. Free admittance. 25 Ford Road. 659-3983, fax 659-9373. Rentals: 659-5287.

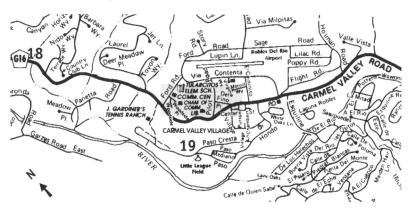

On Cachagua Road East of the Village

1 Galante Vineyards. <u>Free wine tasting</u> by appointment, <u>free tours</u>, Sun-Fri, 11am-3pm. 18181 Cachagua Road. 415/331-1247.

2 Joullian Vineyard. Tasting by appointment, Mon-Fri, 11am-3pm. 20300 Cachagua Road. 659-2800.

3 Carmel Valley Tennis Camp, 20805 Cachagua Road. <u>Free T-shirt</u> to camp participants. Kids: summer; Adults: spring and fall. 659-2615.

4 Cachagua Community Park and Los Padres Reservoir. <u>Free admittance.</u> Follow the signs from the Village to Cachagua, then to Nason Road and the Park. Fishing, ballfield, tot-lot playground, picnic facilities, swimming, row boats, hiking trails past **Los Padres Dam** into the **Los Padres National Forest.** Site of the annual Cachagua Country Fair each May. Open 9am-6pm daily. Dogs on leash or immediate voice command. Cachagua Com. Center, 659-8108.

5 COMSAT Jamesburg Earth Station, past the Village on Cachagua Road, a 34-ton, 10-story antenna dish, focused on a satellite more than 22,000 miles away. Wed 1-3pm, <u>free guided tours.</u>

6 Chews Ridge, 6 miles from Jamesburg, a small town east of the Village. A popular spot for camping and hiking, it is also the location for the MIRA Observatory and Oliver Observing Station.

■ **Oliver Observing Station** on Tassajara Road. 36-inch professional research telescope and mountaintop scientific research that runs on solar and wind power and collected rainwater. Call 883-1000 ext. 58 or e-mail: mira@mira.org to make reservations and get directions. See Calendar of Events for dates of free tours.

7 Tassajara, Zen Buddhist Center. Known for its healthful waters and their restorative benefit, a few days at this retreat will also restore your spirit. Fee. Tassajara is operated as a Soto Zen Buddhist monastery, providing a meditation and work place for monks and students. Guests may participate from early May until the first week in September at five-day retreats, a series of workshops combining Zen practice with poetry, hiking, and yoga, or simply hot soaks in the bathhouse and delicious vegetarian meals. You'll want to explore the surrounding woods and swim in the warm water pool. Shared and private accommodations from stone rooms, cabins, and yurts are available. Day guests are permitted from 8am-5pm. Costs vary. Continue through Carmel Valley Village on Carmel Valley Road and turn right at Tassajara Road to Jamesburg and follow the signs. For reservations: 415/431-3771. For more information: call 415-431-4438, or write Zen Buddhist Center, Tassajara Reservation Office, 300 Page Street, San Francisco, 94102.

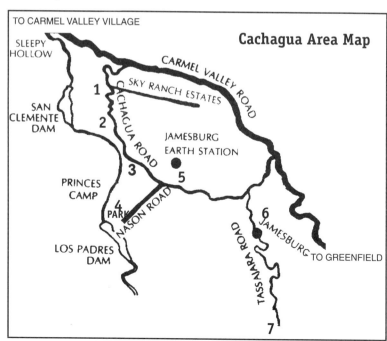

1999 Calendar of Events

Information subject to change. Please call in advance to verify.

JANUARY

January 18   **A VILLAGE AFFAIR**   **$$**
Gourmet food and wine tasting, silent and live auctions to benefit the Community Park Addition Fund. 5:30-8:30pm, Roy Woods Bldg., CV Village, 659-5099.

FEBRUARY

February 13   **AN EVENING AT THE BUCKEYE**   **$$**
Benefit for the CV Library by the Friends of the Library, 65 W. Carmel Valley Rd. Buffet dinner, 6-9pm. Entertainment, 7pm. Live auction. 659-4575.

APRIL

April to October   CLASSIC CARS HOT CHILI NITES   **Free**
Every Thursday, begins and ends with daylight savings time changes. See 30-100+ cars of local Stars: Hot Rods, Classic Cars, and Special Interest Cars. Special $7 barbecue and live music. 6-9pm. Third Thursdays is free raffle and hats. Rhythm and blues bands. Baja Cantina, 7166 Carmel Valley Road, in the Valley Hills Center, next to Quail Lodge. 625-BAJA (2252).

April 30-May 2   CARMEL GARDEN SHOW   **$$**
Showcase of garden materials, entertaining and the latest in interior and exterior room designs. Quail Lodge. <u>Volunteer opportunities</u>. 625-6026.

MAY

May tba   GARDEN ANGEL CRAFTS & BAKE SALE   **Free**
Carmel Valley Community Chapel. Call for info: 659-2278.

May 9   **MOTHERS DAY BRUNCH**   **$$**
11am-2pm, to benefit CV Community Park, at Holman Ranch. 659-2640.

May 16   **GARDEN WALK**   **$$**
Walking tours of Carmel Valley gardens. 624-3671.

May 16   **RUMMAGE SALE**   **Free**
Congregation Beth Israel. Call for more information, 624-2015.

May 23   **OBSERVATORY TOUR**   **Free**
Monterey Institute for Research in Astronomy (MIRA) invites you to experience their very popular free tour of the Oliver Observing Station on Tassajara Road, 1pm and 3pm. See their 36-inch professional research telescope and discover how their mountaintop scientific research runs on solar and wind power and collected rainwater. Call 883-1000 ext. 58 or email mira@mira.org to make reservations and get directions.

JUNE

June 6   **MONTEREY SYMPHONY CONCERT**   Free
Monterey Symphony presents their annual free outdoor community concert at Quail Meadows adjacent to Quail Lodge. 11:30am gates open, concert at 1pm. Gourmet food and beverages sold to benefit the Symphony and the SPCA. 624-8511, fax 624-3837.

June 26   **CACHAGUA COUNTRY FAIR**   Free
Children's games, story-telling, entertainment, horseshoe and softball games, pie-baking contest, silent and live auction, drawing, arts and crafts fair, food booths. 11am-9pm at the Cachagua Community Center on Nason Road. 659-4433.

June 27   **OBSERVATORY TOUR**   Free
See May 23.

JULY

July 10 "GREAT BALLS OF FIRE" STREET DANCE & BARBECUE $$
Mid-Carmel Valley Volunteer Fire Department benefit at Mid-Valley Shopping Center. Barbecue, $10, at 6pm, dancing 8pm-midnight. 624-5907.

July 10-11   **DEL MONTE KENNEL CLUB SHOW**   Free
A comprehensive representation and competition of registered purebred dogs. Carmel Middle School, 8am-4pm. Info, 333-9032.

July 25   **OBSERVATORY TOUR**   Free
See May 23.

AUGUST

August 6-8   **CARMEL VALLEY FIESTA**   Free+$$
Arts and crafts, children's games, swim meet, dog show, and talent contest in the Village Park, noon-5pm Sat-Sun. Live music continuous from noon. Friday night barbecue at Trail & Saddle Club. Clowns and Fiesta Parade, Saturday 11am. www.cvvillage.com/fiesta. 659-2038.

August 15   **WINEMAKER'S CELEBRATION**   Free+$$
25 Monterey, Carmel Valley and Salinas Valley vintners open their doors for a day of complimentary tasting, tours, and fun in the sun. Winemakers' Celebration at the Custom House Plaza Saturday, tickets $18, includes wine tasting, various exhibits, and a food fair prepared by many of the county's finest chefs, plus a souvenir wine glass. Special discounts on cases, tastings of rare wines. Visit A Taste of Monterey Wine Visitors Center on Cannery Row for more complimentary tasting. From 11am to 4pm. For complete information, call Monterey County Vintners and Growers Association at 375-9400; ask them to fax you a brochure.

August 22   **OBSERVATORY TOUR**   Free
See May 23.

August 26-28   **BROOKS USA AUCTION**   **$$**
Classic car auction, Quail Lodge, Carmel Valley. Viewing August 26-28. Auction starts 5pm, Aug. 28. Valerie, 415-391-4000.

August 27   **CONCOURS ITALIANO**   **Free+$$**
100 Years of Fiat. Drive-by presentations, booths of classic car memorabilia, and a corral of non-Italian cars such as Dodge Vipers, Mercedes, Jaguars, and Porsches, Italian fashion show and opera. More than 500 classic Italian cars. You can see these lovely cars touring the Peninsula throughout the weeks before and after the event. 9am-4:30pm. Quail Lodge Resort and Golf Club, 8205 Valley Greens Dr. 624-1581, 425-688-1903.

SEPTEMBER

September tba   **CARMEL VALLEY RANCHER'S DAYS**   **Free**
Cowboys compete for cash prizes at Carmel Valley Trail and Saddle Club, E. Garzas Road. Events include cutting competition, queen contest horsemanship, team roping, stock horse, simulated calf branding with whitewash, open team penning, kids' events. Free admission to all events. Wild boar barbecue, steak/chicken barbecue and snack bar; live music Saturday evening. Proceeds from entry fees and food sales benefit schools, 4 H clubs, fire stations and others. 659-9221.

September 6   **GOSPEL FESTIVAL**   **Free**
"Sweetest Sounds This Side of Heaven." Live performances from soul to blues, jazz and gospel. Reasonably priced barbecue all day, free kids' activities, volleyball, arts & crafts booths. Swimming pool $3. 11am-5pm at Carmel Valley Community Center, 25 Ford Road near the Village. Take Carmel Valley Exit off Highway 1, drive 12 miles, turn left on Ford Road. Barbara Sherman, 625-3492.

September 12   **GARY IBSEN'S TOMATOFEST™**   **$$**
The largest tomato tasting event in the nation featuring more than 200 tomato varieties at Quail Lodge. Music, children's garden project. 12:30-4:30pm, Tickets $40. Children under 16 free. Proceeds benefit Carmel Valley Community Youth Center, Carmel Youth Center and AIWF Children's Garden Project. Reservations: 626-2475, fax 622-9468. Info: call 625-6041.

September 19   **FALL FESTIVAL**   **Free**
Live music, kids' games, crafts, silent auction, farmers' market, country store, rummage sale and raffle prizes. Barbecue. An outdoor Mass at 10:30am, Festival following from noon to 5pm. Our lady of Mt. Carmel Church at 9 El Caminito, just up from Carmel Valley Road in the Village. 659-2224.

September 20   **"GREAT BOWLS OF FIRE"**   **$$**
Chili cookoff at Holman Ranch, 5-8pm. $15. To benefit the Carmel Valley Chamber of Commerce. 659-4000.

September 26   **OBSERVATORY TOUR**   **Free**
See May 23.

OCTOBER

October   **SCENIC DRIVE**   **Free**
Take a scenic drive through the county at Halloween to see the fall colors and visit the pumpkin patches. Farmer Joe's Produce, Carmel Valley Road at Schulte Road, is open daily during the growing season. Decorative pumpkins fill the field next to the parking lot and the white wooden farm stand. Earthbound Farm's Farm Stand, 7230 Carmel Valley Road, open daily 9:30am to 6pm until Halloween. Hacienda Hay and Feed, 7180 Carmel Valley Road just past Earthbound Farms. Maze, petting zoo, and great pumpkins all month, 8:30am to 5:30pm. 624-5119.

Oct tba   **TULARCITOS FALL FESTIVAL**   **Free**
Call for more information, 659-2276.

October 2   **SOUL AND BLUES REVUE**   **Free+$$**
2-10pm at Hidden Valley Music Seminars, Carmel Valley Village. Free seminars on variety of instruments for musicians of all ages until 5pm. Show/barbecue following, $40, under age 21, $20. Net profits for local youth music programs. Gary Luce, 624-0101, Barry Harrow, 659-1234, or Jennifer Hill, 625-5137.

October 3   **JEWISH FOOD FESTIVAL**   **Fee**
Jewish Food Festival & Crafts Faire. Corned beef, kugels, blintzes, lox and bagels, matzo ball soup, chopped liver and cabbage rolls, rugelah, mandelbrot, strudel and cheesecake. Music, entertainment, wandering storytellers, strolling musicians, cooking demonstrations, synagogue tours and more. Crafts booths and exhibits offering jewelry, art, clothing, and other handmade items with a Jewish theme or made in Israel. 10am-3:30pm. Free entrance to seniors over 65 and children under 12. $3 adults, $1 teenagers. Congregation Beth Israel, 5716 Carmel Valley Road. Park at the Carmel Middle School for free shuttle bus. 624-2015, 624-8272.

October 24   **OBSERVATORY TOUR**   **Free**
See May 23.

October 30   **ALL SAINTS' FALL FESTIVAL**   **Free**
Carnival booths, costume parade, karaoke, haunted house, train rides, cake walk, drawings. Barbecue. Free ice cream. 11am-3pm, All Saint's Episcopal School, 8060 Carmel Valley Road. 624-9171.

October 31   **"HOWL-O-WEEN"**   **Spectators free**
"Costume Competition for Man's Best Friend" presented by Del Monte Kennel Club. Costume competition for you and your dog. All ages welcome to participate. Prizes. $10 to enter dog competition (register 8:30-9:30am); $3 to enter the costume contest. CV Community Park, 25 Ford Road. Ruth Edwards, 649-4280 or 333-9021.

October 31   **COSTUME PARTY**   **Free**
Live music, complimentary limousine rides at 9pm, prizes, drink specials. Hosted by Carmel Valley Ranch and Baja Cantina, 7166 Carmel Valley Road, 3.5 miles from Highway 1. 625-2252.

October 31   **TRICK-OR-TREAT**   **Free**
Mid-Valley Shopping Center has free candy for those in costume. 5.5 miles up Carmel Valley Road from Highway 1.

NOVEMBER

November 25   **THANKSGIVING DINNER**   **Free**
Carmel Valley Community Thanksgiving Dinner for all residents, 1-4pm, Carmel Valley Community Center and Cachagua Community Center. The dinners are free and all Carmel Valley residents are invited. Volunteers are needed on Nov. 24, 25 and 26 to help with food preparation, serving, and cleanup. For reservations or information, call 659-2640.

DECEMBER

December 4   **CHRISTMAS TREE LIGHTING**   **Free**
Community gets together to light up the tree, 4-5pm, Carmel Valley Community Park in the Village. 659-2640.

December 11   **SANTA FLY-IN**   **Free**
Santa Claus arrives at the Carmel Valley Airport, 11am, followed by a Christmas Parade to the Community Youth Center. 659-3983.

The Holman Ranch

The Ranch hosts several benefits for the City and other community organizations during the year: "Great Bowls of Fire," chili cookoff, Mon. Sept. 20, 5-8pm, benefits the Chamber of Commerce; Carmel Valley Women's Club "Arabian Nights", May 21, 5-8pm; "Wild Celebration," Oct. 17, 2-5:30pm, to benefit the SPCA; "Life's Greatest Luxuries," Nov. 7, car raffle, wine, jazz, food to benefit Special Olympics. Holman Ranch Road. Call for complete information, 659-6054, 659-2640.

Free & Fun in
Marina & North County

Marina Sculpture Center

Salinas River Wildlife Refuge

Lazzerini Farms, Hwy 1, Moss Landing

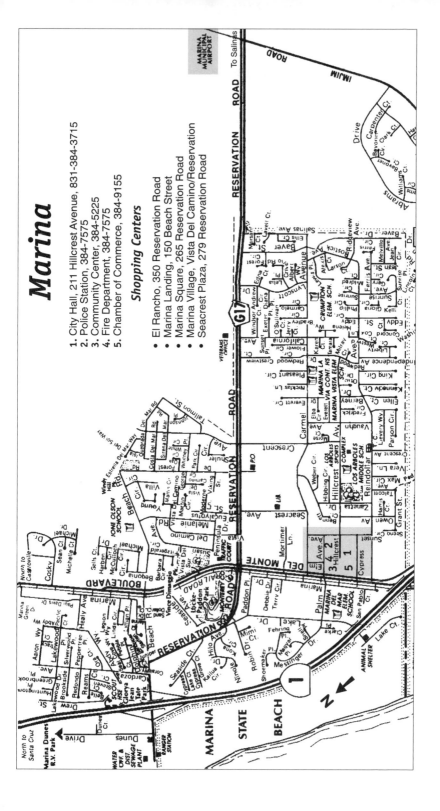

Marina

1. City Hall, 211 Hillcrest Avenue, 831-384-3715
2. Police Station, 384-7575
3. Community Center, 384-5225
4. Fire Department, 384-7575
5. Chamber of Commerce, 384-9155

Shopping Centers

- El Rancho, 350 Reservation Road
- Marina Landing, 150 Beach Street
- Marina Square, 265 Reservation Road
- Marina Village, Vista Del Camino/Reservation
- Seacrest Plaza, 279 Reservation Road

Marina Municipal Airport

Marina Municipal Airport, east on Reservation Rd. off Highway 1, left on Imjim, is alive with activities. Marina is also seeking volunteers to provide services at the airport: tree trimming, weed abatement, litter removal and painting, between 8am-5pm, Wed-Sun. For more information, call the city clerk's office at 384-3715, ext. 7101.

■ **Monterey Sculpture Center** has 45-min. free guided tours from 10:30am-4pm, Mon-Fri. Right, foundrymen pouring molten bronze into ceramic shell molds. Left, welding monumental bronze by sculpture artist Betty Saletta and preparing piece for patina. The Center will also open a free 10 acre Sculpture Park and Nature Walk in 1999. Walk through oak groves to see famous sculptures. For more information, call Christine, 384-2100.

➤ Free Airplane Rides – Youth Orientation Flights at Marina Airport. **Young Eagles Program** of Chapter 204 of The Experimental Aircraft Association. Local pilots and aviators take up kids ages 8-17 for a free 15-20 minute ride that may include hands-on experi-  ence. Worldwide endeavor to fly 1 million kids by 2003, the anniversary of the maiden flight of Wilbur and Orville Wright at Kittyhawk. Adult permission is required. Flights are four times a year at 10am on Saturdays. For information or reservations, call Marv at 373-6587.

➤ **Skydive Monterey Bay**, 3261 Imjim Road. Wear comfortable clothes and just show up – they supply the training and equipment. Reservations are recommended but not required. Skydives daily, weather permitting. www.skydivemontereybay.com. 384-3483, 888-229-5867.

➤ **Balloons-by-the-Sea**, hot air ballooning, 3261 Imjim Rd. 800-464-6420.

➤ Sailplane Rides from $80 to $160 are at the Marina Airport. Call **Monterey Bay Soaring Adventures** at 800-696-SOAR.

1999 Calendar of Events

Information subject to change. Please call in advance to verify.

April 3   **MARINA 5-MILER**   Spectators free
Meet at Vince DiMaggio Park, 8:30am, to register. 9am: children 11 and under, free 1-mile fun run. Adults: 5 miles, fees $15-$20. Under 18 years to 60 years+. Children's Easter Egg Hunt after the run. Free drawing. Dj entertainment by KWAV. Benefit for city recreation programs. Free soda and ribbons. 3200 Del Monte. 384-3715.

June 5-6   **MARINA MOTORSPORTS SWAP MEET**   Free
7am at Marina Airport, Reservation Road. Free admission; free parking for 1972 and older cars (not for sale); general parking $2. Swap spaces $20, car corral $15. Food, music. 384-1200.

August tba   **MULTI-CULTURAL ARTS FESTIVAL**   Free
Presented by Marina Arts Council, 10am-5pm, Opens with a march from the corner of Reservation Road and Del Monte to the festival site at Vince DiMaggio Park on Del Monte Blvd. Dancers, musicians, writers, artists, poetry contest winners, great food and more. Roz Davidson, 883-8750.

September 11-12   **MOTORSPORTS SWAP MEET**   Free
7am at Marina Airport, Reservation Road. Free admission; free parking for 1972 and older cars (not for sale); general parking $2. Swap spaces $20, car corral $15. Food, music. 384-1200.

October   **SUNDAY MUSIC SERIES**   Free
Free Sunday concerts in Vince DiMaggio Park, 12:30-4:30pm. 384-4636.

October 30   **10K RACE/WALK AT FT. ORD**   Free
19th Memorial for Giulio DePetra, founder of the Monterey Peninsula Walk Walk Walk Club. Call Hansi Rigney for time and place, 626-6602.

October 31   **YOUNG LIFE PUMPKIN PATCH**   Free balloons
Pick your own among scarecrows, cartoon characters and bigger-than-life pumpkin carriages. Free balloons on weekends. Davis Road between Reservation Road and the Salinas River, 9am-5:30pm in October. Nonprofit youth organization. Call to verify location, Grace, 422-6441.

October 31   **HALLOWEEN HARVEST PARTY**   Free
An alternative to trick-or-treating from 5-8pm at Bay Believer's Church, 3056 Del Monte Blvd. Booths, games, a cookie walk and other family activities. Call 384-0241.

December   **MRWMD RECYCLED ART FESTIVAL**   Free
Sculptures and artwork created by local artists from reused objects and materials. Monterey Regional Waste Management District, 14201 Del Monte Blvd., two miles north of Marina. Mon-Sat, 8am-4:30pm. 384-5313.

December 3   **CHRISTMAS TREE LIGHTING**   Free
Entertainment, refreshments and Santa Claus treats for the children. 6pm at Marina Village Shopping Center, 265 Reservation Road. Sponsored by the Marina Rotary Club. 384-0425

December 18   **CHILDREN'S CHRISTMAS PARTY**   Free
A visit from Santa Claus is expected (ages 1-10). Sponsored by the Civic Association of Marina, 11am at the Civic Center, 211 Hillcrest Ave.

December 25   POTLUCK CHRISTMAS DINNER   Free
Noon to 5pm at the Marina Community Hall, 221 Hillcrest Ave. Attendees are asked to bring a favorite dish to share, and place settings. People who can't bring food are asked to volunteer their time. The dinner is free and open to everyone. 394-4445.

Entertainment

◆ **Challengers Club**, 223 Reindollar. No cover. Karaoke nightly 9pm-1:30am, except Tues-Wed starts at 10pm; Friday is Ladies Night. Pool tournaments Tue-Thurs, women's pool tournament, Wed. 384-4642.

◆ **Marina Club**, 204 Carmel Ave. (off Del Monte). No cover. Karaoke Thurs, Sat-Sun,Tues. 384-7632.

◆ **Higher Ground Christian Coffeehouse & Bookstore**, 3056 Del Monte Blvd. Contemporary Christian music Fri, 7pm. Donation, $3. 625-3492.

Library & Cultural Council

● **Marina Library**, 266 Reservation Road, Suites K and L, 384-6971. Hours: Tues, 10am-6pm, Wed-Thurs, 12-8pm, Fri-Sat, 10am-5pm. Closed Sun-Mon. Preschool storytime, Tues-Thurs, 2:30-5pm. Homework Center, Tues-Thurs, 2:30-5pm for students in grades 1-12.

● **Marina Arts Council Poetry Competition**, deadline July 1. Countywide, children and youth arts scholarship, to age 16. The Marina Arts Council has lots of cultural activities. Contact Roz Davidson, 883-8750, or write to P.O. Box 429, Marina, CA 93933.

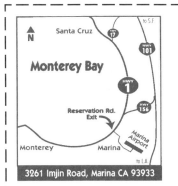

Parks & Recreation

▲ **Marina State Beach**, off Highway 1 at Reservation Road. 170 acres. Dolphins, pelicans, whale watching in season (Dec-Mar), kite flying, sand dunes, boardwalk, fishing, hang-gliding, cafe, observation deck, surfing. Dangerous surf for wading or swimming. Dogs o.k. on beach, not on dunes.

▲ **Marina Dunes Open Space Preserve**, is located off Dunes Dr. just north of Marina State Beach. Most of these 10 acres of coastal dunes are being restored as endangered species habitat for the snowy plover, Smith's blue butterfly, and others, with coastal pedestrian access to the beach. Foundations of an old sand processing plant are still visible. Walking, jogging, dog-walking, exercise, photography, contemplation, fishing, family activities, sunbathing, surfing, and hang-gliding. This site provides a relatively quiet and underutilized access that has not yet been "found" by the crowds. Stay on designated paths and respect dune restoration and habitat closure signs. Open dawn to dusk. 384-7695, 659-4488.

▲ **Glorya Jean Tate Park**, Abdy Way and Cordoza Ave. 4 acres. Ballfield, community building, multiuse field, picnic area, playground, rentable rooms, restrooms. Field use by reservation only. 384-4636.

▲ **Locke-Paddon Park**, on Reservation Road near Del Monte Avenue. Unique vernal ponds, remnant salt marshes created 12,000 years ago in the last glacial retreat, are now a wildlife habitat. Original wetland wildlife preserve. Shoreline trail, picnic tables, restrooms. 384-4636.

▲ **Los Arboles Sports Complex**, Reindollar and Vaughn avenues. 6 acres. Ballfield, community building, trails, multiuse field, tennis, volleyball, restrooms. Snack bar. Field use by reservation only. 384-4636.

▲ **Vince DiMaggio Park**, Del Monte Blvd. and Reservation Rd. 1 acre. Community building (once the United Methodist Church sanctuary), is used for recreation department activities and has rentable rooms. A popular family picnic and playground site. 384-4636.

Bicycling

▲ **Bicycle path** along the beach goes north to Castroville and south to Pacific Grove. Call 384-9155 for other bike paths. **Community Center**, 211 Hillcrest Ave., conducts free bicycle and helmet safety programs. Call 384-5225. Free air and maps at **BoyerSports**, 721 Neeson Road, 883-4644.

Golf Clinic

▲ Free golf clinics with a PGA professional for **Fairway Partners**, the Salvation Army Monterey Peninsula Corp.'s junior golf program. Kids 7-17. Bayonet/Black Horse Golf Course at Ft. Ord driving range. Rides from Seaside available. Call for reservations: 899-4911 ext. 25.

Recreation Centers

▲ **Marina Senior Center.** Free ballroom dancing on Wednesdays, 12:15-2pm. For a modest fee, play bingo on Fridays from 12:15-3pm. Many more activities for seniors, call 384-6009.

▲ **Shea Gymnasium**, 4480 Col. Durham Road (Old Ft. Ord) is open for residents 14 and older to play basketball, Tues-Fri, 3-6pm (Fri 8pm), Sat, 10am-6pm, and Sun, 2-6pm. Registration required for free supervised sports activities Sat, 10-2pm. 899-6270.

▲ **Zaruk "Tak" Takali Teen Center**, 304 Hillcrest Ave., near Los Arboles Middle School, free big-screen TV, games and sports, 3-7pm weekdays. Special events like pizza parties, video nights and field trips. 884-9542.

▲ **Youth Center**, 211 Hillcrest Ave. is open Mon-Fri, 2-6pm, closed weekends and holidays. Variety of activities: ping-pong, pool, foosball, box hockey, tetherball, a merry-go-round, swings and a slide set. Portable basketball goals are available. Two playgrounds at Olson and Crumpton Schools are open after school, Mon-Fri, until 5pm, and supervised by staff. After-school youth sports leagues throughout the year. Monthly Activity Calendars can be picked up at playgrounds or the youth center. Programs are free. To register, call 384-4636 in the am or 384-3715 ext. 7203, 1-5pm.

More Marina Attractions

➤ **Western Hang Gliders**, located at Marina State Beach, offers free ground school for hang-gliding, open dawn to dusk, 384-2622.

➤ **Marina Dunes R.V. Park**, 3300 Dunes Dr. Exit Highway 1 at Reservation, west, to Dunes Dr., right. All sites are attractively landscaped for privacy and beauty. All sites have picnic table; some have cable TV and most have water/electric/sewer. Laundry room, restrooms with hot showers, store, recreation room. 384-6914, fax 384-0285.

➤ **Dunes Restoration, Beach Garden Project**. Volunteers needed to out-plant seedlings for revegetation of sand dunes. Call Joey, 659-1263.

➤ **Ocean Outreach Volunteers** conduct a training course for volunteers who wish to lead beach clean-up programs, assist with community festivals, and much more. 2222 East Cliff Dr. Suite 5A, Santa Cruz. 462-9122.

➤ For great bargains, visit Monterey Regional Waste Management District's Resale Shop, **Last Chance Mercantile**, 14201 Del Monte Blvd., 2 miles north of downtown Marina. Hours: Mon-Sat, 8am-4:30pm. 384-5313.

Moss Landing & Elkhorn Slough

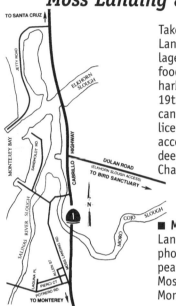

Take Highway 1 north of Monterey to Moss Landing, a New England type fishing village with storefronts, rusting boats, seafood restaurants, antique shops, and a busy harbor, once a thriving whaling station and 19th century shipping port. Wind surfing, canoeing and kayaking, boat ramp, fishing licenses and supplies, restrooms, wheelchair accessible. Port opens onto the 7,500-foot-deep submarine canyon of Monterey Bay. Chamber of Commerce, 633-4501.

Attractions

■ **Moss Landing Post Office**, 8042 Moss Landing Road. Lobby contains historical photos and articles about the first European settlers, whalers, and the founder of Moss Landing, Captain Charles Moss. Open Mon-Fri, 9am-5pm, Sat 9-12.

■ **Phil's Fish Market**, Sandholdt Road. The last remaining cannery, now a very popular restaurant and fish market. Bring your own pot to take home flavorful cioppino. Watch the sea critters in open tanks. Buy T-shirts with famous recipes. Open daily in the summer, 8:30am-8:30pm. Winter: Mon-Thurs, 10:30-6pm, Fri-Sat, 10:30-8pm. 633-2152.

■ **Monterey Bay Aquarium Research Institute**, 7700 Sandholdt Road. Research arm in the Marine Sanctuary for the world-famous Monterey Bay Aquarium. Call for date and time of their open house. 775-1700.

■ **Antique Stores**, an eclectic collection on Moss Landing Road, take you back to yesteryear. Browsing the shops is definitely a fun way to spend an afternoon and take home that inevitable souvenir. Several restaurants in the area will satisfy your appetite too.

Waterfront Activities

▲ **Salinas River State Beach**, on Potrero Rd. off Highway 1. Hiking and equestrian trails, wildflowers, fishing, fires at the north end only. Undercurrents make swimming unsafe. Salinas River National Wildlife Refuge, south of the beach, shelters brown pelicans, least terns and snowy plovers. Small ponds in the area are the remains of the Salinas River. 384-7695.

▲ **Elkhorn Slough National Estuarine Research Reserve**, NE of Moss Landing, 1700 Elkhorn Road, 2 miles north of Dolan Road. 1400 acres. Five miles of trails meander through this estuary area which is an important nursery area for fish, sharks and rays, and home to over 200 species of birds including herons, egrets, and brown pelicans. Rays and sharks can be spotted in the slough's shallow waters in midsummer. Guided trail walks 10am and 1pm weekends, wildflower walk 9am Fridays. Day-use fee $2.50. Closed Mon and Tue. Free Visitor Center with interpretive exhibits, trail maps and brochures. Hikes include: Long Valley Five Fingers Loop, 2.3 miles, easy; South Marsh Loop, 3.3 miles, easy. Special Mother's Day celebration in May and Estuary Day in mid-September. Be a volunteer docent! www.elkhornslough.com, 728-2822/728-5939.

▲ **Kirby Park**, off Elkhorn Road, midway down the slough. Fishing, boating, birding. **Nature Conservancy Preserve** is reached through the park. Wheelchair accessible, on-site guided tours and nature study, 728-5939.

▲ **Zmudowski State Beach** north of Moss Landing, turn on Struve Road and follow the signs to Giberson Road. 175 acres. A popular fishing and surfing spot where the Pajaro River meets the sea. Swimming, picnic, walks. Extends south to Moss Landing State Beach. Sand dunes and wetlands, equestrian trail, restrooms. 384-7695, 649-2836.

▲ **Moss Landing State Beach**, Jetty Rd. off Highway 1, south of Zmudowski. $3/car. Surfing, windsurfing, kayaking, canoeing, surf fishing, hiking, horseback riding, birdwatching, wooden pier, jetty. Restrooms. 384-7695.

▲ **Moss Landing Wildlife Area**, off Highway 1, dirt access road is north of Struve Rd. 649-2870.

Entertainment

◆ **Maloney's Harbor Inn**, live jazz, 6-9pm, Saturday, <u>no cover</u>. 724-9371.

◆ **Moss Landing Inn**, music, Wed-Sun, 9:30pm-1am, <u>no cover</u>. 633-9990.

1999 Calendar of Events

Information subject to change. Please call in advance to verify.

July 24-25   ANTIQUES & COLLECTIBLES FAIRE $$
8am-5pm. Over 200 vendors plus over 20 permanent shops. Pancake Breakfast 7am, fish fry 11am. Admission $2, <u>children under 12 free</u>. Free parking. No dogs. Halfway between Monterey and Santa Cruz on Hwy 1.

October   PUMPKIN PATCHES   Scenic drive
Springfield Farms, Highway 1 just south of Moss Landing, open 8:30am-5pm. 633-8041. Dominic's, Highway 1, 2 miles north of Moss Landing.

October tba   MARINE LABS OPEN HOUSE   Free
With touch tanks, seminars, videos, fish printing, puppet shows, current research, fresh seafood, algae pressing, dune and beach walks, kids' activities and more. Featuring their resident sea lions, Beaver, Sake and Nemo. Sat 11am-5pm, Sun 10am-5pm. Take Moss Landing Road off Highway 1 at Moss Landing. Turn onto Sandholdt Road and follow signs to parking area. No pets please. For more information, call MLML at 755-8650 or visit http://color.mlml.clastate.edu/www/.

October 1-3   MONTEREY BAY BIRD FESTIVAL   Free+$$
Second annual Monterey Bay Birding Festival. Join us for a variety of activities, including: Special tours: Elkhorn Slough (boat and kayak), Big Sur, Carmel River, Watsonville Slough, Moss Landing, Salinas River Wildlife Area and Special Pelagic Trips. Bird banding, bird songs and calls, photography, shorebirds, gulls, native plants, raptors. Live music, exhibits, food, special demonstrations. Free and fee workshops. 10am-5pm. 728-3890, 728-2822. For information, registration packet and schedule, contact the Elkhorn Foundation, 728-5939. e-mail esf@elkhornslough.com. Website: www.elkhornslough.org. <u>Experience Elkhorn Slough free on annual Clean-up Day</u>.

Surfin' Safari Slough

➤ Surfing is good at Moss Landing. Visit the **Moss Landing Surfshop** at 7544 Sandholdt Road for custom made surf boards and private lessons at reasonable prices. Call Richard, 633-6123.

➤ **Elkhorn Slough Safari**, a 2-hour cruise on a 27' pontoon boat, The Safari, with Captain Yohn Gideon. View otters and seals up close. Naturalist guide. Adults $24, Under 14, $18. Reservations. 633-5555, www.elkhornslough.com.

➤ **Annual Clean Up Elkhorn Slough Day**, third Saturday in September, 9am to noon, Kirby Park on Elkhorn Road. <u>Free T-shirts</u> for the first 75 volunteers. Bring your friends, boots or kayak. 622-7651.

Prunedale

Chamber of Commerce 831-663-0965

August 29   FUN DAY AT MANZANITA PARK   Spectators free
Castroville Blvd., off San Miguel, between Highways 101 and 156. Children's Fun Run, 10K/5K runs and 5K walk, softball tournament. Fund-raiser for Manzanita Sports Complex. Info: Diane Carrillo, 663-2108.

October tba   ARTS & CRAFTS FAIRE   Free
Artisans from the Tri-County area. Refreshments, clowns, music, line dancing, door prizes. Sat-Sun, 10am-4pm. Take Highway 101 to San Miguel Canyon Road, right on Moro Road, follow signs to Prunedale Grange Hall. Info: 663-5023.

More to See and Do

◆ **The Office**, Hwys 101-156, Prunedale, 663-4047. Country band for dancing Saturdays, 8:30pm, no cover. **R&O Lounge**, Hwys 101-156, Prunedale, 663-2318. Thurs, 9pm-1am, prizes, drink specials, no cover.

● **Monterey County Public Library**, 17822 Moro Rd. Preschool storytime, ages 2¹/₂-5yrs, Wed 11am. Homework Center, grades 1-12, Mon-Wed, 3-6pm. 663-2292.

▲ **Manzanita Park**, 464 acres of gently rolling hills sprinkled with manzanita, oak, and pine. Quiet, scenic trails are shared by hikers and horses in this multi-use natural center adjacent to Prunedale. Spectacular views of all of North County. 663-2699.

➤ **Mobilastics, Gymnastics**, 8475 Prunedale North Rd. Free trial class in gymnastics to first time students. Events include a Show Day in September, a Halloween Party in October, and a Summer Camp. 663-6028.

Pájaro

● **Monterey Free Library**, 29 Bishop St. Storytime (bilingual) Thurs, 11:30am. Homework Center, grades 1-12, Tues & Thurs, 2-6pm. 761-2545.

➤ **Pájaro Valley Golf Club**, a lush 18 hole course with scenic views. Open to the public, an historic course since 1926. 724-3851.

Aromas

● **Monterey County Free Library**, Blohm & Carpenteria Sts., in the Porter-Vallejo Mansion, historical landmark. Children's storytime Thurs 10am. Homework Center, grades 1-12, Wed 2-6pm, Thurs 1-5pm. Free summer reading program for all ages. 726-3240.

▲ **Royal Oaks County Park**, between Aromas and Prunedale on Maher Road off Echo Valley Road. 122 acres. The oldest park in the county, established in 1966. Softball diamond, tennis courts, basketball court, horseshoe pits, trails, volleyball standards, and picnic areas. Short trails, average .5 miles. Call 755-4895 for picnic reservations (up to 300). 663-2699.

Castroville

Chamber of Commerce 831-633-6545

Founded in 1863 by Juan B. Castro, Castroville is the second oldest town in Monterey County. The artichoke crop, introduced in 1920, made the

town famous. It is now the third largest cash crop in the Salinas Valley, making Castroville the official "Artichoke Center of the World." The annual **Artichoke Festival** draws visitors from all over the world to see the fascinating thistle. Marilyn Monroe was the first Artichoke Queen in 1947. This year's festival will boast more music, including a swing band, country music and a mariachi band; antique and classic automobiles and hot rods; Marilyn Monroe T-shirts, buttons, and other memorabilia. Castroville is busy sprucing up the town with a beautification plan for $25 million worth of improvements over the next decade. For more information: Castroville Festivals, Inc. P.O. Box 1041, Castroville, CA 95012-1041. 831-633-2465.

Castroville Attractions

■ **Giant Artichoke Restaurant**, 11261 Merritt St. See everything artichoke, including a giant 12' statue in front. One million people are rumored to have had their picture taken here. Open Mon-Thurs, 7am-4pm, Fri-Sun, 7am-9pm. 633-3204.

■ **Bing's Diner**, 10961 Merritt St., a "900 Series" streetcar built in the 1920s, used in Oakland, and converted to a diner in Castroville in 1950. Locals claim it's named after Bing Crosby who ate here during his early years of travel to Monterey County. Open 6am-8pm for breakfast, lunch and dinner. Try their famous ribs. 633-0400.

■ **La Scuola Ristorante**, 10700 Merritt St. This Italian restaurant is located in Castroville's original schoolhouse. Decor includes historical pictures of early Castroville. Open Tues-Sat, 11:30-2pm for lunch and 5-9pm for dinner. Sat 5-9 for dinner only. Closed Sun-Mon. 633-3200.

▲ **Castroville-Marina Bike Trail**, newly opened trails for bike enthusiasts take riders from the shore inland. Call 633-6545 or 384-9155.

▲ **Crane Street Park**. Castroville's newest park opened in February, 1999. Tot-lot playground, picnic table, and a small barbecue pit, a large grassy area, and a view of Castroville's artichoke fields.

▲ **North County Recreation**, Castroville Community Center, 11261 Crane St., has many classes for kids and teens. 633-3084.

● **Public Library**, 11266 Merritt St. Open Mon-Thur, 2:15-9pm, summer, Mon-Thur, 9am-9pm. Homework Center for grades 1-12, open Tues-Thurs, 3-6pm. 633-2829.

1999 Calendar of Events

Information subject to change. Please call in advance to verify.

May 15-16   **ARTICHOKE FESTIVAL**   **Free+$$**
Castroville Community Center, 10am. Entertainment, car show, live music, an artichoke-eating contest, arts and crafts, food, celebrity chefs cooking demos, a parade, and the coronation of the Artichoke Queen. Robert Steen, 633-2465.

October tba   **MULTICULTURAL FESTIVAL**   **Free**
Carnival games, international entertainment, jump house, spin art, pumpkin decorating, gold panning, cake walk, costume booth. 11am-3pm, Castroville Elementary, 11161 Merritt St. Fundraiser for school equipment. 633-2570.

November 25   **THANKSGIVING DINNER**   **Free**
12-4pm at Castroville Community Center, 1126 Crane St. (behind Catholic church). Santa will have toys for children. 633-3084

Free & Fun in
Old Monterey

Fisherman's Wharf

Museum of Art

Colton Hall

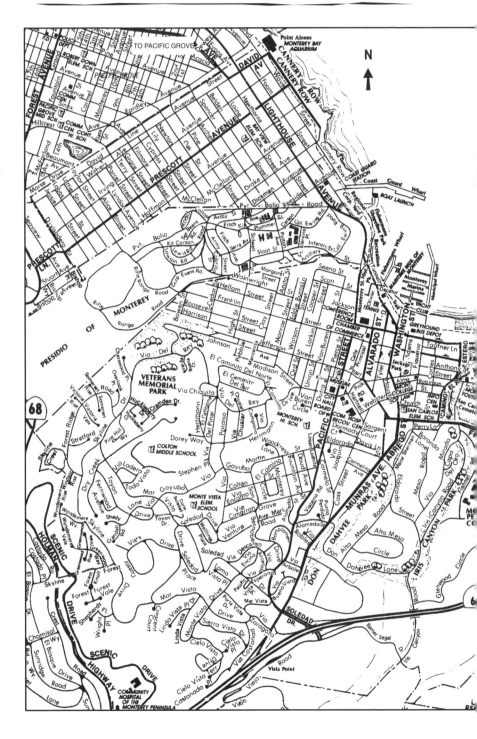

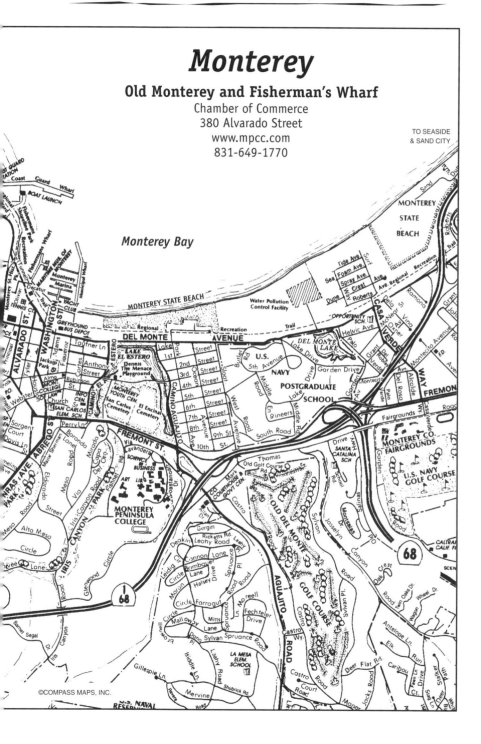

Monterey

Old Monterey and Fisherman's Wharf

Chamber of Commerce
380 Alvarado Street
www.mpcc.com
831-649-1770

©COMPASS MAPS, INC.

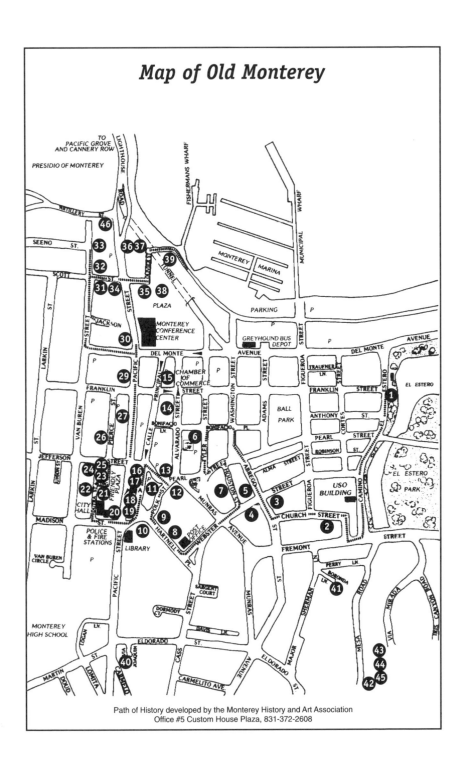

Map of Old Monterey

TO
PACIFIC GROVE
AND CANNERY ROW

PRESIDIO OF MONTEREY

FISHERMANS WHARF

MONTEREY MARINA

MUNICIPAL WHARF

SEENO ST.

SCOTT

PLAZA

MONTEREY
CONFERENCE
CENTER

PARKING

GREYHOUND BUS
DEPOT

DEL MONTE

AVENUE

DEL MONTE

AVENUE

CHAMBER
OF
COMMERCE
STREET

TRAUFNER
LN.

EL ESTERO

FRANKLIN

STREET

FRANKLIN

BONIFACIO

WASHINGTON STREET

ADAMS

BALL
PARK

ANTHONY

ST.

PEARL

STREET

ROBINSON

ST.

EL ESTERO
PARK

JEFFERSON

PEARL

MUNRAS

USO
BUILDING

CAMINO

MADISON

CITY
HALL

POLICE
& FIRE
STATIONS

LIBRARY

POST
OFFICE

WEBSTER

AVENUE

CHURCH STREET

FREMONT

STREET

VAN BUREN
CIRCLE

PERRY LN.

BORONDA
LN.

MONTEREY
HIGH SCHOOL

SARGENT
COURT

DORMODY
CT.

ELDORADO

ST.

MESA

ROAD

VIA
MIRADA

CARMELITO AVE.

MARTIN

Path of History developed by the Monterey History and Art Association
Office #5 Custom House Plaza, 831-372-2608

Historic Sites

1. First French Consulate (P)
2. Royal Presidio Chapel (N, SHL #105)
3. Casa Madariaga (P)
4. Casa Pacheco (P)
5. Casa Abrego (P)
6. Estrada Adobe (P)
7. Stevenson House (SHL #352, MSHP)
8. General Fremont's Quarters (P)
9. First Federal Court (P)
10. Stokes Adobe (P-Restaurant)
11. Casa Amesti (P)
12. Cooper Molera Adobe (MSHP)
13. Alvarado Adobe (SHL #348, P)
14. Casa Sanchez (P)
15. Osio-Rodríguez Adobe
16. Larkin House (N, MSHP, SHL #106)
17. Sherman Headquarters (P)
18. House of the Four Winds (P, SHL #353)
19. Casa Gutiérrez (SHL #713, MSHP)
20. Brown-Underwood House (P)
21. Colton Hall & Old Jail (SHL #126)
22. Casa Vásquez (SHL #351)
23. Gordon House (P)
24. Casa Alvarado (P)
25. Casa de la Torre (P)
26. Casa Jesus Soto (P)
27. Casa Serrano (*)
28. Capitular Hall (P)
29. Merritt House (P-Merritt House Inn)
30. Casa Soberanes (SHL #712, MSHP)
31. Perry House
32. Doud House
33. Old St. James Church
34. California's First Theatre (SHL #136, MSHP)
35. Casa Del Oro (SHL #532, MSHP)
36. Old Whaling Station (P)
37. First Brick House (MSHP)
38. Pacific Building & Memory Garden (SHL #354, MSHP)
39. Custom House (Maritime Museum Of Monterey, N, MSHP)
40. Casa Joaquin Soto (P)
41. Casa Boronda (P)
42. Casa Buelna (P)
43. Casa de Castro (P)
44. Casa Bonifacio (P)
45. Casa de Doud (P)
46. Vizcaino-Serra Landing Site (SHL #128)

Cooper Molera Adobe

LEGEND

(N) National Historical Landmark
(SHL) State Historical Landmark
(MSHP) Monterey State Historic Park
(P) Private Residence, not generally open to public
(*) Monterey History & Art Assn. Headquarters
P Off-Street Parking

CALIFORNIA STATE PARKS

The Path of History in Old Monterey

For outdoor lovers, romantics, artists and shoppers, there is an infinite array of possibilities in Monterey. The bustling, seaside town is best known for its collection of historic buildings, said to be the largest gathering outside Williamsburg, Pennsylvania. The Path of History walking tour will take you through these buildings and their gardens, past the art galleries and museums, the eateries and shops.

From Monterey State Parks: **The Path of History** includes 46 unique nineteenth century historic structures, meticulously restored to their original condition by the Monterey History and Art Assn., the State of California Department of Parks and Recreation, and the City of Monterey. You may follow the line on the map to see all 46 structures, or begin the selected walk below at the Custom House Plaza; it takes about 90 minutes. Numbers in parenthesis indicate their position on the map and their date of construction. There are bronze markers on the sidewalk, illustrated tiles and descriptive signs to guide you. Free admission noted, others by guided tour from the Stanton Center and Cooper-Molera Adobe. The gardens are always open. Watch a free video at the Stanton Center before you go.

■ **Stanton Center & Custom House Plaza (Map#39),** site of the Monterey State Historic Park Visitor's Center, State Park History Theatre, and the Maritime Museum. Free film: 17-minute Monterey history film every 20 minutes, 10am-5pm. Gift shop with local items and books, 649-7118. Walking tours of house interiors and gardens depart from here hourly, $5 for all. A free self-guided kids' treasure hunt daily in the foyer. **The Maritime Museum,** Monterey's fishing history artifacts collection, is open free several times a year, including FirstNight®. Free symposiums with marine themes are occasionally offered. Regular admission is adults $5, seniors, teens, military $3, children 6-12 $2, and under 5 free. 10am-5pm, closed Thanksgiving, Christmas and New Year's. 373-2469. www.mbay.net/~mshp.

■ **Pacific House & Garden (#38)** (1847) Originally built for the storage of U.S. military supplies, it has also been a hotel, law office, church, ballroom, and newspaper office. It now houses the **Monterey Museum of the American Indian** and a new visitor center/museum currently under construction. Watch for its grand opening. Visit the Memory Garden behind the Pacific House, created in 1928 and one of the loveliest of the historic walled gardens. Each year the Merienda celebrating the founding of Monterey in 1770 takes place in this garden.

■ **Custom House & Garden (39)** (1827), Custom House Plaza. Free admission, 10am-5pm daily. During California's Mexican era, the Monterey Custom House presided over Mexico's only port of entry on the Alta California coast, opened to foreign trade in 1822. It was here that Commodore John Drake Sloat raised the American flag in July of 1846, claiming over 600,000 square miles of territory for the United States. Gardens, created in 1827, reflect the Mexican era and are the earliest of the historic gardens with succulents, cacti and other drought-tolerant plants.

■ **First Brick House & Garden (37)** (1847), Heritage Harbor. Free admission, 10am-5pm daily. Briefly inhabited by its builder, Gallant Dickenson, this building represents the kiln fired brick construction method brought to California by settlers in the early American period.

■ **Whaling Station & Garden (36)** (1847), Decatur Street, Heritage Harbor. The Old Whaling Station boasts Monterey's only remaining whalebone sidewalk, a reminder of one of the town's most important industries from 1850-1900. The charming adobe and its gardens are now under the stewardship of the Junior League of Monterey County.

■ **Casa Del Oro & Garden (35)** (1845), **Picket Fence,** Scott and Olivier Streets. Free admission, Thurs-Sun, 11am-3pm. Used as a general store by 19th century businessmen David Jacks and Joseph Boston, the Casa del Oro is open again as the **Boston Store**, operated by the Historic Garden League. Volunteer to help them with the restoration of Monterey's gardens on first Tuesdays and third Saturdays, 9-11am, at various state-owned properties: second Wed 9-11am at Doud House, Scott and Van Buren. Bring gloves, clippers, rake, etc. Call for Tues and Sat locations, 649-6825. The Boston Store, 649-3364.

■ **First Theatre & Garden (34)** (1844), Scott and Pacific Streets. Free admission, Wed-Sat, 1-5pm. Jack Swan's saloon became the first theatre when he let the NY Volunteers, assigned to Monterey at the end of the Mexican War, put on plays. The Troupers of the Gold Coast have been presenting 19th century melodramas here since the 1930's. Call for times, 375-4916.

■ **Mayo Hayes O'Donnell Library** (1876), 155 Van Buren Street. Free admission, Wed, Fri-Sun, 1:30-3:45pm. This little red church was the first Protestant Church in Monterey. It is now a library of "Californiana" and owned by the Monterey History and Art Association. Take a book, settle into a chair with a comforting view of the bay, and absorb some Monterey and California history. Friendly docents answer questions and find books. Brochures and maps available.

■ **Casa Soberanes & Garden (30)** (1842), 336 Pacific Street. With its thick walls, interconnecting rooms, cantilevered balcony and lovely garden, Casa Soberanes tells the story of life in Monterey from its Mexican period beginnings to recent times. Terraced borders of abalone shells, antique bottles and a whalebone grace the garden created in 1907 and once known as "Jade Heaven."

■ **Osio-Rodríguez Adobe (15)**, 380 Alvarado St., built in the early 1840s by Jacinto Rodriguez, a delegate to California's first Constitutional Convention in 1849, now houses the Chamber of Commerce and **Visitors Center**. Mon-Fri, 8am-5pm 649-1770.

■ **Casa Serrano (27)** (1843), 412 Pacific Street. Free admission, Sat-Sun, 2-4pm. It was originally started by Thomas Larkin in 1843, and purchased and finished by Don Florencio Serrano, one of the first school teachers, in 1845. On fourth Saturdays of each month, chat with docent Diana J. Dennett, local author and 9th generation descendant of an early Monterey family that came with Father Serra in 1770. Dennett is pictured at right with Señor Camilo Alonzo-Vega, Consul General of Spain, in 1998 at the Presidio of San Francisco with her enchanting and historical book, *Tell Me More Ancestor Stories, Grandma!*, available at the Boston Store, the National Steinbeck Center, and local bookstores.

■ **Larkin House & Garden (16)** (1834), 510 Calle Principal. This adobe built during Monterey's Mexican period by Thomas O. Larkin, American merchant and U.S. Consul to Alta California, has stood witness to intrigue, business deals, and lively social occasions. Today its early 19th century rooms hold antiques from many parts of the world. Walled garden from 1842 was replanted as an English-style garden in the 1920s with yew, magnolia, redwood, rose arbor, fuschia, rhododendron and foxglove.

■ **Casa Gutierrez (19)** (1846), Madison and Calle Principal. Tucked away alongside other buildings, Casa Gutierrez is one of the few remaining adobes built in the simpler Mexican style which once lined Monterey's streets. Presently, the structure is not open to the public.

■ **Colton Hall (21)** (1849), Pacific Street at Madison. Free admission, daily 10am-5pm. Built and finished as a town hall in March by Walter Colton, by September it was the site of a convention called by Governor Riley to draft California's first Constitution, a copy of which resides inside. It served as Monterey County seat and Court House until 1872. Between 1873 and 1897, it was

a grade school. In 1949, the City of Monterey established the **Colton Hall Museum**, dedicated to the history of the City. A museum attendant is available for tours and information. Colton Hall will be the center of many Sesquicentennial Events in 1999 celebrating 150 years since the signing of the Constitution. Peek through the bars of the **Old Monterey Jail** (1854) just behind the museum. 646-5640.

■ **Cooper-Molera & Garden (12)** (1827), Polk and Munras Streets. The former home of John Rogers Cooper, a New England sea captain who came to Monterey in 1823, and three generations of the Cooper family. He changed

his name to Juan Bautista Rogerio Cooper, his citizenship to Mexico and his religion to Catholic, then married into the prominent Vallejo family. The large complex includes an exhibit room, carriage display, historic period garden and farm animals. The two-acre period garden was planted in the 1980s by the Old Monterey Preservation Society. Chickens, a rooster and sheep freely wander in the Victorian flower garden, vegetable garden and fruit orchard. A museum store is open daily, 10am-4pm, winter, and 10am-5pm, summer (Memorial through Labor Days). Tours of Cooper-Molera interiors begin here. Call for times 649-7118. Special garden tours of Cooper-Molera Adobe, Stevenson and Larkin House gardens from May through Sept, 2nd and 4th Tues & Sat, 1pm, $2. May 7 is Seniors Day at Cooper-Molera, and those 55 years and older gain free admittance to state adobes and walking tours. Oct 8 is John Cooper Lang Day, a special day for the disabled, with a free tour. 647-6226, 649-7111.

■ **Stevenson House & Garden (7)** (1840), 530 Houston. Reading more like a Robert Louis Stevenson tale of travel and romance than real events taking place in Monterey, the story of Stevenson's courtship of Fanny Osbourne, his future wife, comes alive amid period settings and displays of Stevenson memorabilia. Stevenson lived here briefly in 1879. A large Victorian garden hidden behind a high wall is a peaceful oasis with benches, an old Ficus and Angel's Trumpet vine. <u>Free admission on Nov. 14</u>, noon-3pm, on Robert Louis Stevenson's Unbirthday. Docents, Scottish pipers in the garden and Stevenson himself! 649-7172.

■ **Royal Presidio Chapel (2)** (1794), 500 Church. <u>Free admission</u>, 8:30am-6pm daily. Oldest structure in Monterey and an example of Spanish Colonial Architecture. Catholic Gift and Book Store, 373-6711.

■ **First French Consulate (1)** (1848) On Camino El Estero, near Franklin St., former home of the first French Consulate in California, now it is one of Monterey's **Visitor Centers**. Here you will find a knowledgeable staff, maps, brochures, and postcards. Open Mon-Sat, 9-5, Sun 10-4.

Special Adobe Activities

● Each year certain adobes participate in two public tours. April 24, 1999, is "A Signature Year" Adobe Tour, to celebrate 150 years since the signing of California's Constitution in Colton Hall. The 16th Annual Christmas in the Adobes will be Thursday, Dec. 9, and Saturday, Dec 11, 1999. Fee.

● Casa Serrano, Cooper-Molera, Memory Garden, Perry House, Doud House and the Mayo Hayes O'Donnell Library are available for private parties. For more information, call Linda Jaffee, Executive Director Monterey History and Art Association, 625-6103 or 648-7118.

Volunteer Opportunities with Monterey State Parks

➤ **Monterey State Historic Park Docent Training Class** will be Sept. 29, 1999, 6-9pm. Topics include California history, Monterey's historic buildings and gardens, tour techniques and presentation skills, living history, period clothing, school programs, and more. Call 647-6204 for information and to receive an application. For more information, see the Monterey State Historic Park web site at: www.mbay.net/~mshp/.

➤ **Old Monterey Preservation Society** (OMPS) is the nonprofit Cooperating Association with Monterey State Historic Park whose purpose is to provide educational and interpretive programs and activities, give support for various interpretive projects, and foster preservation of Old Monterey. You can help when you join for $10 which entitles you to free entrance to scheduled tours of the Adobes, invitation to programs, docent training, workshops in costumes, crafts and living history, and special events. 647-6226.

Other Interesting Places

■ **Naval Postgraduate School**, off Del Monte Ave., was originally the Del Monte Hotel built in 1887 by Charles Crocker. The Hotel was part of a 20,000 acre complex which included all of Pebble Beach and hundreds of acres of rare botanical gardens and recreational facilities. Visitors may take a <u>free self-guided walking tour of the building and grounds</u> which includes the **Arizona Garden** with a very large collection of cactus and succulents. The original garden required three train cars of succulents from Sonora, Mexico. Pick up a free map in Hermann Hall, the main building. **Eagles Eye Art Gallery**, Rm#24, is in the basement of Hermann Hall, and open <u>free</u> Mon-Fri, 11:30am-3pm, featuring local watercolors. Check out the murals

around the building and the Jo Mora art in the La Novia room. Ask at the quarterdeck in Hermann Hall for a key to the viewing tower and enjoy a spectacular 360-degree view of Monterey and the bay. The Roman Plunge swimming pool is open Tues-Fri, 11am-6pm, Sat, 10am-6pm, Sun, noon-6pm. Fees vary, call 656-2275. <u>Free concerts</u> on the lawn Memorial Day, 4th of July, and Labor Day weekends, plus other free events. Call for dates and times, Public Affairs Office, Mon-Fri, 8am-4:30pm, 656-2023.

■ **State Theatre**, 417 Alvarado. Opened in 1926 as the Golden State Theatre, one of several beautiful theatres built on the Monterey Peninsula during the early 1900s. Of these, the Golden State Theatre was the largest and grandest and today it is the only one left. It was designed by the Reid Brothers architectural firm of San Francisco which also designed the Fairmont Hotel, the Cliff House and the Music Pavilion in Golden Gate Park, plus the Hotel del Coronado in San Diego. The architecture follows a medieval Spanish theme complete with tapestries, wrought-iron chandeliers, colorful heraldic shields and old ornamentation. The auditorium is designed to give the impression of a Castilian courtyard. A nonprofit group, The State Theatre Preservation Group, has been formed to promote and facilitate the restoration of the theatre to its original 1926 appearance. To help, write to them at 395 Del Monte Center, Suite 140, Monterey, CA 93940.

■ **St. John's Chapel**, 1490 Mark Thomas Drive, between Del Monte Golf Club and the Hyatt Regency. This historical church will be open September 11, 10am-3pm, for tours during their annual Bargain Hunt which features antiques, collectables, art, books, clothing, toys, crafts, and much more. Coffee, sandwiches, baked goods and jams, and friendly smiles. 375-4463.

Fisherman's Wharf & Commercial Wharf #2

"Everything for family fun!" A stroll down the wharf brings exciting sights and sounds to your senses. Browse the shops, sample free salt water taffy and clam chowder. Watch the harbor seals, pelicans, cormorants and sea gulls. Take in a whale watch cruise or do some deep sea fishing. Artists are sketching portraits and musicians are strolling among the crowds.

Public Art At the Wharf

Pietro Ferrante, 1969.
Robert H. Hoge (1904-1998).
Bronze.
Gift from Ferrante family, placed at current site in 1989.

Santa Rosalia, 1979.
Richard Lutz. Bronze.
Donated to the City by the Italian Heritage Society.

There's always something going on at Fisherman's Wharf and Commercial Wharf #2. See the boats enter and leave the harbor. Watch fishermen bring in the day's catch and buy the freshest seafood available. There's a variety of excellent restaurants and The Wharf Theatre for

after dinner entertainment. For more information and a schedule of free entertainment and events, call the Fisherman's Wharf Assn., 373-0600.

California Brown Pelican

Tall Ships will dock in Monterey Bay for free+fee tours: February 24-28, May 29-June 7, June 18-21. See Calendar of Events for more information.

Discounts for *Free & Fun* Readers

➤ $5 off/person on fishing trips. $2 off on whale watching trips
Angelo Shake Monterey Sportfishing and Whale Watching Cruises
96 Old Fisherman's Wharf
800/200-2203, 831/372-2203, www.montereysportfishing.com

Benji Shake Monterey Baywatch Cruises
90 Old Fisherman's Wharf
831/372-7153, www.montereybaywatch.com

➤ $1 off/person on Glass Bottom boat tours
Sea Life Tours/Glass Bottom Boat
90 Old Fisherman's Wharf
831/372-7151, www.sealifetours.com

➤ $5 off/person on fishing trips.
$2 off on whale watching trips
Randy's Fishing and Whale Watching
66 Old Fisherman's Wharf
831/372-7440, www.randysfishingtrips.com

Browsing the Shops in Old Monterey

■ While visiting the adobes, you'll have plenty of opportunities to window shop: Christopher Bell Collection, Chivalry Bath Shoppe, Do Re Mi Music & Video, Dudley Doolittle's Travel Shop, The First Noel, A&J Gallery, Aiello Jewelers, Alvarado Mart, The Art Show, Avalon Beads, The Bachelor Shop, Bay Books, Burlwood Gallery, Gasper's Jewelers, Green's Camera World, Hats & Caps, Hellams Tobacco Shop, Pieces of Heaven, Troia's Market, and more. Old Monterey Business Assn., 655-8070. Chamber of Commerce, 648-5360.

■ **Del Monte Shopping Center**, Munras Ave. at Hwy 1. Open air center with lush gardens designed by well-known local artist Elizabeth Murray. Free live entertainment from 2 to 4 every Saturday and Sunday afternoon in the garden. Over 100 stores, shops and restaurants. 373-2705.

r — — — — — — — — — — — — — — — — — — — ┐
| **Attn: Brides & Ice Cream Aficionados** |

| ➤ Getting married? Come in for a free consultation on your Bridal Makeup, or receive a Free Skin Care Kit with every facial service. **Excellent Reflection Therapeutic Skin & Body Care**, 444 Pearl St. #A-18. Tues & Fri, 10-5, Wed & Thurs, 12-6, Sat, 10-3. 648-3305.

| ➤ Come into **Carmel Creamery**, 459 Alvarado St., for a free taste of their gourmet ice cream. You'll be so glad you did - it's out of this world! Open 11-8 daily (Fri-Sat, 11-10). 372-4720.
L — — — — — — — — — — — — — — — — — — — ┘

Farmers & Flea Markets

■ **Monterey Bay Certified Farmers Market**, 2:30-6pm Thursdays at Monterey Peninsula College lower lot, 980 Fremont St. Certified organic produce, honey, bread, and much more. Free food samples. 728-5060.

Old Monterey Market Place

■ **Old Monterey Market Place**, Alvarado Street from Pearl to Del Monte, is lined with over 100 vendors every Tuesday, 4-7pm winter, 4-8pm summer. Go to the Market, it's a great way to get outdoors, learn about the city and its people, and be entertained at the same time. Free food samples, demonstrations and live entertainment. Featuring the Baker's Alley on Bonifacio Place with fresh breads, pastries, pizza. Fresh fish, flowers, produce, herbs, honey, arts, crafts, clothing, food to go. Children's events, Bookmobile 6-7 p.m. (first Tuesday at 6:15: stories, songs and finger plays for all ages). Santa visits early December. 655-2607.

■ **Monterey Fairgrounds Flea Market**, March to December, last weekend of every month, 7am-4:30pm. $1 admission. 2004 Fairgrounds Rd. 372-5873.

Art Galleries

Call each gallery for dates and times of their free artist receptions

- **Monterey Museum of Art at Civic Center**, 559 Pacific St. Open Wed-Sat, 11am-5pm, Sun 1-4pm. Regular admission is $3 general, $1.50 students and military, under 12 free. Free to the public on third Thursdays, with entertainment and refreshments, 7-9pm. Features Monterey and California art, photography, Asian art and international folk art; lectures, films and workshops. The docent program teaches art enthusiasts how to guide children and adults through the exhibitions, plus take part in field trips and lectures. Call Bill at 633-4100 or 372-5477. 372-7591. www.montereyart.org.

- **Eagles Eye Art Gallery**, Rm#24, in the basement of Herrman Hall, Naval Postgraduate School. Mon-Fri, 11:30am-3pm. Local watercolors. 372-3565.

- **Christopher Bell Studio**, 200 Alvarado St. 10am-7pm daily. Sculpture, fountains, other artworks. 649-0214.

- **Spa on the Plaza**, 201 Alvarado St. Local artists. 647-9000.

- **Venture Gallery Coop**, 260 Alvarado St. 10am-6pm daily. 372-6279.

- **Alvarado Gallery**, Monterey Conference Center. Mon-Fri, 9:30am-4:30pm.

- **Burlwood Gallery of Monterey**, 271 Alvarado Mall, 372-7756.

- **LeBlanc Gallery-Metal Sculpture**, 271 Alvarado Mall, 372-7756.

- **Lallapalooza**, 474 Alvarado St. Mon-Fri, 11am-10:30pm, Sat-Sun, 4pm-12:45am. Dan Koffman originals in a restaurant setting. 645-9036.

- **Levin Gallery Inc.**, 408 Calle Principal. 9:30am-5pm, or by appt. daily. Photography - Westons, Ansel Adams and others. 649-1166.

- **A Woman's Wellspring**, 575 Calle Principal. Tues-Fri, 10am-6pm, Sat 9am-3pm. Women's art. 649-2320.

- **Morgan's Coffee & Tea**, 498 Washington St. Mon-Thurs, 6:30am-10pm, Fri 6:30am-12am, Sat 7am-12am, Sun 6:30am-10pm. 373-5601.

- **Monterey College of Law Art Gallery**, 404 W. Franklin. 373-3301.

- **Gold Leaf Frame Design**, 620 Munras Ave. Tues-Sat, 8am-5pm. Local artists. 649-3520.

- **Thomas Kinkade Gallery**, 692 Del Monte Shopping Center. Mon-Fri, 10am-9pm, Sat 10am-7pm, Sun 11am-5pm. 657-1210.

- **Marsh's Oriental Art & Antiques**, 599 Fremont St. Tues-Sat, 9:30am-4:30pm. 372-3547.

● **Monterey Peninsula College**, 980 Fremont. Art gallery showcases student art from the college and from local high schools. Call for dates and times of free art shows and receptions, 646-4200.

● **Monterey Museum of Art at La Mirada**, La Mirada Adobe, 720 Via Mirada off Fremont Blvd. Located in an adobe built in the 1800s, this museum is surrounded by rose gardens, the Peden Rhododendron Garden, picturesque stone walls, and a beautiful view of the bay. Always free admission to the gardens. Museum is open Thurs-Sat, 11am-5pm; Sunday 1-4pm. First Sundays are free to the public, with guest musicians from 1:30-3:30pm, and complimentary hors d'oeuvres. 372-3689. Annual Monte Carlo Night, last Saturday in February, features gaming, live music, and silent auction. 372-5477.

● **Mezzanine and Upstairs Galleries** at the Monterey Peninsula Airport Terminal, 200 Fred Kane Drive, 8am-10pm daily. 624-7910.

● **Upstairs Gallery**, Fisherman's Wharf. 12-5pm daily. Local artists and others. 372-1373.

● **Balesteri's Wharf Front**, #6 Fisherman's Wharf. 9:30-8pm daily. Amazing collection of wood and metal, natural handcrafts and art. 375-6411.

● **Sea N Tree Gallery**, #15 Fishermans Wharf. Antique reproductions, local art, sculpture, glass, handcrafts. 9am-9pm daily. 649-6222.

● **Santa Catalina School Gallery**, 1500 Mark Thomas Dr. Local artists. Mon-Fri, 9am-5pm, Sat-Sun, 11am-5pm. 655-9300.

Become a Docent at the Monterey Museum of Art

As a volunteer you will find it a rewarding experience. You may spend a few hours a month sharing the exhibitions with the visitors, providing groups of adults or school children with an appreciation of both fine and decorative arts, and personally experience a program of art education through visits to other museums and studios and in presentations by artists. You will also enjoy a wealth of activities available to you as a member of the Monterey Museum of Art.

If you are interested in this opportunity for voluntary service in one of the nation's premier small city art museums, please call the Museum at 372-5477.

Public Art in Monterey

Clockwise from top left, at the **DoubleTree, Portolá**, 1986, Fausto Blazques (b. 1944), bronze, dedicated by King Juan Carlos I of Spain in 1987; parking lot mural of jazz musicians, Washington St.; **Two Cougars**, 1910, Arthur Putnam (1873-1930), bronze cougars as top decoration on the Berthold Monument in the Friendly Garden; parking lot mural on Pacific St. of early Monterey buildings.

This mural painted on the side of the Fire and Police Station building on Pacific Street at Madison depicts life in Monterey under Mexican rule and shows El Cuartel, the former military barracks and government headquarters. Painted by Monterey County teens in the "One Voice" Mural Project.

A Self-Guided Tour of Public Art pamphlet by Colton Hall Museum and Cultural Arts Commission, with the location of more public art displays in Monterey, is available at the Visitors Center, 380 Alvarado St.

Monterey Public Library

Monterey Public Library, 625 Pacific St., 646-3932, Reference 646-3933, bookmobile 646-3710. Mon-Thur 9am-9pm, Fri 9am-6pm, Sat 9am-5pm, Sun 1-5pm. California's first public library, it was organized as a subscription library in 1849. Free library card with proof of local residence. Check out <u>free books, magazines, CDs, books on tape, video and audio cassettes</u>. <u>Free access to the Internet</u> from five workstations. Visit the California Room for an extensive collection of Californiana. Comfortable chairs and a polite, knowledgeable staff. Web site at http://monterey.org/lib/lib.html has Kid's Page. Internet services, contact Library Director Paula Simpson, e-mail: simpson@ci.monterey.ca.us, or 646-5601.

Free Youth & Children's Programs

Teen Voices, second Monday, 7pm, features high school poetry and Open Mic poetry reading for teens in a coffeehouse setting.
Pajama Storytime, last Tuesday, 7pm, ages 3-7 and family.
Baby & Me, last Friday 10am, babies to age 2, siblings 2-5, adults.
Old Monterey Marketplace - 6:15pm first Tuesday, look for Bookmobile on Alvarado Street at Pearl. All ages.
Preschool Storytimes, Tue-Wed, 11am, ages 3-5.
Toddler Storytime, Wed 10am, 2 year-olds. One child on one adult lap.

Persons with disabilities who require assistance to attend programs, please contact the Administrative Office at 646-5603.

1999 Meeting Calendar for Literary Circle

It's a monthly book discussion group, not a club, facilitated by Stuart and Paula Walzer. <u>Free and newcomers are always welcome</u>. Meets Thursday, 7-8:45pm, with these selections on these dates:

January 28	*Corelli's Mandolin: A Novel* by Louis De Bernieres
February 25	*The Samurai's Garden* by Gail Tsukiyama
March 25	*Roughing It* by Mark Twain
April 29	*How the Garcia Girls Lost Their Accents* by Julia Alvarez
May 27	*The Age of Innocence* by Edith Wharton
June 24	*The Cunning Man* by Robertson Davies

All selections are currently in print and may be borrowed from the library or purchased at local book stores. Some selections may require special order, so contact your bookseller early. Call for dates after June.

Bookmobile Schedule, Jan-June 1999

Casanova/Oak Knoll: Casanova Plaza Apts.. (800 Casanova)...alternate Wed 10:30-11:30; Casanova/Oak Knoll Park Center Preschool...alternate Tues 11-11:30; Lerwick Dr...every Fri 4:30-5:45; Ralston Dr. near Casanova Ave...alternate Wed 5-5:45.

Deer Flats: Deer Forest Drive near Deer Flats Park...every Thurs 4:45-5:45.

Del Monte Beach: Surf Way near Sea Foam Ave...alternate Tues 4:45-5:45.

Downtown: Old Monterey Market Place, Alvarado St. at Pearl...every Tues 6-8pm. (Nov-Mar, 6-7pm only)

East Downtown/El Estero: Youth Center Preschool, Pearl St., between Camino El Estero and Camino Aguajito...alternate Fri 11-11:30.

Fisherman's Flats: Via Isola at Trapani Cir...every Thurs 3:30-4:30.

Glenwood Circle: Park Lane #200...every Fri 1-2:30; Glenwood Cir.... near Kimberly Place #300...alternate Sat 1:45-2:30.

La Mesa Village: Leahy Rd., between Shubrick and tennis courts...every Wed 1-4:15.

Monte Vista: Monte Vista Center...alternate Sat 11:15-12; Mar Vista Dr. between Via Gayuba & Toda Vista...alternate Fri 3-4.

Montecito: Hannon St. at Montecito Ave...alternate Tues 4:45-5:45; Montecito Pk., Montecito Ave., between Dela Vina and Ramona...alternate Sat 11:15-12:15.

New Monterey:

Archer Park, on McClellan St. near Archer...alternate Fri 3-4

Archer Park Preschool...alternate Tues 11-11:30

Bay View School...alternate Tues 11:35-12:30

Grace St. between Withers & David...alternate Wed 5-5:45

Hilltop Park Center, 871 Jessie, at Withers...every Tues 3:15-4:15

Hilltop Park Preschool...alternate Fri 11-11:30

Oak Newton Park on Newton St. at McClellan...alternate Sat 3-3:45

Oak Grove: 2nd St. at Park Ave. by El Estero Apts...alternate Sat 2:45-3:45

Old Town: Portola Vista Apts, Del Monte between Pacific and Van Buren...alternate Wed 10:30-11:30.

Villa Del Monte: Encina Ave., between Palo Verde & Del Robles...alternate Sat 1:30-2:15.

For more information, exact dates of alternating stops (or a complete daily schedule), or to request a particular item, call 646-3710.

Local Bookstores

● **The Book Tree.** Books of uncommon interest for discerning readers...local authors galore. Mon-Fri 10am-5:30pm, Sat 10am-2pm. 118 Webster St. 373-0228.

● **Monterey Bible Bookstore.** Oldest bookstore on the Monterey Peninsula, founded in 1951. Providing Bibles, books, music, and gift items. MST bus passes. Mon-Sat 10am-5:30pm. 487 Alvarado St. 375-6487.

● **Old Monterey Book Co.** Wed-Sat 10am-5pm. 136 Bonifacio Place. e-mail: montbook@mbay.net. 372-3111.

● **The Book End.** Large stock of used books including foreign and children's books. Mon-Sat 10:20am-5:30pm, Sun 11am-3pm. 245 Pearl St. 373-4046.

● **The Bookhaven.** 10am-10pm daily. Book searches, storytelling, reading and study group access. 559 Tyler St. 333-0383.

● **Waldenbooks Kids.** 222 Del Monte Center. Mon-Thurs, Sat, 10-9, Fri 10-10, Sun 10-6. 373-0987.

● **Bay Books.** Free lectures, speakers and events regularly scheduled. New book club forming in Spring 1999. Call for dates and times. Coffeehouse with comfortable browsing, large selection and friendly service. Locally-baked cakes, muffins and freshly-roasted coffees and espresso. Sun-Thurs 7:30am-10pm, Fri-Sat 7:30am-11pm. 316 Alvarado. 375-1855.

● **Monterey Institute of International Studies Book Store.** 434 Pacific Street, 647-8288. Occasional free lectures; call 647-4100.

Lectures & Book Related Happenings

● Free Storytime, music, crafts, games plus dinner for ages 4-11, Tuesdays 6-7:45pm at **Monterey United Methodist Church**, Soledad Dr. 375-8285.

● Free Storytime at noon every Wednesday at **Thinker Toys.** Weekend activities include face painting, magic, balloons and more! Del Monte Shopping Center, between Starbucks & Gymboree. 643-0907, fax 643-0534.

● **Lyceum of Monterey County.** Educational programs on science and nature, arts and crafts, sports and hobbies, computers, humanities and life skills. Free on special occasions. Call for a free copy of their newsletter, "The Scroll." 1073 6th Street. 372-6098, fax 372-6065.

● **Gentrain Society of the Monterey Peninsula** presents speakers at 1:30 first and third Wed, Lecture Forum 102, MPC. Refreshments at 1:15. Free. 373-7254.

● Free classes for adults at **Monterey Adult School.** Call 899-1615.

> ➤ **Own-A-Book Annual Book Drive**, sponsored by **The Herald** each November. Donate your clean, gently-read books for children from birth to 14 years. Call 649-4409 for drop off points, to participate or be a recipient.

1999 Calendar of Events

Information subject to change. Please call in advance to verify.

JANUARY

January 13   DINE OUT FOR DAFFODILS $$
30+ restaurants will donate a portion of their sales to benefit local cancer patients. Call 372-4521 for list.

January 14-17   MONTEREY SWINGFEST $$
Swing dance workshops, contest and open dancing. 805-937-1574.

January 15-31   WHALEFEST 1999   Free+$$
Celebrate as gray whales take their annual migration from Alaska to Baja California and back. An estimated 15,000 to 20,000 whales pass by Monterey Bay, south and northbound. Pick up your passport and schedule of Whalefest 1999 events at the Monterey Association of Cultural Institutions (MACI) booth in Custom House Plaza on Saturday the 16th at 10am. Also Saturday, free educational and entertaining hands-on exhibits and activities related to whales, continuous live music, cool whale stuff; free admission to the Maritime Museum. Live Dixieland music at the plaza throughout the day and continuous live music at Fisherman's Wharf. Sunday, Jan. 24, the Monterey Bay Aquarium will host a free open house from 7-9:30pm. California Gray Whale Migration continues through March. 372-2203, 644-7588. www.monterey.com.

FEBRUARY

February 11   INTERNATIONAL JAZZ PARTY   Free
All-star jazz bands from Japan and the U.S. led by trumpter Bill Berry and clarinetist Eiji Kitamura. Doubletree Hotel, 7:30pm. 659-5373.

February 14   A DAY OF ROMANCE IN OLD MONTEREY   Free
10am-2pm. Experience four living history reenactments of love stories in Monterey State Historic Park's most renowned homes - Stevenson, Larkin House, Diaz Adobe and Cooper-Molera Adobe. Food, music and period dances. Free but tickets are limited. www.mbay.net/~mshp. 647-6226, 647-6204.

February 14   A WHALE OF AN ART SHOW   Free
Contemporary arts and crafts, 10-5pm at Custom House Plaza, near Fisherman's Wharf. Classical music entertainment. Gourmet coffee, fine paintings, handmade paper, jewelry, ceramics, wood, clothing, accessories, photography. 625-0931.

February 23   POST OFFICE CELEBRATION   Free
150th anniversary. Monterey's Post Office was the first to be established west of the Mississippi. Call 646-3991 for more information.

February 24-28   TALL SHIPS IN THE HARBOR   Free+$$
Grand arrival at Fisherman's Wharf, 2pm, Wed. Feb 24. Historic tall ships, *Hawaiian Chieftain and Lady Washington*, will sail the coast of California on the third annual six month long Voyages of ReDiscovery. The costumed crew will be giving tours, teaching classes, participating in gun battles and sailing the ships. Free tours for the public on the 24th from 2:30-6pm. Other tours, Thurs & Fri, 4pm and 6pm. Sat from 10am and 1pm. Cost is $7 family, $3 adult, $2 student/ senior, $1 child. Reservations not required. Exciting 3 hour sails with costumed crew, Sat 2- 5pm, Sun 10am-1pm & 2-5pm. Cost is $40 adult, $25 child. Reservations required. Call 800/200-LADY. Next stop, Santa Cruz, March 1-7.

February 27   JOHN STEINBECK'S BIRTHDAY PARTY   Free+$$
Free exhibits, entertainment, music and lectures at the Aquarium and free birthday cake at the rail car on the recreation trail, near the carousel. Fee events include walking tours of Cannery Row and Doc Ricketts Lab and a bus tour of Steinbeck country in Salinas. 372-8512, fax 375-4982.

February 27-28   EAST OF EDEN CAT SHOW $$
Annual feline show in the Salinas Room (agriculture building) at the Monterey Fairgrounds. 150+ felines. $5 general, $3 seniors, $2 children/students. 372-7018. Benefits the Monterey County SPCA. Spectators welcome free to SPCA Dog Games every third Thursday: "My Dog Can Do That," at 7pm, Highway 68 across from Laguna Seca. Monthly prizes, year-end tournament. $5 monthly entry is tax-deductible. 726-1918.

MARCH

March 5-7   DIXIELAND MONTEREY   Free+$$
National and international bands of traditional Dixieland jazz. Free Jazz parade and cabarets downtown. Call 443-5260, 888/349-6879.

March 5-7   ART, CRAFTS, & ALL THAT DIXIELAND JAZZ   Free
Eighty artists and crafts people with paper art, paintings, photography, stoneware, leather, sculpture in glass, metal and wood, wearable art, jewelry, lamps, garden accessories, toys. Custom House Plaza, near Fisherman's Wharf, 10am-5pm. Carmel Art Guild, www.dixiejazz/monterey.html, 625-0931.

March 8   COLTON HALL BIRTHDAY   Free
Living history, birthday cake and punch. Open House 2-4pm at Colton Hall Museum, Pacific Street between Madison and Jefferson. 646-5640.

March 18-21   SEA OTTER CLASSIC CYCLING FESTIVAL   Free
Road cycling and mountain biking. $6 per vehicle park entrance fee. Family activities include interactive games, a huge expo and great food. Saturday ride 10 miles through the rolling green, wildflower covered hills. Enjoy refreshment stops and the chance to win great prizes. Laguna Seca, Highway 68, east of Monterey. www.seaotter.org. 373-1839, fax 373-1089.

March 20   CHOCOLATE ABALONE DIVE   Spectators free
Watch divers search for 500 numbered chocolate abalone and win prizes. Breakwater Cove. Diver entry fees: $20-$23. 375-1933.

March 20-21   CELEBRATION SIDEWALK SALE   Free
Arts, handmade crafts and downtown merchants. 10am-5pm on Alvarado Street from Del Monte to Pearl St. Old Monterey Business Assn. 655-8070.

March 27-28   MONTEREY BAY SPRING FAIRE   Free
Crafts faire, live Pacific Repertory Theatre, Actors-in-the-Adobes, and a Human Chess Game with a theme. Custom House Plaza. www.pacrep.org, 622-0700.

March 27-28   SPRING HOME SHOW $$
New items for the home: roofing, flooring, security systems, patios, sunrooms, spas, saunas, tile, marble, custom closets. Wildlife education program and product demonstrations. Barbecue, live musical entertainment. Admission $2, children under 12 free. Sat 10am-7pm, Sun 10am-5pm. Monterey Fairgrounds. 800/237-0551.

APRIL

April 4   **EASTER EGG HUNT**   **Free**
Easter Sunday hunt for pre-schoolers through third graders. Bring a basket and look for over 5,000 eggs and 100 golden prize eggs. Frank Sollecito Ballpark, 777 Pearl St., 646-3866.

April 15-17   **MONTEREY WINE FESTIVAL** $$
Various Peninsula locations. Free cooking demonstrations with the finest chefs working their culinary magic. Call for locations and times. "New Release" Party, wine tasting, big bottle auction, wine brunch, workshops. Tickets from $10-$150. 800/656-4282, 656-9463, fax 649-4124, www.montereywine.com. More wine info: www.wine.brats.org/

April 17-18   **SEAFOOD AND MUSIC FESTIVAL**   **Free**
Continuous music from three professional sound stages highlights this celebration of bounty from the sea. Craft booths. Custom House Plaza, Mall and Alvarado Street, 10am-5pm. Old Monterey Business Assn., 655-8070.

April 18   **BOOK FESTIVAL** $$
Meet authors, attend seminars, enjoy live music at the Fairgrounds. 624-8886.

April 24   **"A SIGNATURE YEAR" ADOBE TOUR**   **Free+**$$
Historic downtown adobes, 12am-7pm. 52nd Annual event with a Sesquicentennial theme: living history, food entertainment, 23 adobes linked to the California Constitution signers. Tour free to children younger than 16, adults $10. Party 5-7pm is free and open to the public. Tickets at Bay Books, the Cooper Store, Maritime Museum. Monterey History and Art Assn., 372-2608, 375-9175.

Apr30-May 2   **HONDA CHALLENGE OF LAGUNA SECA** $$
AMA National Superbike Races. Volunteer opportunities to attend free. 800/327-SECA, 648-5111, fax 373-0533. www.laguna-seca.com.

MAY

May 1   **INTERNATIONAL DAY**   **Free**
Graduate students from around the world present food, dancing, crafts and educational displays. Naval Postgraduate School. 12-4pm. 656-2186.

May 1   **ANNUAL WAG 'N WALK**   **Spectators free**
Breakwater Cove. Watch people with their leashed dogs walk the 2 to 4 mile course along the Recreational Trail at Shoreline Park. Benefit for the SPCA. $50 pledge to walk. 373-2631 ext. 231, 422-4721 ext. 223.

May 7   **COOPER-MOLERA ADOBE**   **Seniors free**
11am-1pm. Free to seniors 55+. Refreshments. 525 Polk St. 649-7118.

May 13   **TASTE OF OLD MONTEREY** $$
4-9pm at Ferrante's in the Marriott. Food and entertainment; a fun-filled epicurean extravaganza of downtown's international delights. Sponsored by The Old Monterey Business Assn., 655-8070.

May 15   **GARDEN DAY AT COOPER-MOLERA ADOBE**   **Free**
Free refreshments and an opportunity to see the adobe gardens in full bloom and to buy cuttings from the garden. Bring containers and any plants, bulbs or softwood cuttings to exchange. Free seedling trees from the Monterey Parks Dept., 525 Polk St., 649-7118.

May 29-30   GREAT MONTEREY SQUID FESTIVAL   Free+$$
Entertainment, educational displays, cooking demonstrations, and arts and crafts.
Call for prices. Monterey County Fairgrounds. 649-6544.

May 29-June 7   TALL SHIP IN THE HARBOR   Free+$$
H.M. Bark Endeavour, a replica of Capt. Cook's ship, will dock at the Coast Guard
Pier. Call 800/432-2201 for more information.

May 31   CONCERTS ON THE LAWN   Free
Free concert at 2pm by the Monterey Bay Symphony at the Naval Postgraduate
School. Public is also invited to attend 1pm rehearsal. Free tours of the former
Del Monte Hotel and Arizona Cactus Garden. 656-2023.

JUNE

June/July   THEATREFEST   Free
Four weekends. Pacific Repertory Theatre's annual gift to the communities of
the Central Coast includes Fairytale Theatre, Actors in the Adobes, Arts & Crafts,
Music, Human Chess Game, International Foods at Custom House Plaza. Support their Theatre Season March-October at the Golden Bough, Circle Theatre
and Forest Theatre. Box office 622-0100. www.pacrep.org.

June 11-13   SIDEWALK FINE ARTS FESTIVAL   Free
Sidewalk Show on Alvarado Street. 10am-5pm. Handcrafted ceramics, paintings
and sculpture. Old Monterey Business Assn., 655-8070.

June 18-21   TALL SHIPS IN THE HARBOR   Free+$$
Tall Ships *Bill of Rights*, *Pilgrim of Newport*, *Hawaiian Chieftain*, and *The Californian*
will anchor in Monterey. Call for info, Nautical Heritage Society, 800/432-2201.

June 19, 20   DOWNTOWN CELEBRATION   Free
Artisans, crafters, food. Call 655-8070 for more information.

June 25-27   MONTEREY BAY BLUES FESTIVAL $$
Continuous entertainment from 10:30am to 10:30pm. Merchandise booths and
great food. For more information, call Bonnie Adams at 394-2652. Tickets $15 to
$70 for a 2 day festival pass. Monterey Fairgrounds. 649-6544. Numerous free
blues around the Peninsula: Blue Fin Cafe, Doc's Lab, The Jazz Store (fee).

JULY

July 2   CALIFORNIA BREWMASTERS' CLASSIC $$
Restaurants and caterers provide gourmet food and nonalcoholic beverages.
More than twenty breweries pour microbrews and answer questions. Tasting until
9:30pm, complimentary pilsner glass to first 600 arrivals. Dance, silent auction,
gifts. 6:30pm at DoubleTree Hotel. Benefit for KAZU Public Radio. 375-7275.

July 4   ANNUAL SALMON DERBY   Free+$$
Monterey Bay Salmon & Trout Project, Monterey Bay Veterans, noon-9pm. Cash
& raffle prizes. Open to the public; stay to watch the fireworks from the Breakwater Cove Marina. Volunteers are always needed to help with the physically-challenged at Salmon Derby, Rock Cod Derby, and at Laguna Seca. John, 646-8324.

July 4   FOURTH OF JULY CELEBRATIONS   Free
After military units raise American flags in downtown Monterey, the annual parade will run from 10-11am on Alvarado Street and Calle Principal. Alcohol-free
Big Little Backyard Barbecue at 11am-5pm at City Hall, Pacific Street at Madison. Nonstop music, games, entertainment. Free cake for Monterey's birthday.

Bring picnic or purchase food from nonprofit vendors. 20 minute fireworks at 9:15pm off Commercial Wharf#2, with a Sesquicentennial theme and choreographed to music on KWAV 97FM. 646-3866, 646-3427.

July 4   **LIVING HISTORY FESTIVAL**   **Free+$$**

9am-4pm, Custom House Plaza, Memory Garden and California's First Theatre. Free activities: flag raising, smugglers, military, demonstrations, cannons, horses...and more! Children's games and crafts, corn cob dolls, weaving, rope making, Jacob's ladders, marbles, spinners ...and more! Living history demonstrations are $2 for adults, $1 for children. Other events include a black-powder marksmanship contest, pie, cider, souvenir tin cup...and more! www.mbay.net/~mshp/ 372-2608, 647-6204, 647-6226.

July 4 weekend   **CONCERT ON THE LAWN SERIES**   **Free**

Free concert at 2pm by the Monterey Bay Symphony at the Naval Postgraduate School. Free tours of the former Del Monte Hotel and Arizona Cactus Garden. Bring a picnic lunch. Call for day of event, 656-2023.

July 5   **MONTEREY BEACH CLEANUP**   **Free**

Time to clean the beach again. Meet at 9am at Monterey Beach near Wharf#2. Call to register or just show up. 646-3719.

July 6-Oct 26   **OLD MONTEREY MARKETPLACE**   **Free+$$**

Gold mining exhibits and more. 4-8pm, every Tuesday. Celebrate California's sesquicentennial by panning for gold with instruction from California State Park Rangers, $2.25. For more information, call 655-8070.

July 9-11   **MCGRAW SUPERBIKE**   **$$**

World Superbike event at Laguna Seca. www.laguna-seca.com. 800-327-SECA.

July 10   **SLOAT'S LANDING**   **Free**

Ceremony commemorating the landing of Commodore Sloat in Monterey, and the U.S. claiming of California from Mexico. Presidio of Monterey. Sponsored by the Monterey History and Art Assn. 372-2608, 373-2469.

July 16   **JUNIOR OLYMPIC TRACK AND FIELD**   **Spectators free**

Parade at 10am followed by track and field events and a traditional awards ceremony with medals, ribbons and gold certificates for the Playground Program children, ages 5-14. Ice cream bars at the end for everyone! Monterey High Football Stadium at the end of Larkin Street. 646-3866.

July 22-25   **MONTEREY NATIONAL HORSE SHOW**   **Free**

Week long celebration of jumping, roping, team penning, barrel racing, stock horse class and cutting class, musical entertainment, cowboy poetry, barbecue, country-western dance, and silent auction. Pattee Arena at the Monterey Fairgrounds, 372-5863.

July 24, 25   **SCOTTISH/IRISH FESTIVAL AND GAMES**   **Free+$$**

Scottish athletic events, historical reenactments, Highland & Irish step dancing, Celtic music, crafts, food, drinks and more! Tickets $9-$14. Monterey Fairgrounds. Free Caber Parade at 5:30pm, Friday, July 23, on Ocean Ave. at Devendorf Park, Carmel. Celtic Concert Friday, too. Call for time and place. http://Montereyscotgames.com. 455-9640, 626-3551.

AUGUST

August tba   **GREAT TOMATO CONTEST AND PARTY**   **Free**

Vote on the best tomatoes around. Last year over 150 varieties were represented. 3-7pm. Monterey Fairgrounds, 375-4505.

Aug 7-8   **TURKISH ARTS & CULTURE FESTIVAL**   Free
Turkish art, crafts, music, folk and belly dancing, children's activities. Sat-Sun 11am-6pm. Festival free, post festival concert/dance $15-$20. Custom House Plaza. www.turkiye.net. 646-1916.

Aug 7-8   **CELEBRATION SIDEWALK SALE**   Free
Arts, handmade crafts and downtown merchants. 10m-5pm on Alvarado & Mall. 655-8070.

August 17-22   **MONTEREY COUNTY FAIR**   Free+$$
Food, entertainment, competitive and commercial exhibits, livestock, floriculture, 4-H, carnival rides and more. Specials and discounts include:

● Tues. 17th - $1 off admission, 12-1pm, with canned food donation.

● Tues. 17th - Senior's Day. 65+, $1 off admission & special activities.

● Wed. 18th - Kids under 12 admitted free to enjoy a variety of activities and entertainment designed just for them at Munchkin Meadows, with fun and safe rides, magic shows, singalongs, hands-on entertainment.

● Thurs. 19th - Special Friends' Day for individuals faced with physical and mental challenges. They are invited to enjoy the fair with free admission, before the crowds, starting at 11am, and free carnival rides throughout the day. A complimentary lunch, sponsored by the Rotary Clubs of the Monterey Peninsula will be served for the first 250 friends. Wheelchairs are available and may be reserved by calling Sue Houser at 372-5863 and 757-3110.

● Free admission every day for those in military uniforms.

● $1 and $3 off coupons available at local bookstores and merchants.

● The Fair Xpress Bus Tour brings performers to cities two days before the Fair; including: Goldie the Scarecrow, Elvis and McGruff the Crime Dog. They entertain onlookers and hand out Fair admission discount coupons. Call for locations 372-5863.

● Free shuttle service, provided by MST, is available from the Del Monte Shopping Center parking lot.

● Hours: Tue-Fri, noon-11pm, Sat 10am-11pm, Sun 10am-10pm. www.montereycountyfair.com. 372-5863.

August 27-28   **MONTEREY SPORTS CAR AUCTION** $$
Cars on display in the Custom House Plaza at noon on both days. Open to the public with an entrance fee. Auction at the DoubleTree Hotel at Fisherman's Wharf. Call for information, 800/211-4371.

August 27-29   **HISTORIC AUTOMOBILE RACES** $$
Races for seven groups, broken down by years (pre-1928 sport and racing cars through 1981 championship cars). 400 historic racing Ferraris, Alfa Romeos, Porsches and Cobras.   Tickets $25-$40. Volunteer opportunities. Laguna Seca on Highway 68. www.laguna-seca.com. 800/327-SECA.

August 28   **FAMILY FUN DAY**   Free
Musical entertainment, martial arts, theater and computer demonstrations, storytelling, face-painting, crafts, soccer contests, sack races, prizes. 10am-4pm. Monterey Peninsula College softball field, gymnasium, adjacent classrooms. Free parking. A Community of Caring event. 373-0154.

SEPTEMBER

September tba   DISCOVERY DAY   Free
Hands-on science activities for youth of all ages, 10am-3pm at the Naval Postgraduate School. Call for date. 656-3346.

September 4   ANNUAL REGGAEFEST $$
Reggae music, food and crafts. 10am-10pm. <u>Children 10 and under free</u> with
paid adult. Monterey Fairgrounds. Information: 394-6534. Tickets 372-5863.

September 4-6   ANNUAL GREEK FESTIVAL   Free
Live traditional music and costumed dancing. Food booths will serve Greek sal-
ads, mousaka, lamb and beef gyros, barbecued chicken, baklava and drinks.
Arts and crafts, children's games (a mini-carousel), drawing. Benefit for building
of a new church and other charities. Sat-Sun, 11am-7pm, Mon 11am-4pm, Cus-
tom House Plaza. Presented by Saint John the Baptist Greek Orthodox Church
of Monterey County, 424-4434.

September 4-6   PERUVIAN PASO HORSE SHOW   Free
"A Rolls Royce Ride, a Really Classy Horse Show." Sat-Sun 9am-5pm. Special
evening performance Sunday 6:30-9pm: champagne challenge, costumes, spe-
cial demonstrations. Monterey Fairgrounds. 484-2849.

September 6   CONCERT ON THE LAWN SERIES   Free
Special Sesquicentennial concert by the Monterey Bay Symphony at the Naval
Postgraduate School at 2pm. Come early and bring a picnic lunch. Orchestra
rehearsal at 1pm is open to the public. Free tours of the former Del Monte Hotel
and Arizona Cactus Garden. 656-2023.

September 10-12   GRAND PRIX OF MONTEREY $$
Featuring the Texaco/Havoline 300. <u>Volunteer opportunities</u>. Laguna Seca Race-
way, Highway 68. www.laguna-seca.com. 800/327-SECA.

September 11-12   FESTA ITALIA SANTA ROSALIA   Free
To honor the fishermen of this community and to keep the Italian culture alive.
Procession from San Carlos Cathedral through downtown Monterey to Custom
House Plaza with children dressed in colorful Italian traditional dress, a float
carrying Santa Rosalia, queen and princesses, Grand Marshall and wife, Monterey
High School Band, Peace Makers Drill Team, Presidio color guard. 2 day Na-
tional Bocce Ball Tournament with 60 teams and a $3,000 prize. Italian food
booths, dancers doing traditional Italian dances and arts and crafts fair. <u>Free
admission to the Maritime Museum</u>. Blessing of the Fleet. Sat-Sun, 10am-5pm.
Custom House Plaza. 649-6544.

September 17-19   MONTEREY JAZZ FESTIVAL   Free+$$
The longest continuously running jazz festival in the world. 42st year. 6pm-mid-
night Friday, 12:30pm to midnight Saturday, and noon-midnight Sunday. Monterey
Fairgrounds. www.montereyjazzfestival.org. 373-3366, 372-5863, 800-307-3378.
Tickets $12-$27. <u>Free jazz around town</u>: Jazz Mass at San Carlos Church, in the
San Carlos Cathedral Hall, on Church Street, just off Abrego. Celebrate faith
through a progressive jazz style Mass in which the hymns and acclamations will
be sung by choir and congregation accompanied by jazz organ, keyboard, wind,
bass, and drums. Plaza Linda Restaurant in Carmel Valley, 6-9pm Saturday.
Hyatt Lounge and Casa Munras Hotel in downtown Monterey will have jazz per-
formances Friday and Saturday.

September 18   **FALL FESTIVAL**   Free
Children's procession at 10am at Bay View Elementary School and continuing along Lighthouse Ave. to Scholze Park. Live music, face painting, clowns, jugglers, silent auction, sidewalk sales and food booths 'til 2pm. Call New Monterey Business Association president Kathi DeMaria at 375-0818.

September 18   **COASTAL CLEANUP**   Free
You've been enjoying those free beaches all year and now's the time to show your appreciation, earn free T-shirts and other rewards. Call 415/904-5210 for places and times to meet.

September 24-26   **CHERRY'S JUBILEE**   Free+$$
Restored hotrod and other classic car owners get together to celebrate with parties, dancing, food and souvenir booths. Free viewing: More than 800 restored classic cars cruise Monterey and settle on Cannery Row for a "Show and Shine" Friday 5-10pm; cars parade and are judged for "People's Choice Awards" at Steinbeck Plaza, with live blues band. Saturday and Sunday the cars cruise the track at Laguna Seca. The annual event is a fund-raiser for the Salinas Valley Memorial Hospital. Laguna Seca is free to children younger than 6, otherwise $8 for teens and adults, seniors $5, and $2 children 6-12. Volunteer opportunities. Laguna Seca Recreation Area, Highway 68. www.laguna-seca.com. 759-1836.

September 26   **FIRST NY VOLUNTEER REGIMENT**   Free
Re-enactments by the original regiment assigned to protect Monterey after the U.S. took California in 1846. The regiment will march, drill and shoot muskets at the Custom House from 11am-3pm. 647-6204.

OCTOBER

October 1   **LIBRARY ANNIVERSARY CELEBRATION**   Free
The first public library in California will celebrate its 150th anniversary. Monterey Public Library, 625 Pacific St. For information, call 646-3930.

October 2   **SESQUICENTENNIAL PARADE**   Free
9am parade to begin the major sesquicentennial month for Monterey. For more information, call 646-3991 or 646-5648.

October 2   **MOON FESTIVAL/NATIONAL HOLIDAYS**   Free
Chinese art, music, Kung Fu Martial art and video films. A special Chinese Cultural Program, 12-3pm in the DLI-REC Center, Presidio of Monterey, in Bldg. 843. Refreshments will be served. 394-2965.

October 4   **BLESSING OF THE ANIMALS SERVICES**   Free
Coinciding with the birthday of St. Francis of Assisi, at the following churches: 9:45am at St. John's Chapel, 1490 Mark Thomas Dr., co-sponsored by the SPCA. Dogs should be on leashes; cats, birds and others should be in cages. Church, 375-4463, SPCA, 373-2631. St. James Episcopal Church, 381 High St., at 9:45am, followed at 10am by Mass in honor of St. Francis and 11:30am by a festive Italian barbecue to celebrate the birthday of Christendom's beloved saint of "All things bright and beautiful!" Fun for children.

October 6   **CHILDREN'S DAY**   Free
Happy Birthday, Library! Sesquicentennial event. For more information, call 646-3930.

October 9   **MCAP AIDS WALK**   Spectators free
Registration-breakfast at 8:30am at Monterey High School (Hermann Drive). Walk through downtown, along the recreation trail to Lovers Point in Pacific Grove for

awards at 11:30. Food, music, prizes, massages, children's activities. Return shuttles available. 394-4747. Also in Santa Cruz: start in San Lorenzo Park, circular route along West Cliff Drive and return to the park. 408/427-3900.

October 9   **PARADE OF BOATS**   **Free**
Sesquicentennial event. (Or 10/8 date tbd). For more information, call 646-3991.

October 13   **CALIFORNIA CONSTITUTION DAY**   **Free**
Anniversary Celebration of California's 1849 Constitution, presented by City of Monterey, Colton Hall Museum, and Cultural Arts Commission. Reenactment by local thespians. Reception and refreshments. 6pm at Colton Hall Museum on Pacific Street. Reservations required. 646-5640.

October 13   **HISTORIC DANCE CONCERT**   **Free**
Sesquicentennial event. Special emphasis on dances of the 1840s and 1850s, both American and Californiano, followed by Fandango (Public Street Dance). City Hall. Sponsored by the City of Monterey, Monterey State Historic Park, and Monterey Museum of Art. Unveiling of Sesquicentennial public art and stamp cachet (Philatelic Club) at Colton Hall. 646-3991.

October 23   **MAKE A DIFFERENCE DAY IN MONTEREY**   **Free**
One-day community service project for local residents to help clean up, repair city parks and enjoy a free picnic. Register by calling the city volunteer program at 646-3719. Walk-in registration on the day will also be accepted. 9am-1pm. For other communities, call 800/776-9176.

October 31   **HALLOWEEN ACTIVITIES**   **Free**
Thinker Toys offers a Pumpkin Coloring Contest with a $25 gift certificate prize, Oct 20-31. Del Monte Shopping Center. 643-0907.

Del Monte Shopping Center, Highway 1 at Munras, costumed kids can Trick or Treat from 4-6pm. Chris, 373-2705.

Self-guided tours of **El Encinal Cemetery**, Fremont Blvd. and Aquajito Blvd. Brochures will be available from 8am-4pm that day at the office between Pearl and Fremont at El Estero. Look for headstones of Ed Ricketts, Flora Adams (Woods), cartoonist Jimmy Hatlo, actor Steve Cochran. 646-3864.

Halloween Pumpkin Carving Contest, ages 3-12, 10am at Archer Park Center, 542 Archer. Call for info, 646-3870.

The **Monterey Police Department**, 351 Madison, and three **Fire Departments**: Pacific and Madison Streets, 500 block of Hawthorne, Dela Vina & Montecito, will give away 22" glow-in-the-dark bands from 3:30pm until they run out. 646-3800.

Monterey Bay Urgent Care Medical Center will X-ray trick-or-treat candy tonight. Parents, kids and candy may drop by the center between 5-9pm at 245 Washington Street. For more information, call 372-2273.

NOVEMBER

November tba   **SOUTHWESTERN INDIAN SHOW**   **Free**
Jewelry, sand paintings, sculptures, kachinas, baskets, prints, art, rugs, pottery, gift items. Fri 5-8pm, Sat 11am-7pm, Sun 11am-5pm. Monterey Fairgrounds. 372-5863.

November tba   "HOLIDAY SURVIVAL WORKSHOP"   Free
How to streamline festivities, reduce stress, timesaving tips, inexpensive gift ideas, holiday spending plan. 6-8pm. Call for date and place, 800- 969-PLAN ext. 327.

November 11   VETERAN'S DAY ACTIVITIES   Free
Marine Corps Detachment at the Presidio of Monterey will hold a U.S. Marine Corps Birthday Proclamation ceremony at 10am at Custom House Plaza. A pass in review and retreat ceremony at 4:15 at the Presidio of Monterey's Soldiers Field will honor U.S. veterans of all wars. An open house at the Edge Club, Bldg. 221 on Patton Ave. The public is invited to attend.

November 11-14   R.L.S. UN-BIRTHDAY   Free
Storytelling, Scottish music, Stevenson House tours and un-birthday cake with costumed docents, actors, writers, musicians and refreshments. Sponsored by the California State Parks, the Robert Louis Stevenson Club of Monterey and the Old Monterey Preservation Society. Stevenson House, 530 Houston St. Call for times, 649-7118.

November 25   THANKSGIVING COMMUNITY DINNER   Free
Thanksgiving Day Dinner for anyone who doesn't want to be alone on the holiday. Or help serve Thanksgiving dinner to those in need. Call ahead or just show up. Monterey Fairgrounds. 372-5863.

November 26-28   WINTER GIFT FAIRE   Free
Food, arts, crafts. All artists on-site. Custom House Plaza. 622-0700.

DECEMBER

December 3   MONTEREY TREE LIGHTING CEREMONY   Free
Apple cider and refreshments are served after choral groups and bands and the 35' live fir tree is lighted. Santa Claus will be there to greet the children. In case of rain, ceremony will be held inside Colton Hall. 6:30-8pm, Colton Hall Museum, 351 Pacific Ave., 646-3866.

December 6   HOLIDAY ARTS & CRAFTS FESTIVAL   Free
Entertainment, local artists and vendors, refreshments, a visit from Santa. 10am-4pm, Monterey Sports Center Gymnasium, 301 E. Franklin St. Monterey Recreation and Community Services Department. 646-3866.

December 7   SANTA'S ARRIVAL   Free
Visits and activity on Alvarado Street at the Old Monterey Market Place, 5pm. Free pictures with Santa, 5-7pm, by Green's Camera.

December 7-9   HOSPICE TREES OF LIFE $$
Lightings and ceremonies in Monterey, Salinas and Hollister to honor the people we love who have passed on. Call Jennifer Joseph at the Hospice Foundation for more information. 333-9023.

December 9, 11   CHRISTMAS IN THE ADOBES $$
Candlelight luminaria, period decorations, musical entertainment, costumed volunteers, variety of refreshments in more than 20 adobes. Docents and military guard await your pleasure, 5-9pm. Tickets at Cooper-Molera store and Bay Books. Tickets are limited and reservations are encouraged. www.mbay.net/~mshp. 649-7118 (or 647-6226 after Oct. 15).

Dec 10-Jan 3   SPECIAL CHRISTMAS FESTIVITIES $$
Free for members and children under 12, $3 for nonmembers. Special exhibitions, miniature works of art, and decorated trees. Monterey Museum of Art, 599 Pacific Ave., 372-5477.

December 10   **LA POSADA**   **Free**
A traditional Christmas candlelight parade which reenacts the search of Mary and Joseph for lodging via the Larkin House, Stokes Adobe and Colton Hall. 6:30pm. at the Monterey Conference Center. For the whole family. Bring a candle or flashlight, join the procession, and sing Posada songs and Spanish Christmas carols. 646-3866.

December 12   **"BRIGHTEN THE HARBOR"**   **Spectators free**
Lighted boat parade begins at 5pm from the U.S. Coast Guard Pier, proceeding to Lovers Point and then returning to the Monterey Harbor. Free to watchers on shore or in boats, $25 entry per boat. Pick up entry forms at the Harbormaster's office, or call 645-1980. Sponsorships are tax deductible, proceeds to the Monterey Peninsula Youth Sailing Foundation. Refreshments and trophies afterwards at the pier. Drawings for prizes. 393-0303.

December 25   **CHRISTMAS COMMUNITY DINNER**   **Free**
Noon-3pm, everyone is welcome, sponsored by community businesses and individuals. Free food, entertainment and clothing for attendees as well as a visit from Santa and toys for the kids. Volunteers needed to donate items and time; call Barbara May, 375-8179. Monterey Fairgrounds. 372-5863, 373-3720. Homebound people may phone Sand City Police Chief Michael Klein at 394-1451 to arrange for dinner delivery.

December 31   **FIRST NIGHT® MONTEREY**   **Free+$$**
Millennium theme, 3pm to midnight. A non-alcoholic New Year's Eve celebration including music, entertainment, dancing, food and art exhibits. Over 100 groups from opera to rock, folk dancers to poets, actors to clowns. Mission is to strengthen our families and unite our community through the arts. Downtown Monterey is closed to traffic and cultural events take place on the street and inside the businesses. Buttons to admit to inside events $10, under 5 free. Plenty of things to see and do on the street. Support the arts and enjoy all of the entertainment. Free parking at Del Monte Shopping Center and shuttle service to downtown. All bus service will be free, 2pm-2am, to anyone wearing a First Night button. Free shuttle service for all passengers–button or not–between Del Monte Center and the Monterey Transit Plaza from 1pm-12:30am. Call 899-2555 for extra free routes. Call the Volunteer Center of Monterey to help with this event: 1-800-776-9176. Volunteers receive free admission to the event and a free T-shirt. www.firstnightmonterey.org. 373-4778.

Dec/Jan   **THE CALIFORNIA CHALLENGE**   **Free**
Designated driver program. Sly McFly's, The Mucky Duck, Bulldog Pub, Doc's Night Club, Whitey's Place, Cuz's Sportsman's Club, and the American Legion Hall participate by offering free entry and free sodas to designated drivers who fill out a RADD card available from participating establishments or downloaded from www.ubl.com/radd. This yearly event is sponsored by Recording Artists, Actors and Athletes Against Drunk Driving (RADD). Couch Distributing, 724-0649.

Coupon Savings Without Coupons

Pick up your free Safeway Club Card on your next visit to any Safeway and receive coupon savings on your purchases.

Carmel: Ask at your child's public school about a free way to earn money for the school using SCRIP currency at Safeway.

Entertainment

Music, Dancing, Karaoke and Pub Games

◆ **The Crown Anchor**, British pub and restaurant. Live music, Fri-Sat 9:30pm-1am. No cover. Free Quizgo trivia game, Wed 8:30pm. Happy Hour, Mon-Fri 4-6:30pm, special drink prices. 150 W. Franklin St. 649-6496.

◆ **Characters Sports Bar & Grill.** Live music, Sat 9:30pm-1am. No cover. Mon-Fri 4:30-6:30pm, complimentary appetizers with beverage purchase. Drink specials from 4pm. In the Marriott, 350 Calle Principal. 647-4023.

◆ **Long Bar.** Music and dancing, Thurs-Sun 9pm-1:30am. Karaoke, Thurs and Mon, special drink prices. Happy Hour, Mon-Wed/Fri 4-7pm, special drink prices. No cover. 180 E. Franklin. 372-2244.

◆ **Cibo Ristorante Italiano.** Live music, Tue-Sat, 9:30pm-1:30am. Sundays 8:30pm-12:30am. Jazz Happy Hour, Fridays 5-7pm. KSDC Happy Hour, Tuesdays 5-7pm, Soul/R&B, 9pm-12:30am. Wednesdays, World Beat 9pm-12:30am. No cover. 301 Alvarado. www.cibo.com. 649-8151.

◆ **McGarrett's' Club.** Free swing dance lessons Fri 8-9:30pm, dancing after, no cover. Wed 8-9pm, free line dancing lessons. 321 D Alvarado at Del Monte Ave., upstairs. Hospitality employees always get in free. 646-9244.

◆ **Viva Monterey.** Live DJ music & dancing 7 nights a week, 9pm-1:30am. No cover. 414 Alvarado St. Open 4pm-2am. 646-1415.

◆ **Ye Admiral Benbow Tavern.** Live music every other Friday, 9pm-midnight. No cover. Full lunch and dinner menu. 444 Alvarado St. 656-9543.

◆ **The Mucky Duck.** A bit of Britain in downtown Monterey. Tuesday is Quiz Night, $1 to play, 8-10pm with cash prizes. Live music outside Fri-Sat, 9pm. No cover. Happy Hour, Tues & Fri 4:30-8:30pm, discount drinks, half price appetizers. 479 Alvarado St., 655-3031.

◆ **Knuckles Historical Sports Bar.** Free munchies, free parking, children are welcome. Mon-Fri 4pm-1am, Sat 10am-1am, Sun 9:30am-1am.

◆ **Peninsula Lounge.** Jazz piano, Tues-Thurs 7-10pm; jazz band, Fri-Sat 8-midnight. No cover. At the Hyatt Regency, 372-1234.

◆ **El Indio**, Fresh Mexican Cantina. Happy Hour, Mon-Fri from 4-6pm with $2 Margaritas and $2 Drafts. Complimentary appetizers 5-6pm. Del Monte Shopping Center. 375-4446.

◆ **Casa Cafe & Bar.** Live music, no cover, Thurs 6-10pm, Fri-Sat 7-11pm. Mon-Fri 4:30-6:30pm, complimentary hors d'oeuvres, cocktails at Happy Hour prices. Casa Munras Garden Hotel, 700 Munras Ave. 375-2411.

◆ **The Safari Club.** Large screen. Mon-Fri 5-7pm, complimentary hors d'oeuvres, Happy Hour beer prices. The Bay Park Hotel, 1425 Munras Ave. 649-1020.

◆ **Wharfside.** Joe Lucido, jazz guitar, Fri 6:30-9:30pm. No cover and complimentary hors d'oeuvres. Fisherman's Wharf. 375-3956, fax 375-2967.

◆ **London Bridge Pub.** Seamus Kennedy will perform four times in 1999. April, June, July and October. No cover. Call for days and times. Free Celtic Jam, first Sundays at 6:30pm. At the entrance to Wharf #2. 655-2879.

◆ **Monterey Joe's.** Roger Eddy live, Thurs 5:30-8pm. No cover. 149 N. Fremont St., 655-3355.

◆ **Cafe of Controversy**, serves coffee, soda, candy and pastries, along with politics in the spirit of Jeffersonian democracy. Open Mic, Wed 8-11. 600 East Franklin St. 333-9134.

◆ **Good Vibrations DJs.** Free entry at various Monterey "hot spots" when Good Vibrations DJs are performing. Specializing in weddings, corporate events, and private parties. Call for schedule or to book, 647-9234.

Dance Groups

◆ **Dance lesson** free at the Monterey Peninsula Dance Association. Dances every Friday, 7-10pm. Learn to Lindy Hop, Shag, West Coast and East Coast Swing. Bring a friend, come have fun, call for your free lesson. 71 Soledad Drive, Mon-Fri, 11am-9pm, 648-8725.

◆ **Line Dancing**, free on Mondays, 6-8:30pm at the American Legion, top of Jefferson Street. First hour for beginners. 646-4035.

◆ **Scottish Country Dancing** on Mondays, 7-9pm, Monterey Senior Center, 18 and older, $1. 646-3873.

◆ **Contra Dancing,** 1st and 3rd Saturdays, 7:30pm, at the YMCA, 600 Camino El Estero. $7. www.nuthouse.com/contra/. 479-4059.

Dinner & Coffeehouse Entertainment

◆ **El Palomar.** Live Mexican music with dinner, Sat-Sun, 6:30-9pm. 724 Abrego St. 372-1032.

◆ **Lallapalooza Restaurant.** Sunday Jazz Series, 6-9pm, features Dennis Murphy & Friends. No cover. 474 Alvarado St.. 645-9036.

◆ **Morgan's Coffee and Tea**. Musical acts, some free. Saturday children's programs. 498 Washington St., 373-5601. Recorded schedule, 655-6868.

Movies and Theatre

◆ **Galaxy Six Cinemas.** Free refill on large popcorn and drinks. Seniors (55+), children, and matinees before 3pm, $4.50. Regular $7.50. 280 Del Monte Shopping Center, 655-4617 (777-FILM x135). www.cinemacal.com.

◆ **State Theater.** Free refill on large popcorn and drinks. Seniors (60+), & matinees before 6pm, $4.50. Regular $7.25. 417 Alvarado St, 372-4555.

◆ **MPC Theatre Company.** Children ages 5-17, accompanied by adult, are admitted free. Season tickets $45. MPC box office, 646-4213.

Play and Pray Together

◆ Join the Monterey **Community Band**, directed and conducted by Dick Robins. Performs at the City's Christmas Tree Lighting Ceremony, Spring Concert, and other community events. No auditions but you must be able to read music and provide your own instrument. Weekly rehearsals: Mondays, September through June, 7:15pm-9:15pm, Monterey High School Band Room (lower parking lot, off Martin Street). Sponsored by the Monterey Recreation and Community Services Dept. Call Cindy Vierra 646-3866.

◆ **Taize Services.** A candlelight service for prayer and meditation draws on the music and style of worship in Taize, an ecumenical Christian community in France. Instruments accompany the congregation in simple, chant-like prayerful song. Silent meditation and reflection. Infant care is provided (0 to 3 yrs.) Held 7:30pm, second Fridays, at the First Presbyterian Church of Monterey, 501 El Dorado, alternating months with St. Angela's in Pacific Grove. Other churches participate during Lent. 373-3031.

Jonathon Lee at the Big Sur Marathon

Jonathon Lee is one of Monterey's most beloved musicians. He volunteers every year to play at the International Big Sur Marathon and thousands are thrilled at his inspirational music on the edge of the Pacific Ocean. Jonathon is also available for day and evening functions. Two free offers for *Free & Fun Guide* owners: Buy a CD and get a free autographed photograph of Jonathon Lee – or – book and prepay a major event, such as a corporate meeting, wedding or concert, and receive a complete autographed set of Jonathon's CDs. Expires 7-1-99. 525 Hartnell St., 800-533-8233, fax 648-3333. www.redshift.com/~jlm.

Waterfront Parks & Activities

▲ **El Estero Park and Lake**, Aguajito Road and Del Monte Avenue. 45 acres. Dennis the Menace Playground is the City's most popular and most famous, being the result of creative efforts donated by Hank Ketcham, creator of the Dennis the Menace comic strip, local sculptor Arch Gardner, and the Monterey Peninsula Jaycees. Unusual playground equipment includes a real steam engine, Dennis the Menace sculpture and climbing structure, umbrella tree, the Thing, giant swing ride, balancing bridge, lion drinking fountain, suspension bridge,

giant slide, the maze, giant roller slide, moon bridge, circular slide and bell tower, coil spring with slide, and adventure ship. Harry Greene Island, a bird refuge in the middle of the lake, is named for the father of modern Monterey. Lake fishing (license required), barbecue/picnic, walking paths, benches, youth center, playing field, dance studio, boat concession and snack bar. Restrooms. Open 10 to dusk. 646-3866. Group picnic area 646-3866. Ballpark 646-3969. Snack Bar 372-8446. Youth Center 646-3873. Boating concession, paddle boats, 375-1484.

▲ **Skate Park.** A new skateboard park, to open sometime in 1999, will be located in the turnaround area of the parking lot behind Frank E. Sollecito, Jr. Ballpark and Dennis the Menace Park.

▲ **Fisherman's Shoreline Park**. Starts at Fisherman's Wharf, west to the Coast Guard Pier. Dogs on leash on the trail. 5 acres of grassy areas and bay view benches. Fine view of the wharf and boats in the marina. Gulls, pelicans, otters, seals, cormorants, paths to shore. Walk onto the Coast Guard pier to see the many sea lions at the end. Open dawn to dusk. 646-3866.

Other Fun Activities at El Estero Park

➤ **Monterey Peninsula Walking Club** meets at the Dennis the Menace parking lot every Sunday at 9am for a "Fun Walk" and the public is invited. Different levels of walkers: 1½ hrs. to 3 hrs. for a 10k or less. Variety of walks: into Pacific Grove, downtown Monterey, to Seaside or meet at Pt. Lobos. Call Will Lyon for more information, 375-5732.

➤ **Volunteer gardeners** meet 9am to noon, Tues and Thurs, in the French Consulate building, Franklin and Camino El Estero. Tools provided. To join the fun, contact the Monterey Parks Department, 755-4899.

▲ **Monterey State Beach** stretches along the Bay from Monterey's Municipal Wharf#2 east to Seaside. Handicapped access to trails. Fishing from pier requires no license, scuba diving, kayaking, swimming, hiking, biking, volleyball and kite flying. Wading, sunbathing, picnics, restrooms at the wharf. Dune restoration. Dogs on leash. Open dawn to dusk. Call to reserve the volleyball court, 646-3866.

More Ways to Have Fun at the Beach

➤ **Tidepooling**. Pick up a free High-Low Tide Book at any Longs Drug Store for a year's worth of high and low tide times, plus a wind chill factor table, times of sunrise and sunset, a highway and shore map from Pt. Año Nuevo to Lucia, phases of the moon, and 2 recipes for clam chowder. There are two Long's Drug Stores on the Monterey Peninsula: 686 Lighthouse Ave., New Monterey, and at 2170 Fremont St., Monterey.

HIGH **LOW TIDES** 1999

Compliments of —

Longs Drugs
"The Best Drug Store In Town"

686 LIGHTHOUSE AVENUE
MONTEREY, CA 93940
(408) 655-5404

— HEADQUARTERS FOR —

Prescriptions	Boxed Chocolates	Hardware
Photo Supplies	Baby Needs	Automotive Supplies
Film Processing	Small Appliances	Tobacco
Sporting Goods	Toiletries	Toys
Party Goods	Housewares	Medicines
Greeting Cards	Liquor - Wine	Cosmetics

Other California Locations on Back

➤ **Tips for Tidepooling**: Remain with your group—don't go off alone. Don't fool around on the rocks. Walk slowly and carefully as the rocks are very slippery. Wear tennis shoes. Don't get trapped by the rising tide. Waves can knock you down, so always watch for them. Don't bring glass containers in the tidepool areas. Don't pry animals from the rocks. Return animals to the same area from which you removed them. Return each rock to the exact spot you took it from. Sea animals don't like being stepped on or having fingers poked at them. Leave empty shells on the beach—they may be some animal's future home. Remember that all tidepool life is protected by law. (Courtesy Monterey Visitor and Convention Bureau)

➤ **Breakwater Cove Marina**, between Fisherman's Wharf and Wharf #2, has two concrete ramps for your boats or kayaks, restrooms, benches, restaurants. 646-3950

➤ July 5 is **Monterey Beach Cleanup Day**. Call 646-3719.

➤ September 18 is the **Annual Monterey Bay Coastal Cleanup** at the following beaches: Asilomar State Beach, Bay Street, Carmel Beach, Carmel River, Coast Guard Pier, Fort Ord, Garrapata, Kirby Park/Elkhorn Slough, Lovers Point, Marina State Beach, MacAbee Beach, Molera, Monastery Beach, Monterey Dunes, Monterey State Beach, Moss Landing, Naval Postgraduate School, Pfeiffer, Rocky Shores, Salinas River, Seaside State Beach, Spanish Bay, Tioga Road, Wharf #1, Wharf #2, Zmudowski. Volunteers will collect and document debris found in the ocean, on beaches, inland waterways and dunes. Volunteers will also receive a free Brita pitcher. Call 800-Coast4U.

➤ **Ocean Outreach Volunteers** conduct a training course for volunteers who wish to lead beach clean up programs, assist with community festivals, and much more. 2222 East Cliff Dr. Suite 5A, Santa Cruz. 408-462-9122.

➤ **Maritime Museum of Monterey** is looking for about 100 volunteers to act as docents during the late May visit of *H.M. Bark Endeavour*, scheduled to visit Monterey from May 29 to June 7 as a fund-raiser for the museum. Volunteers will receive two or three days of training. Call 372-2608, ext. 18.

Other City & County Parks

▲ **Casanova-Oak Knoll Park**, corner of Ramona and Euclid avenues. Fenced and nicely-maintained. Large barbecue area, grassy area and gigantic shade trees. Multipurpose rooms to rent. 646-3866.

▲ **Deer Flats Park**, on Deer Forest Road. Fenced in playground, small basketball court, quiet reading area.

▲ **Don Dahvee Greenbelt**. Munras Avenue between Del Monte Shopping Center and El Dorado Street. 35.8 acres with trails and picnic tables. Bicycle path. Open dawn to dusk.

▲ **Fisherman Flats Park**, San Vito Street. Grassy area and a well-maintained sandy play area with benches for parents.

▲ **Jack's Peak County Park**, 2.5 miles east of Monterey on Jack's Peak Drive south of Highway 68. 755-4899. Entry fee: Fri-Sun $3/car, Mon-Thurs $2/car. Call Monterey County Parks Administration Office for free entrance days: 888/588-CAMP, 755-4899 (undecided at press time). 1068 ft. summit, highest peak on the Peninsula. 525 acres of wildflower meadows and pine and oak forests. Grasslands, hiking and equestrian trails. Dogs on leash. The Skyline Self-Guided Nature Trail offers a view of Carmel Bay and Point Lobos. Picnic areas with barbecues. Trails include: Skyline and Rhus Trail Loop, 2.8 miles, easy; Coffeeberry Lower Ridge Loop, 2.5 miles, easy; Madrone Trail Loop, 2.3 miles, moderate.

▲ **Larkin Park**, at the northern ends of Monroe and Clay Streets. Everything you need including a basketball court. Busy and noisy.

▲ **Quarry Park**, on Via Del Pinar near Via Gayuba. Hiking trails.

▲ **Veterans Memorial Park**, Jefferson St. and Skyline Dr. 50 acres hiking trails, picnic areas, playing fields and restrooms. Camping with no hookups for $15/vehicle/night; hikers & bikers, $2/night. Access to Huckleberry Hill Nature Preserve, 81 acres of trails with good bay views. 646-3865.

▲ **Via Paraiso Park**, corner of Via Paraiso and Martin streets. 11 acres. Barbecue, picnic area, baseball diamond, large play area, tennis courts, basketball and volleyball. Trees and trails, clean restrooms. 646-3866.

▲ **Laguna Seca**, off Highway 68, 8 miles east of Monterey. $5 day/car use fee. Campsites with hookups, showers, restrooms. Fishing, rifle range, hiking trails, nature preserve. Monterey County Parks, 755-4899.

Laguna Seca Raceway

Laguna Seca is the site of a world class race track with special events throughout the year: The Sea Otter Classic, Cherry's Jubilee and more. Write to the Sports Car Racing Assn. of the Monterey Peninsula (SCRAMP) for event information and how you can volunteer to be involved (all proceeds to local charities): P.O. Box SCRAMP, Monterey, CA 93942. 648-5111. See Calendar of Events.

▲ **Presidio of Monterey**, site of the original Spanish Royal Presidential fortress in 1770, today home of the Defense Language Institute. Enter on Artillery St. from Pacific St. Turn right on Cpl. Ewing Rd. to see the Bouchard Monument, El Castillo site, and site of the first California Mass performed by Father Serra. Turn left at the end of Cpl. Ewing Rd. to see the Sloat Monument, Indian Village, and Serra Monument. Bay views. Site of an Ohlone Indian Village and burial ground. You can see the Indian Ceremonial Rock here and some artifacts at the Pacific Grove Museum of Natural History. Free walking tour map at the Public Affairs Office in Rasmussen Hall weekdays.

Left, Sloat Monument
Center, History markers
Right, Father Serra

Parks and Recreation Departments

▲ **Monterey Youth Center**, 777 Pearl St. Mon-Thurs 9am-9pm, Fri 9am-5pm, Sat 1-5pm. Closed Sunday. Call or visit today for a free catalog of activities. 646-3873.

▲ **Monterey City Parks & Recreation Departments**, Main office, 546 Dutra St. has many special events and programs and on-going activities for the entire family, such as: arts, crafts, cooking, dance, exercise, gymnastics, music, aquatics, aerobics, field sports. Pick up a current Activities Guide at the Dutra St. office, located in the old Vasquez Adobe behind Colton Hall; open 9am-4pm, 646-3866. Other centers: Archer Park Center, 542 Archer St., 646-3870; Monterey Senior Center, 280 Dickman Ave., 646-3878; Hilltop Park Center, 871 Jessie St., 646-3975; Casanova Oak Knoll Park Center, 735 Ramona Ave, 646-5665. For Monterey and other city residents. Monterey Parks Div. Office, 23 Ryan Ranch Rd. 646-3860.

Walks & Hikes

▲ **The Recreation Trail** along the coastline from Seaside to Pacific Grove follows the old railroad tracks and offers a wide avenue for walkers, bikers, rollerblades and strollers. Start at **Roberts Lake** in Seaside where there is ample parking and follow the path through a grove of Eucalyptus trees, past Del Monte beach, to Fisherman's Wharf where you can rest under the shade trees of **Peace Park**, visit the historic **Custom House**, and the shops of the Wharf. Downtown Monterey is just steps away. Follow the Trail again to the **Coast Guard Pier** and watch the seals and sea lions play. Next you'll pass through **Cannery Row** with all of its restaurants, sites and amenities. At the end of Cannery Row, you'll see the world famous **Monterey Bay Aquarium**, built on the site of Hovden's Cannery. Continue on the path past **The American Tin Cannery Outlet Stores, Hopkins Marine Station**, and follow the coastline to **Lovers Point** in Pacific Grove. Approx. 6 miles.

▲ Take a fun morning walk to the **Coast Guard Pier** to see the harbor seals, or to either of the Wharves to watch fishermen unload their catch and the markets open for business. Fabulous place to watch the sunrise.

Hiking & Biking

➤ **Monterey Bay Hash House Harriers** have noncompetitive 4-5 mile cross country fun runs at various locations in the Monterey Bay area every other Sunday at 1pm. Call Tim Thomas 728-2117, 267-1504.

➤ **Trail Runners of the Monterey Peninsula**, a new group for weekend and evening runs. All ages and levels welcome; beginners and slow runners are especially encouraged to participate. 384-0353.

➤ **Bicycle Rentals:** Adventures-by-the-Sea, 201 Alvarado Mall near the Maritime Museum, 648-7235. Group sales 648-7236, fax 372-4103, www.adventuresbythesea.com. Offers some free pickup and delivery. They also rent kayaks and in-line skates.

➤ Bikes ride free on **Monterey-Salinas Transit Buses**, 899-2555, 424-7695, www.mst.org.

➤ **Naturalist-led Hikes,** guided nature walks for outdoor enthusiasts and families. Ventana Wilderness, Carmel River Valley, State Parks of Big Sur, Monterey and Big Sur Coast. $10 per adult, $5 per child (no charge for children in backpacks or 2nd children). To make reservations, call 375-9831.

Fitness & Sports

▲ **Workout station** at El Estero Park. There are three exercise stations in the World Trail around Lake El Estero. Enjoy your workout surrounded by the beauty of the trees and lake, while Canadian geese, American coots and other sea fowl witness your effort.

▲ **Workout trail** at Monterey Peninsula College. Wells Fargo Game Field Walking Course. Park on Glenwood Circle and enter the campus through a gate by the National Guard Armory and football field. Equipment is old but usable for a good workout among the oak trees, with a beautiful view of the bay.

▲ **Bocce Ball.** There are three bocce ball courts at Custom House Plaza with free access to play this very old Italian game. The game is gaining in popularity and more courts are scheduled to be built soon.

More Fitness & Exercise

➤ **NFL Gatorade Punt, Pass & Kick** contest for boys and girls ages 8-15, usually in October. Free entry. Call 646-3969 for details.

➤ **Bicycle Rodeos** are held twice a year by the Monterey Police Department at several local schools. Safety inspection, presentations and a written and skills test, plus free gifts and prizes. Call Officer Michael Sargent at 646-3808 for dates.

➤ **Bay Physical Therapy** offers free sports injury evaluations, 1st and 3rd Wednesdays. 5-7pm. 787 Munras. Call for appt. 375-5909.

➤ **"Rideshare Week"** hosted by the Association of Monterey Bay Area Governments (AMBAG). Participants pledge to carpool, vanpool, take a bus, walk or telecommute at least one day during that week, and are eligible to win prizes. Call 422-POOL, 429-POOL OR 637-POOL.

➤ **"Exercise: A Guide From the National Institute on Aging,"** is a free 100-page manual that includes the latest research on the benefits of exercise, how to develop an exercise routine, and resource lists for older exercisers. To order, call 800-222-2225.

1999 Audubon Society Trips

The Society has a very dedicated and active group in the county. They welcome all newcomers to join them on these fun and educational outings. Call ahead for more details.

January 23   Lake San Antonio Boat Trip. Chris Tenney, 753-1656, Robert Horn, 372-4608.

February 21   Los Banos Field Trip. Sandhill cranes, ducks, owls, geese. Bring lunch. Meet at Los Banos Wildlife area on map at 9am. 2 hrs.... from Monterey. Paul Eastman, 624-8669.

February 27   Fort Hunter Liggett and South County. Details tba.

March 6   Beginner's Field Trip: Crespi Pond, near Asilomar, Pacific Grove, 9am. Robert Horn, 372-4608.

March 20   Monterey Peninsula coastline habitats. Brian Weed 373-2019. 8am at Wharf#2 base.

April 10   Pinnacles National Monument. 8:30am in the park. 7:30am Del Monte Center at Cinema #70. Vitaly Volmensky, 375-3906.

April 23-25   Salton Sea and Morongo Valley. Rick Fournier, 633-0572.

May 8   Bird songs of upper Carmel Valley. Jim Booker, 624-1202.

May 15-16   Cosumnes River Preserve, Sacramento River System. Tim Amaral, 663-4712.

May 22   California condors at Ventana Wilderness Sanctuary. Kelly Sorenson, 624-1202.

June 5   Pt. Lobos, meet at the park entrance 9am. Brian Weed, 373-2019.

June 12   Annual meeting/bird banding demonstration. Andrew Molera State Park. Details tba.

June 27   Kern River Preserve tentative.

Monterey Peninsula Audubon Society
Box 5656, Carmel, CA 93921.
831-645-6617. Rare Bird Alert 375-2577.

Free & Fun in
New Monterey
& Cannery Row

Steinbeck Plaza

San Carlos Beach

The Fish Hopper

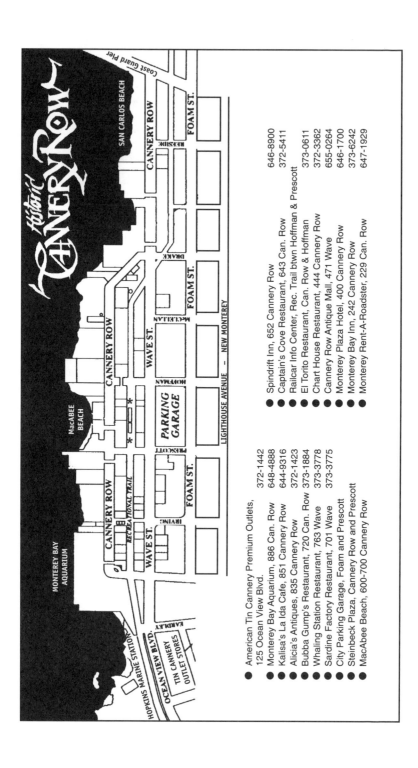

Historic Cannery Row

- American Tin Cannery Premium Outlets, 125 Ocean View Blvd. — 372-1442
- Monterey Bay Aquarium, 886 Can. Row — 648-4888
- Kalisa's La Ida Cafe, 851 Cannery Row — 644-9316
- Alicia's Antiques, 835 Cannery Row — 372-1423
- Bubba Gump's Restaurant, 720 Can. Row — 373-1884
- Whaling Station Restaurant, 763 Wave — 373-3778
- Sardine Factory Restaurant, 701 Wave — 373-3775
- City Parking Garage, Foam and Prescott
- Steinbeck Plaza, Cannery Row and Prescott
- MacAbee Beach, 600-700 Cannery Row

- Spindrift Inn, 652 Cannery Row — 646-8900
- Captain's Cove Restaurant, 643 Can. Row — 372-5411
- Railcar Info Center, Rec. Trail btwn Hoffman & Prescott
- El Torito Restaurant, Can. Row & Hoffman — 373-0611
- Chart House Restaurant, 444 Cannery Row — 372-3362
- Cannery Row Antique Mall, 471 Wave — 655-0264
- Monterey Plaza Hotel, 400 Cannery Row — 646-1700
- Monterey Bay Inn, 242 Cannery Row — 373-6242
- Monterey Rent-A-Roadster, 229 Can. Row — 647-1929

Historic Cannery Row
Walking Tour of Shops & Attractions

Cannery Row, originally called Old Ocean View Avenue, and often referred to as "America's Most Famous Street," was made famous by local author John Steinbeck in his book of the same name. He depicted the hardworking inhabitants – the Spanish, Chinese, Portuguese, Italians, Japanese and Scandinavians – who were the whalers, fishermen, and cannery workers. There were 21 canneries operating during the heydey years of 1921-1946.

Start your walking tour at the east end of Cannery Row near San Carlos Beach, at the entrance to the Breakwater Cove Marina and Coast Guard Pier. There is plenty of parking in this area.

The large concrete structure at 225, now home to **Adventures-by-the-Sea** and other shops, was the **Aeneas Packing Company**, built in 1945. It was one of the last canneries to be built.

Where to "Spot" Sea Otters
Municipal & Fisherman's Wharf, Coast Guard Breakwater, Cannery Row, Lovers Pt, Otter Pt, Pt Piños, Pt Joe, Bird Rock, Cypress Pt, Pescadero Pt, Carmel Pt, Pt Lobos.

The **Friends of the Sea Otter**, Retail and Educational Center, 381 Cannery Row Suite Q, is open daily, 10am-8pm, (9pm summer). Pick up free map for best places to spot otters, and educational material. 642-9037, www.seaotters.org.

At Drake and Wave Streets, look for the Jessie Cursault bronze memorial by the recreation path to **Edward F. 'Doc' Ricketts**, Steinbeck's friend and inspiration for several major characters in his books. Ricketts was a revolu-

tionary in marine biology and made tremendous contributions to modernizing the science. He was killed on this spot by the evening Del Monte Express train on May 8th, 1948. Daily an unknown admirer puts fresh flowers in Ed's outstretched hand.

At 425, you see the **Tevis Estate Carriage Houses**, part of an estate on 1000 feet of coastal frontage built in 1902. Major cannery figures Ben Senderman (owner, Carmel Canning Co.), Knute Hovden (owner, Hovden Food Products Corp.), and Frank Crispo (revitalization), also lived in these homes.

Encore Espresso, with homemade goodies and al fresco seating on the Recreation Trail, across from Doc Ricketts memorial, invites you to bring in your *Free & Fun Guide* and <u>receive one free coffee refill</u> of the coffee of the day with any purchase. Open daily, 6:30am-5pm. 655-3001.

At 471 Wave, the **Cannery Row Antique Mall**, once Carmel Canning Co. Warehouse, is listed on the National Register of Historic Places. Open Mon-Sat 10am-6pm, Sun 10am-5pm. 21,000 sq.ft. Venture to the second floor lounge to view <u>free changing displays</u> of people's collections. Toy trains, 40s and 50s fashions, antique fishing tackle, toys from yesteryear, and James Bond are examples of past displays. Lalique crystal shows, Jan-Feb, 1999. Free off-street parking. Call Claudia to find out what's next, 655-0264. antiques@redshift.com.

The pillars at 508 are all that remain of Cannery Row's first rudimentary canning shed opened on Ocean View Avenue in 1902 and sold in 1908 to become the Pacific Fish Company.

Edgewater Packing Company, 640 Wave St., is near the Recreation Trail and 600 Cannery Row. Watch the turn-of-the-century carousel and Dr. Leghorn C. Einstein (two pampered chickens who alternate shifts) play tic-tac-toe. Kids in costume ride the carousel for <u>free on Halloween</u>. 649-1899. There's a good bicycle map on the side of this building. Adjacent is an information center in the Heritage Railroad cars. Pick up <u>free maps and brochures</u>.

Restaurants, shops and offices now inhabit the old <u>Marina Apartments at 651,</u> which were built by the Wu family in 1929.

MacAbee Beach, at **Steinbeck Plaza**, Cannery Row and Prescott, was a lively whaling site for the Portuguese whalers in the 1870s and 1880s. Today there are many <u>free events</u> in the plaza and <u>live music</u> on weekends. The beach access affords views of the bay and steps to the water, favorite kayaking and diving spot; many benches to sit and relax. Follow the walkway next to the Spindrift Inn, open dawn to dusk, <u>no fee</u>.

Adjacent to the plaza, at 711, sits a replica of the **Monterey Canning Company**
building, which was a major canning en-
terprise owned by George Harper and
A.M. Allen. Today it's home to 40 businesses, restaurants and the second floor
Artist Colony.

685 Cannery Row: Check out: **Boyz Toyz**, a unique and fun shop for boyz
and girlz of all ages. 333-1060. boyztoyz@juno.com. **Riley Golf**, Free swing
analysis and advice on how to play better and enjoy the game more. 373-
8855. www.rileygolf.com.

Spirit of Monterey Wax Museum, 700 Cannery Row at Prescott Avenue.
California history is reenacted in life-like prominent characters. A self-
guided tour covers 400 years of history in about 20 minutes: scenes from
John Steinbeck novels, dioramas of Kit Carson, Native Americans, friars
and conquistadors. Open daily, 9am-9pm. Children 6 and under free; free
to all costumed children, ages 10 and under, on Halloween. 375-3770.

A Taste of Monterey is upstairs over the water at 700 Cannery Row. Features over 30 local wineries, Monterey theme gift center, winery maps and
tour information. The visitors' center has a panoramic view of the entire
bay from Monterey to Santa Cruz, with entertaining and educational exhibits. Relax at one of their window tables, enjoy a glass of Monterey County
wine; sample local produce plates and appetizers. 11-6 daily. 646-5446.

At 720, **Bubba Gump's Restaurant**
occupies a rebuilt reduction plant
which turned sardines into fertil-
izer and fishmeal. *"Forrest Gump"*
greets and charms visitors on the
bench, with his box of chocolates,
in front of the restaurant, Saturday, 1-6pm. Gift shop of movie
paraphernalia. Open 11am-10pm
daily. 373-1884.

The two walls of murals on either side of Cannery Row depict scenes from
its heyday. At **Bruce Ariss Way** and Cannery Row, peek into the preserved
cannery workers' shacks which are furnished in 1930s style. Here again is
the recreation
trail which runs
from Seaside to
Pacific Grove,
through the Row
- a good venue for
walking, bicy-
cling or skating.

Mackerel Jack's Trading Company at 799 is the site of Flora Woods' Lone Star Cafe and house of ill repute. John Steinbeck renamed it The Bear Flag Restaurant, owned by 'Dora Flood,' in his novel, *Cannery Row*.

The brown board building at 800 was Doc Rickett's **Pacific Biological Laboratories**, known as 'Doc's Lab' in *Cannery Row*. The Lab is occasionally open to the public by the Cannery Row Foundation. Call 649-6690.

The Sea Pride Canning Company built in 1917, at 807, is now the Cannery Row Trading Company. **Old Cannery Row Fudge Company** gives free fudge samples made the old-fashioned way. Mail order available. 373-6672.

Wing Chong Market, 835, was built in 1918 by Won Yee, who became 'Lee Chong' in Steinbeck's *Cannery Row*. **Alicia's Antiques** houses the Steinbeck Remembrance Room of memorabilia, in the rear of the building, which is open free to the public.

Kalisa's, next door at 851, was originally a boarding house built in 1929, and renamed the 'La Ida Cafe' in Chapter 7 of *Cannery Row*. Kalisa Moore has run the little cafe since the 1960s. Drumming and dancing free, Fridays, 8-10pm. Call for other entertainment and events, 656-0967, 644-9316.

Monterey Bay National Marine Sanctuary

➤ Interpretive Center for the Sanctuary. Free admission, Mon-Fri, 9am-5pm. Special events and programs. 299 Foam Street at D Street. Call for information, 647-4201. www.bonita.mbnms.nos.noaa.gov/

Free "Presenting Cannery Row" Forums

➤ Held the second Thursday of each month at The Monterey Bay Aquarium Education Center by the Cannery Row Foundation. Forums present all the facts on aquarium exhibits, research, conservation efforts, education programs and membership–along with a cyber-tour of the bay, from the tidepools to the depths of a vast underwater canyon. Call 375-4982 or 372-8512.

Otter-Mobile Tours and Charters

Free with mention of *Free & Fun Guide*: One Monterey Bay Aquarium ticket for every two paying people on the Monterey Peninsula tour which includes, in detail, Monterey, Pacific Grove, Pebble Beach and Carmel. Highly recommended tour with historic and current narrative. 9am-5pm. Paula DiCarlo, 649-4523, fax 333-0832.

Tours & Charters

Monterey
Carmel
Pacific Grove
Pebble Beach
17 Mile Drive
Big Sur
Point Lobos
Steinbeck/
Winery Tour

Groups and Individuals

OTTER - MOBILE

CA tcp 4865-S-P (831) 649-4523 Fax 333-0832

The Monterey Bay Aquarium

At 886, the end of Cannery Row, the world famous **Monterey Bay Aquarium**, formerly the site of Hovden Food Products Corp., is the most visited aquarium in the U.S.

● Open 10am-6pm daily; closed Christmas. (9:30am-6pm during summer and holiday periods).

● There are more than 100 galleries and exhibits to see and touch the sea life of Monterey Bay, including sea turtles, fish and shrimp and video and hands-on displays.

● The three-story Kelp Forest exhibit, a dynamic, living kelp forest community has feeding shows by divers daily at 11:30 and 4.

● "Sea Otters along the Rocky Coast," is a nose-to-nose encounter with California sea otters swimming in a 55,000 gallon, naturalistic exhibit; three feeding shows daily at 10:30, 1:30 and 3:30.

● The new Outer Bay exhibit has what is said to be the largest window in the world. It's 54' long, 15' tall and 13" thick.

● Current exhibit on threats facing fish populations, "Fishing for Solutions: What's the Catch?" is ongoing through January 2000. "The Inside Story: Behind the Scenes," is a special exhibit until January 3, 2000. For exhibit info, call Ken Peterson, 648-4922.

● The Aquarium offers several <u>free educational events, free admission to residents once a year, and volunteer opportunities</u>. Guide training classes include the cultural and natural history of the Monterey Bay region, basic marine science and techniques for sharing information with the public. <u>Discount admission rates for seniors, youth and groups</u>. For more information, call 648-4800. Automated information 648-4888; education 648-4850; volunteer office 648-4867; tickets 800-756-3737.

Art Galleries, Museums & Bookstores

● **Thomas Kinkade Archives**, 550 Wave St., 10-5 daily. 657-1554; 400 Cannery Row, Mon-Sat, 10-8, Sun, 10-5, 657-2350; 685 Cannery Row, 10-8 daily, 657-2365.

● **Crystal Fox**, 400 Cannery Row. Mon-Sat, 10-8, Sun 10-5, 655-3905.

● **Robert Lyn Nelson Studios**, 660 Cannery Row#105. 9-9 daily, 655-8500.

● **Sculptures by the Sea**, 685 Cannery Row. Mark Hopkins bronzes, Boehm, Armani and Lladro porcelain, and Swarovski crystal. 11-7 daily, 649-5250.

● **The Happy Store**, 700 Cannery Row. Happy Art by Sally Huss and others. Pick up The Happy Store's Guide to Dining on Cannery Row with a coupon for free appetizers. Mon-Thurs, 10-6, Fri-Sat, 10-9, Sun 10-7. 649-4877.

● **The Artist Colony**, second floor at 700 Cannery Row:

   Frank Sunseri Sculpture. Welded-metal, stone and cast bronze sculptures by Frank Sunseri, since 1976 on the Row. 372-6345.

   Enchanted Angels. #RR. Store of, by and for angels. Channeling lessons, Wed & Sun, 7pm. $10 first two times, then free. Doris, 655-8408.

● **A Book Search by McWilliams & Chee,** Old and Rare Books, 471 Wave. email: abooksearch@redshift.com. www.abooksearch.com. 656-9264.

● **Monterey Cypress Stained Glass,** 400 Foam St. Original designs. Open Mon-Sat, 10am-5:30pm. Sundays by appointment. 373-1989.

● **John Steinbeck Bookstore & Museum**, 551 Foam St. Free admission 10-6pm daily. Visit the past of Steinbeck and learn about the myths and legends of Cannery Row. Walking and lecture tours. Movies, memorabilia, gifts, first editions, new and used books. Closed some Sundays. 646-9117.

● **Books and Things**, 224 Lighthouse. Large and varied stock of old, used, out-of-print and rare titles. Mon-Sat, 11am-6pm, 655-8784.

● **O'Reilly's Antiques & Books**, 600 Lighthouse. Books, silver, furniture. Estates bought...1 item to a houseful. 656-9600.

● **Basset Books**, 626 Lighthouse. Large, varied selection of old, aged, and out-of-print books. Cafe, Sun-Fri, 10am-6pm., Sat, 10am-10pm, 655-3433.

● **Old Capitol Book Co.**, 639-A Lighthouse. Large and varied stock of old, used, out-of-print & rare titles. Mon-Sat, 10am-6pm, 375-2665.

● **Cross Roads International Bible Bookstore**, 699 Lighthouse. 10am-7pm daily. 372-3860, fax 372-4042.

● **Lighthouse Books**, 801 Lighthouse. Specializing in Steinbeck, photography, modern first editions. Wed-Mon, 10:30am-6:30pm. 372-0653.

● **The Monterey Bay Sports Museum**, 883 Lighthouse. 11am-6pm daily. Free admission. 2 blocks from the Aquarium. Enter this museum through a turnstile installed at Pittsburgh's Forbes Field in 1909. Baseball, boxing and football exhibits. 655-2363.

Nature & Activities

Cannery Row Parks & Beaches

▲ **San Carlos Beach**, at the entrance to Cannery Row at the foot of Reeside Avenue and the Coast Guard pier. Site of one of Cannery Row's famous sardine canneries: the San Carlos Canning Co. Swimming, world-renowned scuba diving, picnic tables, grassy areas, restrooms. Check out the bronze starfish and seashells on the rocks. Open dawn to dusk. 646-3860.

▲ **MacAbee Beach**, narrow entry next to the Spindrift Inn, 652 Cannery Row. Popular with scuba divers. Open dawn to dusk. Grassy area, benches, restrooms. Kayaking takes you out on the water to enjoy the many marine birds and mammals: sea otters, seals, sea lions, giant brown pelican, cormorant, common meurre, grebes, seagulls, surf scoters, Canadian geese, American coot, mallards, and many more.

New Monterey Parks

▲ **Cypress Park**, corner of Cypress Street and Hoffman Avenue. Full-size tennis court, grassy area and benches. Rocky area.

▲ **Scholze Park**, Dickman and Lighthouse avenues. Grassy areas, big trees, picnic tables. Location of Senior Center and Friday **MarketFest**, 4-7pm.

▲ **Archer Park Center and Hoffman Park**, on Archer Street between Hoffman and McClellan avenues. Clean play area and spacious, tree-lined barbecue area and multi-purpose rooms. Nice view of Monterey Bay.

▲ **Hilltop Park and Hilltop Park Center**, 871 Jessie Street. 2.8 acres with barbecue/picnic, lawn, play equipment, playground, basketball, baseball, tennis. Open dawn to dusk. 646-3975.

▲ **Oak-Newton Park**, between Oak and Newton streets. Quiet and well-equipped for children. Large grassy area, picnic areas, shade trees, basketball court. Clean rest rooms. A pedestrian gate on the eastern end connects the park to the Presidio.

Dive, Surf and Bike Free Offers

➤ **Bamboo Dive Shop,** 614 Lighthouse. Free air on Fridays. Mon-Fri 9-6. Sat-Sun 7-6. 372-1685.

➤ **On the Beach Surf Shop**, 693 Lighthouse, 646-9283. Free wax and stickers with any purchase.

➤ Free air and same day repairs at **Joselyn's Bicycles**, 638 Lighthouse, 649-8520.

1999 Calendar of Events

Information subject to change. Please call in advance to verify.

February 16   **MARDI GRAS**   **Free**
"Fat Tuesday" with live broadcasts from New Wave radio stations and a "Doo Dah" parade. Entertainment throughout the evening. 649-6640.

February 27   **STEINBECK'S BIRTHDAY PARTY**   **Free**
Cannery Row Birthday Party commemorating the famed author and Salinas' native son, John Steinbeck. 372-8512.

May 1   **HONDA CHALLENGE ON CANNERY ROW**   **Free**
AMA National Superbike Championships. Street closure, cycle displays, autograph sessions and musical entertainment on Cannery Row in celebration of Laguna Seca's motorcycle championships. 373-2259.

May 14   **ED RICKETTS BIRTHDAY CELEBRATION**   **Free**
Call 372-8512.

June tba   **MY MUSEUM BIRTHDAY CELEBRATION**   **Free**
Free prizes and birthday cake; kids entertainment, bounce house, bungee run, coloring contest. Free MY Museum T-shirts to the first 100 kids entering MY Museum. A fun place for kids with a creation center, magnetic center, giant loom, build a house plus lots and lots of other things to do. 601 Wave between Hoffman and Prescott. 3rd floor, 10am-5pm, closed Wednesdays. 649-6444.

July 10   **WORLD SUPERBIKE RACE NITE**   **Free**
6-10pm Saturday to honor Laguna Seca's McGraw Insurance U.S. World Superbike championship races. Cannery Row will be closed between Hoffman and David avenue; open to motorcycles for cruising, parking, exhibits. Live music, stunt shows, riders and racers. Volunteer with the Cannery Row Company to help out with this event if you like bikes. 372-2259.

August 28   **HISTORIC AUTOMOBILE RACES**   **Free**
Vintage car displays and musical entertainment to welcome racers. 372-2259.

September 24-26   **CHERRY'S JUBILEE**   **Free**
Restored hotrod and other classic car owners get together to celebrate with parties, dancing, food and souvenir booths. More than 800 restored classic cars cruise Monterey and settle on Cannery Row for a "Show and Shine" Friday from 5-10pm as cars parade and are judged for "People's Choice Awards" at Steinbeck Plaza, complete with a live band.

October 31   **HALLOWEEN ACTIVITIES ON THE ROW**   **Free**
Halloween Costume Contest, 7-12pm. Free admission, food, parking. **Schooners Bistro on the Bay** in the Monterey Plaza Hotel, 400 Cannery Row. 372-BOAT.

Trick or treat the merchants on Cannery Row (4-7pm) for free candy, balloons, coffee and hot chocolate, free face painting, free carousel rides for children under 10 and in costume at the **Edgewater Packing Company**, free admission to the **Spirit of Monterey Wax Museum**, free or discounted meals for every two children with one adult ordering from the regular menu, at participating restaurants. 649-6690. **The American Tin Cannery** also holds its "Safe & Sane Trick or Treat" from 3-5pm at 45 store locations.

<u>Ghoulish fun</u> at **Hilltop Park Center**'s Halloween Celebration. Activities throughout the day, including a mini-Halloween Carnival and a costume contest. Families welcome, 10am-2pm. 646-3866.

November 26   CHRISTMAS TREE LIGHTING CEREMONY   Free
6pm. "Snow on the Row". Tons of real snow will decorate Steinbeck Plaza for the annual Cannery Row Christmas tree lighting. Music and caroling with the arrival of Santa Claus. Free pictures of kids with Santa. 649-6690.

Row Rats Wanted

Cannery Row's corps of volunteers, the "Row Rats," are seeking additional volunteers for public projects and events on the Row. Hard work, camaraderie and special perks from Cannery Row businesses and restaurants for jobs such as marshalls, vehicle control, communications, traffic barricade monitors. New "Row Rat" volunteers can call 648-8132 for more info.

Public Art at San Carlos Beach

Entertainment
Cannery Row

◆ **Schooners**, Friday, 5:30-8:30pm, live music for Happy Hour, <u>no cover</u>, full bar, validated valet parking. Martini Monday, enjoy specialty martinis and chef's complimentary hors d'oeuvres, 5-10pm. Monterey Plaza Hotel, 400 Cannery Row. 646-BOAT, fax 647-5937, www.montereyplaza.com.

◆ **Planet Gemini**, 625 Cannery Row, comedy club, 373-1449. Cover.

◆ **Blue Fin Cafe & Billiards**, 685 Cannery Row, Steinbeck Plaza, 3rd floor. <u>Free pool</u> while you eat lunch 11am-4pm, Mon-Fri. Happy Hour, 4-7pm, Mon-Fri. <u>Free swing lessons,</u> 8pm, Thurs. Music, Mon-Tues, from 7pm; Wed-Sat, from 9pm; Sun, 10pm-1am. Two for Tuesday, 2 for 1 well drinks and appetizers, 7pm-close. 375-7000, www.bluefin-billiards.com.

◆ **Fish Hopper Restaurant**, 700 Cannery Row. Tues-Fri, Happy Hour, 4-6:30, <u>complimentary</u> tropical hors d'oeuvres, live music. 372-8543.

◆ **Sly McFly's Refueling Station**, 700 Cannery Row. The hottest Blues & Jazz Club in Monterey. Happy Hour, Mon-Fri, 4-7pm. Open Mic and Hot Jazz Jam, Tues, Fri, Sat & Sun, 1-3pm. Piano bar sing along. <u>No cover</u>. 649-8050.

◆ Drum and Dance class, Friday, 8-10pm, **Kalisa's La Ida Cafe**, 851 Cannery Row. Everyone welcome, <u>no cover</u>, donations accepted. Other events, call 625-2111.

◆ **Doc's Nightclub**, at 95 Prescott. Music six nights a week, open 8pm, shows at 9, cover charge varies. Call for information, 649-4241.

New Monterey

◆ **Gianni's Pizza**, 725 Lighthouse Ave. <u>Dinner music</u>, Saturday, 6-8pm, and the best pizza in town anytime. 649-1500.

◆ **El Nido**, 794 Lighthouse Ave. Live music, Friday, 9:30pm-1am. <u>No cover</u>.

◆ Horon Turkish Fold Ensemble offers <u>free dance classes</u> from different provinces of Turkey every Thurs from 7-9pm at the **Monterey Senior Center**, Lighthouse and Dickman avenues. 646-1916.

◆ **Dream Theater**, 301 Prescott. Matinee price until 6pm. Tues, all seats $2.50; come early! <u>Free refill</u> on large popcorn & soda. 372-1494. www.movie-tickets.com.

◆ **Hoffman Playhouse**, 320 Hoffman Ave. Call for info, 649-0259.

Free & Fun in
Pacific Grove

Lighthouse Keepers

Lovers Point

Victorian Houses

Pacific Grove, winter haven to thousands of Monarch butterflies, is a year 'round paradise for visitors and residents, with lots of free and fun things to see and do. Visit Victorian homes and gardens; browse the shops, free museums, and art galleries; enjoy the parks and beaches. Ocean View Boulevard around the point of the Monterey Peninsula takes you past some of the most beautiful scenery in the world, including sea birds and sea mammals, Pt. Piños Lighthouse, and Asilomar State Beach.

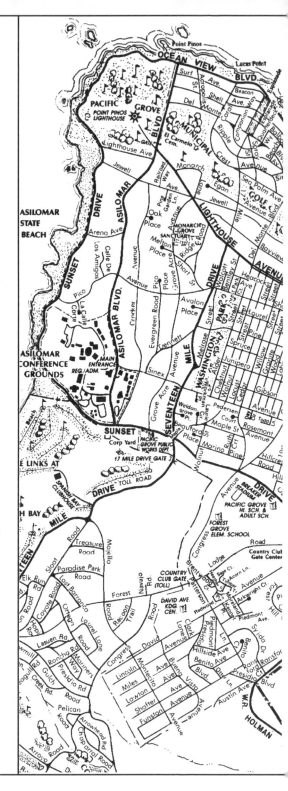

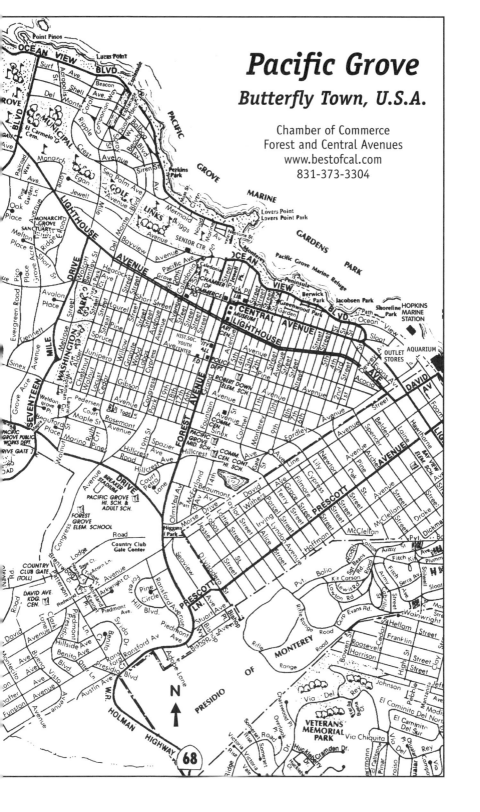

Pacific Grove
Butterfly Town, U.S.A.

Chamber of Commerce
Forest and Central Avenues
www.bestofcal.com
831-373-3304

Historic Downtown Walking Tour

Get oriented with a leisurely stroll through this historic seaside village. The town had its beginning in 1875 as a summer Methodist camp, where several hundred people assembled to worship amidst rough tents. The first camp meeting of the Pacific Coast branch of the Chautauqua Literary and Scientific Circle was held here in June 1879. Fashioned after the Methodist Sunday school teachers' training camp established in 1874 at Lake Chautauqua, N.Y., this location was part of a nationwide educational/cultural network. In 1889, the resort was incorporated, becoming the City of Pacific Grove. The following is adapted from an historic walking tour prepared by local resident and historian Alice Trosow.

Begin your walking tour at the **Chamber of Commerce** building on the corner of Central and Forest Avenues. Here you'll find a lodging referral system, brochures, maps, postcards, and other helpful information. If you're staying in P.G., October to March, pick up your free packet of gifts including coupons for a T-shirt, pizza, 17-Mile Drive admission, Monarch magnet and film developing. Buy aquarium tickets here. Mon-Fri, 9:30am-5pm, Sat 10am-3pm. 373-3304, fax 373-3317, www.bestofcal.com.

Walk across the street to the **Museum of Natural History**, a 1932 adobe-style at 165 Forest, with Larry Foster's life-sized sculpture of Sandy the Gray Whale in front. The museum exhibits include local birds, mammals, reptiles, amphibians, insects, Indian lore and geology. There  is also a relief map of Monterey Bay showing the great canyon plunging to 8400 feet. The native plant garden contains many rare species whose total life range is confined to the Monterey Peninsula. Watch a short video on the overwintering Monarch butterflies. Gift shop merchandise pertains to natural history: shells, minerals, posters, books, etc. Rub the mammoth jade stone sculptures in the entrance and garden. Several local groups hold free & open to the public meetings here, including the P.G. Eco-Corps, second Wednesdays at 7:30pm. <u>Free admission</u> to the museum, Tues-Sun, 10am-5pm. Call for other free events and how you can volunteer to help, 648-3116.

Museum of Natural History 1999 Exhibits

February 13–April 25	Mysterious Manatees
April 16–18	Wildflower Show
May 8–July 4	Landforms Photographs by Mr. Hertzbach
July 17–October 17	Madagascar's Biodiversity
October 30–Dec. 31	Editor's Choice of Nature Photographs

Continue on Central; turn left at Fountain: 100 BLOCK OF FOUNTAIN AV-
ENUE. Below Central. An early residential street in the Retreat, this block
retains many of its original structures. 138 & 138¹/₂, Mrs. Myretta Steiner
House, built in 1892 for A.J. Steiner (who owned a grocery store at Lighthouse and Forest in the 1880s and 90s), this house displays both Queen
Anne and Stick details. The smaller house, originally detached, may have
been a storage shed or servants' quarters. 122-124 – Paris Kilburn House –
Built in 1889, this unusual boat-like house features an eclectic array of
detail work. 116 – "Bathhouse" Smith House – This 2-story barn-like house
was built around 1910, and originally stood at Lovers Point. It features a
gambrel roof, shed dormers, and a variety of paned windows.

At the foot of Fountain is: SEVEN
GABLES, 555 Ocean View. Built in
1886. First owner Jane Page came
from Salem, MA, and named her
home after Hawthorne's novel. Mrs.
Page and later owner Lucy Chase
were civic leaders involved with the
Museum of Natural History. It has
recently been remodeled.

Next door is: GRAND VIEW INN, 105 Grand Ave. Once called "Roserox," this
house was built in 1910 for Dr. Julia B. Platt, a pioneer neurobiologist and
the town's first woman mayor. Now an elegant inn, the house boasts a
commanding view of Lovers Point.

On Ocean View, walk one block to 15th, turn right: MRS. L.H. CODDINGTON'S
HOUSE, 109 15th Street. Built in 1888, this is a pretty example of early
P.G. camp meeting style. The facade's decorative frieze is especially pleas-
ing. The cottage's careful restoration earned a Heritage House Award.

*Continue up to Central, turn left, go one
block to*: ST. MARY'S BY-THE-SEA, 12th
& Central. P.G.'s first formal church, cop-
ied in 1887 from a Gothic church in
Bath, England. Cyrus McCormick (the
inventor's nephew) donated two Tiffany
windows in memory of his wife, whom
he married here in 1889. Sunday Eucha-
rist is at 8am and 10am. You'll find bargains in their thrift store, Mon-Wed-Fri-
Sat, 1-4pm. Watch for their Antique
Show in July. The chapel is open free to

visitors, 12:30-2pm, Mon-Wed-Fri. 373-4441.

Walk up 12th to Lighthouse, turn right to Fountain: STOREFRONTS, 541-553
Lighthouse. These detailed pre-1900 storefronts include 549 and 551 built
in 1888; the Grove's first pharmacy, operated by pharmacist/photographer
C.K. Tuttle, and 553 (originally a tobacco store).

Continue along Lighthouse to Forest:
BRATTY REAL ESTATE, 574 Lighthouse. Built in 1904 by Watsonville
architect W.H. Weeks, this was originally the Bank of Pacific Grove. It
features simulated stone block siding, and is the only example of Ro-
manesque revival style on the Peninsula. _Free rental services_, Mon-Fri
9-5, Sat 10-4, Sun 11-2.

Turn left at Forest, go one block to Laurel,
CITY HALL, 300 Forest Ave. This structure originally served as both police and fire station.
The tower housed hoses and the old fire bell
(now in front of the fire station at 580 Pine).
Plans are underway to make this building the
cornerstone of a new Civic Center that would
encompass the entire block and provide
needed facilities to serve the Council and the
community.

Turn right on Laurel and go to 17th:
KETCHUM'S BARN, Laurel and 17th. Built
in 1891 by H.C. Ketchum, animals were
kept on the ground floor and hay and
other provisions stored in the loft. This
square board and batten barn is now the
home of the P.G. Heritage Society. _Free
and open to the public_ Saturday, 1-4pm.

Across 17th and Laurel is: OLD 17TH STREET. Above Lighthouse. Most of the
cottages on this block were built in the 1880s; a few were built around
1900. Most of these cottages have been converted for commercial uses,
yet the street retains its charming flavor.

Follow Laurel to 18th, turn right to Lighthouse: GOSBY HOUSE, 643 Lighthouse. In 1888, J.S. Gosbey, owner of P.G.'s first shoe store, opened his
home to summer boarders. To house more guests, he added to the Queen
Anne building several times, resulting in the inn's irregular plan.

Next door is: HART MANSION, 649 Lighthouse. This Queen Anne structure
has not changed significantly since it was built in 1894 by Dr. Andrew J.
Hart. The first floor was used for his medical practice, and the 2nd and 3rd
floors for his residence, now a popular restaurant.

Continue 1 block on Lighthouse to 16th: WINSTON HOTEL, 16th and Lighthouse. Built in 1904 by B.C. Winston, a showman who brought buffalo and
trained sea lions to P.G. The hotel boasted rooms on the 2nd and 3rd floors
and a restaurant and shops on the ground floor.

Turn left down 16th: ELMARIE H. DYKE OPEN SPACE, 16th below Lighthouse. Dedicated to the woman affectionately dubbed "Mrs. Pacific Grove." Educator, civic leader and radio personality, her efforts ensured that P.G. remained (until 1969) the last dry town in California.

Next door, at the corner of Central is: CHAUTAUQUA HALL, 16th and Central. Since 1881, this has been a vital part of the community, serving as storage space for the Retreat's tents, church, school, gym, youth center, and meeting place. Last Chautagua was August 1926. In 1970, it became California Landmark #839.

Across Central is: CENTRELLA HOTEL, 612 Central. Built in 1889 to house Chautauqua-goers, the building originally faced 17th St. 1892 saw the addition of the square corner towers and porch. Completely restored.

Continue down 16th: 100 BLOCK OF 16TH ST. Below Central. Several tiny tent cottages line this street. 152 & 154 – Mrs. Eliza Beighle Houses, built in 1901 and 1892. 137 – Mrs. Caroline Thorton House. This Carpenter Gothic cottage was built in 1883. Its lower level has horizontal siding, while the upper portion has vertical siding. 122 – J. Kirk House. This Heritage House Award winner was built in 1891. It features decorative shingles in the gables; the segmented windows still have the original colored-glass panels. 118 – P.B. Chandler House was built almost entirely of redwood by the Pacific Improvement Co. in 1890. It features balloon framing, which is said to be very earthquake resistant.

Turn right on Ocean View, turn right on Forest. 100 BLOCK OF FOREST AVENUE. Below Central. An important residential street in the early Retreat grounds, it is lined with a variety of Victorian-era styles. 112 – W.H. Stephens House was built in 1892, and is quite elaborate, featuring stained-glass windows, gables, fish-scale shingles, and decorative bargeboard. In contrast, 119 – Mary Wilbur House is quite simple in style. Little altered since it was built in 1885, it features redwood siding and a gabled roof with sunbursts. 123 – Grove Hall was built in 1886 for Dr. Carrie Roe, one of the town's first physicians. She opened the house as a sanitarium, renting to and caring for invalids. 132 – Daffodil House – this gingerbread is a few years old, but replicates the era so well it was awarded a Heritage Design Award.

Other noteworthy sites beyond the range of a walking tour include:

Beacon House (circa 1907) 468 Pine Ave., Lacey House/Green Gables (1888) 104 5th St., Langford House (1884) 225 Central Ave., Trimmer Hill (1893) 230 6th St., Pacific Street houses, Palmer House (1887) 489 Lighthouse Ave., Pinehurst Manor (c.1890) 1030 Lighthouse Ave., Pomeroy House (1883) 106 7th St., Pryor House (1906) 429 Ocean View Blvd., Tennant House (1885) 312 Central Ave., Julia Morgan house (1917) at the triangle of 1st and 2nd streets.

Browsing The Shops

The American Tin Cannery Premium Outlets

In this historic cannery building, at the 80-foot History Wall, you'll see pictures of Cannery Row's past. Take their self-guided historical exhibit and walking tour; look for signs throughout the center. There's also an

information center with brochures, maps, and a <u>free coupon book</u>. Restaurants include Archie's American Diner, First Awakenings, Inaka Japanese, P.J.'s Deli and Whitey's Place Cafe & Bar. Apparel stores include Anne Klein, Bass, Big Dog, Carole Little, London Fog, Reebok. Shoes: Banister, Bass, Reebok, Rockport. Also, accessories and intimate apparel, gifts and specialty items, children's wear, luggage and leather goods, jewelry. ATM, KOCN Radio. Sun-Thurs, 10-6; Fri-Sat, 10-8. Across from the Aquarium at 125 Ocean View Blvd., 372-1442.

➤ Nob Hill Foods, Tillie Gort's Restaurant, The Clothing Store, Vivoli's Chowder House, Reincarnation Clothing, and Patrick's Consignment Store invite you to stroll on Lighthouse Ave., up two blocks from the outlet stores.

Historic Downtown

Pacific Grove is known for its home furnishings and home and garden stores. There's free parking all over the city, with an extended hours parking lot behind the theater on Light-

house Ave. Park there to begin your walk at **The Grove Homescapes**, 472 Lighthouse, in the renovated old Grove Laundry building. Enjoy the sweeping staircase, local artworks, and natural fish pond, with colorful Koi and bass, in the garden. Pick up a newsletter with dates and times for <u>free events</u>. Try their <u>free testers</u> of exotic perfumes and lotions from around the world. Daily 10am-6pm. 656-0864.

Next door is **Hambrook's Auction House** at 480 Lighthouse Ave. There's always an interesting collection in the windows, and the auctioneers are very entertaining to watch. If you want to bid, get a number at the service counter in the rear. You may pick up purchased items at the end of the auction, around 5pm. **1999 Auction Schedule:** Jan 8-9, 29-30; Feb 12-20; March 12-13; April 2-3, 23-24; May 14-15; June 4-5, 25-26; July 16-17; August 6-7, 27-28; Sept 17-18; Oct 8-9, 29-30; Nov 19-20; Dec 10-11. Preview auction items, 12-8pm, Thursday before auction dates. 373-2101.

● **Pier 1 Imports,** 490 Lighthouse Ave. Mon-Fri, 10am-9pm; Sat 10am-7pm; Sun 11am-7pm. Third largest sales store in California. 373-5955.

● **Central Avenue Pharmacy**, 133 15th St. <u>Free bottle of Vitamin C</u> with every purchase. Ask Dana Gordon, owner and compounding pharmacist, about his customized prescriptions, sold locally and nationally. 373-1225.

● **Chatterbaux Children's Shoppe**, 157 Fountain, offers <u>free baby registry</u>, birthday club and customer appreciation days. Come see Mr. McGee, their petting rabbit. Mon-Fri, 10am-5pm; Sat 11am-3pm, 647-8701.

● **Pacific Grove Jewelers**, 311A Forest Ave., gives a <u>free jewelry cleaning</u> and checking of prongs. Tues-Fri, 10am-5pm; Sat 10am-4pm. 649-6258.

● **The Holman Building**, across the street, is now an antique collective that will give hours of pleasant browsing and many historical perspectives. When Rensselaer Luther Holman constructed the building in 1924, as Holman's Department Store, it was the largest department store between Los Angeles and San Francisco. On the lower floor is the newly-opened **Harvest Natural Foods**, open daily 9am-8pm.

Interesting shops, many in Victorian homes, line both sides of Lighthouse all the way to Miss Trawick's Garden Shop near the Post Office. Side streets offer their own treasures; check out **Grove Market** on Forest for picnic supplies. See the new city directory on the outside wall of **Lasting Memories** at Forest and Lighthouse to plan your next move.

Fairway Center, Forest Hill & Country Club Gate

Take David Ave. up the hill to another major shopping area between Prescott and David, where Highway 68 enters the city from the south and becomes Forest Ave. Safeway, Lucky's, Trader Joe's, Blockbuster Video, Fifi's Cafe, Rite-Aid Pharmacy, Wells Fargo Bank, Bagel Bakery, B. Dalton Bookseller, Brick Oven Pizza and many other stores are waiting to serve you.

■ **The Discovery Shops** is a thrift store operated by the American Cancer Society, where you will find wonderful bargains and support a worthy cause. 182 Country Club Gate Shopping Center, 372-0866.

➤ **1999 Special Sales:**
February 13 – Tiny Treasures
March 15 – MadHatter Tea Party
        & Spring Fashion show
April 23 – Spring Grab Baskets
May 22 – Jewelry Extravaganza
June 16 – Men's Night
August 7 – Cookbook & Kitchen Sale.

Art Galleries & Receptions

● **Pacific Grove Art Center.** Free admission, Wed-Sat, 12-5pm, Sun, 1-4pm. Four galleries in a variety of media; exhibits change frequently and free receptions are given for the new artists. Adults and children 7 and older can enroll in visual arts courses. Local artists have studios in the center. Each year the Center hosts a collection of art on the free Artists' Studio Tour and distributes tour maps. 568 Lighthouse, 375-2208.

Art Center 1999 Opening Night Receptions, Fridays 7-9pm

Jan. 15	The Edward Weston family celebrates son Cole Weston's 80th birthday with family photographs in all four galleries.
Feb. 26	David Stroup, Marian Whitney, Mary Gould, Diana Jacobs
April 9	A Day in P.G., Gail Hodin Reeves, Molly Martin
May 21	Kent Alexander, Barbara Redding, Steve Aubrey, Andrea Rich
June 20	A. Wiesenseld, Janet McKaig, Jill Lackman, Judith Dunsworth
July 30	30th Anniv., Dantè Rondo, Carolyn Mitchell, Roger Fremier
Sept. 3	Artists Studio Tour exhibit
Oct. 1	Patrons show and juried show; fund raiser
Oct. 29	Monterey Peninsula Art Foundation Group Show
Dec. 3	Christmas show with children and teen class work

● **The Grove Homescapes**, 472 Lighthouse Ave., featuring local paintings, photography, sculpture and ceramics, will host an artist reception from 5-7pm on Feb 26, April 9, June 25, July 30, and Oct 29. Store is open daily 10am-6pm. Sunday Salon Artist Seminar Series, 1-3pm, monthly. Call for those dates, 656-0864. Left, Anita Benson, resident artist at the Pacific Grove Art Center, and Thompson Lange, in front of a Homescapes' mural by Benson.

● **Stowitts Museum & Library**, 591 Lighthouse Ave., Wed-Sat, 1-5pm. Changing exhibitions. Free admission. 655-4488. www.stowitts.org

● **Handcrafters Showcase & Boutique**, 227 Grand Ave., Mon-Sat 10-5:30. Come in for your free handcrafted item with any purchase. 372-8224.

● **Artists Forum Gallery**, 223 Forest Ave. Mon-Sat, 11am-5pm. Arts and crafts, art nouveau, art deco and decorative and fine arts. 375-4278.

● **Back Porch Fabrics**, 157 Grand Ave. Mon-Sat, 10am-5pm; Sun 12-4pm. Local quilters exhibits, including wearable art, and receptions. 375-4453.

- **Claypoole-Freese Gallery**, 216 Grand Ave. Fine art, framing, restoration, water gilding, and carving. 373-7179.
- **Hauk Fine Arts**, 206 Fountain Ave. Belle Yang, Gregory Kondos, Johnny Apodaca and other local artists. 373-6007.
- **Sally Judd Griffin Senior Center**, 700 Jewell Ave. 8am-5pm, 375-4454.
- **Vest Pocket Gallery** in Forest Hill Manor, 551 Gibson. Daily 7:30am-7pm. Local artists, change monthly. 657-5200.
- **Spanish Bay Galleries**, 2108 Sunset Drive. Tues-Fri, 9am-5pm. Sat by appt. Skip Kadish bronze casting figure sculptures, limited edition botanicals posters, and custom picture framing. 373-0554.

Public Art

"P.G. Historic Mural Project," **The Irene Masteller Mural**, 1998, by John Ton and volunteers, beside the Recreation Trail at Berwick Park. Scenes depicting the settling of the area. Next mural will be on the wall of a Grand Ave. cleaners. If you have a wall downtown and would like a turn-of-the-century mural, please donate your space by calling Irene, project advisor, at 375-6430.

Life at the Top, sea otter bronze, Berwick Park, Chrisopher Bell and Pacific Grove Rotary International, 1994.

Butterfly, Marble Granite, a gift of Hilda Van Sickle; Gordon Newell, sculptor, 1964, at Lovers Point.

Pictorial History of California in fresco by Bernard McDonagh & Richard Still, 1968, on the outside wall of Central Avenue Pharmacy, at Central & 15th.

"Once I saw two Victorian ladies rafting on Lake Majella that used to be down by Asilomar, before the Sand Plant ate all of the sand dunes." (Now Crespi Pond on Ocean View near Asilomar Ave.) May 1987 by the **Mural School**: Kate, Ramie, Sherry, Gerrica. On outside wall of the patio at Carrow's Restaurant, 300 David Ave.

John Steinbeck Homes in Pacific Grove

PHOTO: PAT HATHAWAY COLLECTION

147 11th St., built by Steinbeck's father as a summer home for the family. Steinbeck lived here with his bride, Carol, from 1930-1941. After the failure of his second marriage he returned briefly in 1948 before he moved to New York City in 1949.

425 Eardley Ave., purchased by Steinbeck in 1941.

222 Central Ave., home of Steinbeck's maternal grandmother, Elizabeth Hamilton from 1915-1918.

800 Asilomar Blvd., a cottage owned by Steinbeck's sister Esther and her husband from the 1930s to the 1950s, and now part of the Asilomar State Park.

Edward Rickett's Laboratory and Home

165 Fountain Ave. is the site of Rickett's first laboratory, opened in 1923. Dedicated by the City in 1994, Ricketts Row, between Lighthouse and Central avenues, goes from his lab on Fountain Ave. to 9th St., passing Steinbeck's home on 11th St.

331 Lighthouse Ave., where Ed lived with his family in the 1920s.

Please do not disturb the occupants of these private homes. Thank you.

Pacific Grove Public Library
"The Ultimate Source of Intelligent Fun"

● **Pacific Grove Public Library,** at Central and Fountain avenues, was built with Carnegie funds in 1907-08. Hours: Mon-Thur 10am-9pm, Fri-Sat 10am-5pm, Sun 1-5pm. <u>Library cards are free</u> to residents of Monterey, Santa Cruz and San Benito counties who present proof of local address. The library is an intriguing and stimulating place to spend an afternoon or evening, with a helpful staff, comfortable chairs and desks. The newspaper/magazine rack provides something for everyone with nearly 280 titles. There is a wide range of literature in foreign languages: Spanish, French, German, Japanese, Russian, and Italian. Access the library catalog from your personal computer and modem: Dial 646-5680: 9600, none, 8, 1 dot, full duplex, emu VT100. 2-week check out items include: books, books on tapes, videos, CDs, cassettes, and art prints to hang on your wall. 648-3162.

◆ **1st Pacific Grove Adult Spelling Bee**, sponsored by the library board, and organized by the Director, Bobbie Morrison, is March 5, 6:30-9:30pm, St. Angela's Hall, Lighthouse and 9th. Small fee. Adrienne Laurent, emcee.

> **Storytimes, Songs, and Crafts for Children**
>
> Toddler Storytime
> Wed 10:30am, ages 2-3
> Pre-School Storytime
> Thur 10:30am, ages 3-5
> After School Storytime
> Wed 3:30pm, ages 4-8
> Tue 3:30pm, grades 4-6
> Junior Friends of the Library
> ages 9 and up, Tuesdays (except summer months) at 3:30pm.
> Children's librarian
> Lisa Maddalena, 648-3160.

Bookstores

● **Bookmark.** This entire store is devoted to the performing arts. Tickets are available here for **Dance Kids** productions, a nonprofit children's theater and dance organization, which offers <u>free tickets</u> to all of its productions for groups dealing with at-risk children, seniors and physically-challenged adults. Reserve at 624-3729. 307 Forest Ave., 648-0508.

● **Bookworks and Mulberry's for Children.** Large selection of books and magazines, children's area, cafe with espresso, local art on the walls, restrooms. Sun-Thurs 9:30-9:30, Fri-Sat 9:30-10. 667 Lighthouse. 372-2242.

● **Learning Depot.** Bring your child in to explore the <u>free play areas</u>. Mon-Wed 10-5, Thurs-Sat 10-6. 168 Central Ave. 372-8697.

● **B. Dalton Bookseller**, 198 Country Club Gate. 375-9961.

● **Book Warehouse** in American Tin Cannery, 125 Ocean View. 375-1840.

1999 Calendar of Events

Information subject to change. Please call in advance to verify.

FEBRUARY

February 7   **A TASTE OF PACIFIC GROVE** $$
Local restaurants donate food and more than 12 vineyards provide the wine at an elegant setting at the Inn at Spanish Bay. $35 per person. Benefit for schools. Sponsored by P.G. Pride, 373-2891.

February 14   **TOGETHER WITH LOVE**   Spectators free
12th Annual 10K Run/5K Fitness Walk, Lovers Point to Asilomar Beach. 8am register, run/walk 9-10am. Benefits Rape Crisis Center, 373-3389.

APRIL

April 9-11   **GOOD OLD DAYS**   Free
A downtown celebration of the late 1800s includes a crafts fair with over 225 exhibitors, parade, police officer's motorcycle competition and drill team. Pie eating, bubble gum blowing and other contests. Jaws of Life and Fire Departments' Muster-Hose Cart Race, Victorian Fashion Show, entertainment and golf tournament. Fun for the whole family. 373-3304.

April 9-11   **QUILT SHOW** $$
Antique and contemporary works on display at the historic Chautauqua Hall on 16th St. at Central Ave. Co-sponsored by the Monterey Peninsula Quilters Guild and the Heritage Society of Pacific Grove. 372-2898.

April 16-18   **WILDFLOWER SHOW**   Free
Museum of Natural History, Forest and Central avenues, 10am-5pm. Local enthusiasts gather from the wild and present over 500 varieties of local wildflowers for your viewing pleasure. 648-3116.

MAY

May 2   **MONTEREY PENINSULA BRITISH CAR-MEET**   Free
Annual event downtown, 8am - 5pm. Over 200 classic/vintage and racing British cars on display. Saturday's events include a tour of the Monterey Peninsula for car entrants. Entrants' fees benefit local Monterey Peninsula charities. Exhibits, vendors, food. 373-3304, 649-5846.

May 8   **THE HUMAN RACE**   Spectators free
Annual event, Lovers Point to Lake El Estero and back. 8K Walkathon to benefit walker's charity of choice. Entrants, $25. 800-776-9176.

May 9, 30   **CONCERTS IN THE PARK**   Free
Jewell Park, Central and Forest avenues, 1-3pm. Bring a blanket and enjoy local musicians in the gazebo, presented by Friends of the Arts. Meredith, 647-1719.

JULY

July 4   **COMMEMORATION TO HONOR VETERANS**   Free
Jewell Park, Central and Forest avenues, at 11am. Following is a city barbecue ($5) with a variety of free activities for adults and children. 373-3304.

July 20-24   **FEAST OF LANTERNS**   Free
In keeping with a tradition as old as the city of Pacific Grove, the community celebrates with the Feast of Salads ($6 all you can eat) Thursday 11:30-2pm, Chautauqua Hall; Pet Parade Friday, 2pm, Caledonia Park; Street Dancing, Friday, 6:30pm on Lighthouse near the post office; barbecue and entertainment on Saturday at Lovers Point, followed by the Feast of Lanterns Pageant and fireworks display at 8pm. Closing ceremonies on Sunday at the First United Methodist Church on Sunset Drive include a free concert and ice cream for 25¢ a scoop. Volunteers are always welcome. 372-7625, 373-3304.

AUGUST

Aug 27   **CONCOURS AUTO RALLY**   Spectators free
Over 200 classic and sports cars line up on Lighthouse Avenue around 1pm, tour Pacific Grove, Carmel, Monterey and Pebble Beach. Barbecue ($20) and rally benefit Pacific Grove Youth Action, Inc., 372-6585.

SEPTEMBER

Sept/Oct   CONCERTS SUNDAYS   Free
4pm, First United Methodist Church, Sunset and 17-Mile drives. Features a choral and instrumental music in the Chapel. Pacific Grove began as a Methodist retreat, and that tradition is reflected today in the large congregation of this church and its many community events and activities. For more information, call Mary, 372-5875.

September 11   TRIATHLON AT LOVERS POINT   Free+$$
Annual Olympic swim-bike-run event. Friday "Ride the Tri or Tri the Ride" 6pm. A family fun ride from Lovers Point to Asilomar and back. Saturday: free exposition with entertainment and activities. P.G. Pasta Party Friday at 5pm $4-$8. Sponsored by Tri-California, www.tricalifornia.com, 373-0678, fax 373-0679.

September 12, 26   CONCERTS IN THE PARK   Free
Jewell Park, Central and Forest avenues, 1-3pm. Bring a blanket and enjoy local musicians in the gazebo, presented by Friends of the Arts. Meredith, 647-1719.

September 26   RUN FOR THE BEACON   Spectators free
A scenic 10K run follows P.G.'s picturesque coastal reserve to benefit the Beacon House, a residential alcohol/drug rehabilitation center. Details, 372-2334.

OCTOBER

Oct/Mar   MONARCH DAYS CELEBRATION   Free
Coinciding with the butterflies' stay in the city. P.G. businesses offer special promotions, packages of free gifts and discount vouchers. Free seminars and special exhibits at the Museum of Natural History. More than 30,000 visitors each year from all over the world inquire about the Monarch butterfly habitat, one of the world's last remaining. 373-3304.

October 2   BUTTERFLY KIDS PARADE   Free
Children dress in costumes and march through downtown, followed by a Butterfly Bazaar at Robert Down School. Parade begins at Pine and Fountain avenues, Fountain to Lighthouse, down Lighthouse to 17th Street, back to Robert Down on Pine for games, food, arts and crafts. 646-6540, 373-3304.

October 3   **HISTORIC HOME TOUR**   **Fee**
A tour of prime and selected Victorian and historic homes, bed & breakfast inns, churches. Hostesses dressed in Victorian era provide a history of each location. Co-sponsored by the Chamber of Commerce, P.G. Art Center, and the Heritage Society. Volunteer opportunities, call 373-3304.

October 3   **WALK TO CURE DIABETES**   **Spectators free**
Sponsored by the Juvenile Diabetes Foundation. Two mile corporate and family walk to raise money to help find a cure for diabetes. Activities start at 8am, walk begins at 9am at Lovers Point. (800) WALK-JDF, 626-6254.

October 12th   **COUNTRY AUCTION JAMBOREE**   **$$**
Chautauqua Hall, 5-8pm. Annual fund-raiser for the Chamber of Commerce includes the best little hors d'oeurves contest, barbecue, live and silent auctions, western music and line dancing. Admission $15. 373-3304.

October 31   **HALLOWEEN ACTIVITIES**   **Free**
Halloween week storytelling at Bookworks, 667 Lighthouse Ave. Free prizes, treats for kids in costume. Call for date and time, 372-2242. Free candies will be given out by The American Tin Cannery businesses to all children in costume, 3-5pm. Berwick Park neighbors put on a free pumpkin show every year, "Pacific Grove Pumpkins on the Path." Come by just to see or bring your own jack-o-lantern with a lit candle. Trick-or-treaters in costume may go to the P.G. Police Station, Pine and Forest avenues, to pick up their free glow necklaces at dusk.

NOVEMBER

November 6   **MARCHING BAND FESTIVAL**   **Free**
Approximately 30 bands from around California parade and perform downtown, starting at 11am on Pine Avenue. In the afternoon, at the P.G. High School Stadium, watch a field show and competition. 646-6595.

November 29   **TREE LIGHTING CEREMONY**   **Free**
Jewell Park, Central and Forest avenues, 5pm. Entertainment by local school bands, followed by caroling at the museum and a visit from Santa. 373-3304.

DECEMBER

December 7   **CHRISTMAS AT THE INNS**   **$$**
Visit several bed and breakfast inns decorated in Victorian splendor for the holidays. A limited number of tickets are sold. Entertainment and refreshments served. Volunteer opportunities to dress up and greet the public, call 373-3304.

December 11   **STILLWELL'S SNOW IN THE PARK**   **Free**
Caledonia Park, on Central Ave. behind the post office, is transformed into a winter wonderland with snow and twinkling lights. There's a Santa's workshop and the Snow Queen, Frosty the Snowman, hayrides, carolling and more. Plenty of snow to play in! 373-3304.

December 15-31   **CANDY CANE LANE**   **Free**
The entire neighborhood puts up elaborate lawn and rooftop Christmas and Hannukah scenes. Drive in on Morse Drive or Beaumont, off Forest Avenue near David. Park and walk or join the nightly procession of cars.

December 18   **LIVING NATIVITY**   **Free**
Outdoor tableau of scenes from the story of the birth of Jesus Christ with angels, shepherds and live baby lambs. 7-9pm, pageant repeats every 15 minutes. First United Methodist Church, Sunset at 17 Mile Drive, 372-5875.

Entertainment

◆ **The Tinnery**, at Lovers Point, is open for breakfast, lunch and dinner. Entertainment in the Lounge, Wed-Fri-Sat nights. No cover. Happy Hour, Mon-Tues-Thurs-Fri. Free hors d'oeuvres during the Jazz Happy Hour, Wed 5-7pm. Ocean View and 17th, 646-1040.

◆ **Mariposa Grill.** Fri-Sat, free music with dinner, 5:30-9pm; Sunday music with breakfast-lunch, 10am-1pm. 1120 Lighthouse Ave., 642-9303.

◆ **Juice 'n' Java.** Fridays, 7:30-10pm. Free Open Mic night with host Rama P. Jama, all styles of performing arts, from comedy and poetry to music; sign up early. Fireplace, sofa and chairs, local newspapers, sidewalk seating. Other entertainment, call for times, 599 Lighthouse Ave., 373-8652.

◆ **Bookworks and Mulberry's for Children.** Comfortable chairs, children's area, cafe with espresso, pastries and sandwiches, restrooms. Free live guitar music, Tues-Fri-Sun, 7-9pm. 667 Lighthouse Ave., 372-2242.

◆ **Hootenanny**, bi-monthly at the P.G. Art Center. Free group sing-along (song books provided), blues to folk, rock and country, vintage sounds of 1920s to '50s and today's music. Bring snacks and beverages to share. Any contributions benefit the Center, 568 Lighthouse Ave., 375-2208.

◆ **Senior Poetry Readings** every fourth Thursday at 3pm at Sally Griffin Center, 700 Jewell Ave., 373-5602. Free.

◆ **Community Chorus** meets every Friday at 7pm, Sally Griffin Center, 700 Jewell Ave. Non-Pacific Grove residents also welcome. Come and sing! Call Scott Getline, 372-4897. Free.

◆ **Taize Services**, a free candlelight service for prayer and meditation draws on the music and style of worship in Taize, an ecumenical Christian community in France. Instruments accompany you in simple, chant-like prayerful song. There is also time for silent meditation and reflection. Infant care is provided (0 to 3 yrs.). 7:30pm, first Fridays at St. Angela's Catholic Church in the church hall, Lighthouse Ave. and 9th St., 373-3031.

◆ **Chautauqua Hall Ballroom Dancing.** All ages, 7-10pm, every Saturday, $5 includes refreshments. Dick Robins Quintet first and third Saturdays. Dance lessons $2 at 6:15pm. 16th at Central. 375-2903. Not free, but fun!

◆ **Lighthouse Cinema.** Regular admission $7.50; children, seniors (65+) and matinees before 6pm, $4.50. Every Tuesday is discount Tuesday. Movies running longer than 2 weeks are $4.50 all showings. Free refill on large popcorn and drink. 525 Lighthouse Ave., 372-7300 (call 777-FILM x139).

Waterfront Recreation

Scenic Drive Around the Peninsula

Begin your scenic drive on Ocean View Blvd. at the **Monterey Bay Aquarium**. Follow the coastline beside the **Recreation Trail** to **Lovers Point**, where the trail ends. Continue around the point of the Peninsula, past Asilomar, to the P.G. gate into the **17-Mile Drive** at Pebble Beach. Along the way you may see harbor seals, sea otters, sea lions, whales (Dec-Mar), deer, squirrels, raccoons, and many kinds of birds. There are several turnouts with benches where you can park, watch the sunset, or explore the shore.

Walk, Run, Skate or Bicycle

▲ **The Recreation Trail** continues from the Highway 1 bicycle path at Castroville, north of Marina, through Seaside and Monterey, along old railroad tracks and the coastline of Pacific Grove to **Lovers Point Park**. Be aware that bicycles and skaters share the trail with walkers and runners. The trail is always open.

Parks and Attractions

▲ **Hopkins Marine Station**, at China Point, owned by Stanford University since 1891, has <u>free talks</u> on marine mammals and fisheries by the Ameri-

can Cetacean Society, Monterey Bay Chapter, which meets at 7:30pm, last Thursdays, for slide/lecture presentations on the grounds in the **Monterey Boatworks**. 130 Ocean View Blvd., (across from **The American Tin Cannery**). Call Allan Baldridge for info, 663-9488.

▲ **Jacobson Park**, Ocean View Blvd. and 7th St., a very small park with native plants, benches facing the Bay and rocky outcrops to climb.

▲ **Berwick Park**, Ocean View Blvd. and 10th St., one acre with a large lawn, a natural landscape with native vegetation, and spectacular bay views. Plenty of room for picnics and a game of frisbee. Dawn to dusk.

Explore the Tidepools

There are several turnouts along the shore where you can climb among the rocks and view the sea creatures in the tidepools. The Great Tidepool where "Doc" Ricketts collected specimens for his laboratory is located off Ocean View Blvd. at the foot of the Lighthouse. Unlawful to remove any marine life.

▲ **Lovers Point Park**, Ocean View Blvd. and 17th St., is a very popular spot that juts out into the bay with rocks to climb, barbecue/picnic facilities, large lawn area, sand volleyball court, sandy beaches, toddler's swimming pool, snack bar and restrooms. Fishing, surfing, swimming, diving. Site for weddings and city events including the Feast of Lanterns. Open dawn to dusk. Call 648-3130 to rent volleyball kits for $20.

▲ **Perkins Park** is the section of dramatically beautiful shoreline west of Lovers Point, where walking trails meander among the pink ice plant first planted by Hayes Perkins. Benches and stairways to the water.

▲ **Crespi Pond** on Ocean View near Asilomar Ave. is a haven for sea birds of all kinds: gulls, mallards, coots, and an occasional heron. Off-street parking, restrooms.

▲ **Point Piños Lighthouse** (c. 1855) is the oldest functioning light station on the California coast. <u>Free admission</u>. Recently restored, its Civil War-era kitchen, parlor and Victorian bedrooms are furnished with antiques. Expert Bruce Handy, Fri-Sat, 1-4pm. Local theater actress, Roo Hornady, appears as Emily Fish, the socialite lighthouse keeper from 1893-1914, Sat-Sun, 1-4pm. 648-3116.

Join a Walking Club

➤ Meet at the **Recreation Trail** behind the snack shop at Lovers Point, 2 pm Tues and Thur. All walking levels.

➤ The **Monterey Peninsula Walk Walk Walk Club**, Sat-Sun 8am, starting from the parking lot at the Senior Center, 700 Jewell Ave. near Lovers Point. All levels accommodated. Visitors welcome. Hansi, 626-6602.

➤ **Walk for Fitness** Tues 7-8am, at 207-16th St. Paul Haider, 641-9220.

Bicycle and Skate Vendors

➤ **Pacific Rim Cycling**, 214 Forest Ave. 372-2552. <u>Free air, info, & maps</u>.

➤ **In-Line Retrofit**, 171 Forest, 642-0355, 800/701-7000, has <u>free stickers</u>. Mon-Sat, 11-6, Sun 11-4. www.inline-retrofit.com.

▲ **Asilomar State Park and Beach** at the end of Highway 68, on the border of P.G. and Pebble Beach. No entrance fee. Swimming, surfing, walking, kite flying, beautiful sunsets, fishing (license required), scuba diving, tidepools, picnics, boardwalk, native plants, wildlife viewing of harbor seals, sea lions, sea otters, cormorants, pelicans and other bird and marine species. Open dawn to dusk. Ocean danger, water subject to large waves. No lifeguard. Information center, 372-4076.

■ **Asilomar Conference Center**, 800 Asilomar Avenue, off Highway 68. No entrance fee. The early buildings, such as the Visitor's Lodge, Mary A. Crocker Dining Hall, Merrill Hall, and the entrance gates, opposite, were designed by Julia Morgan of Hearst Castle fame, from 1915 to 1928, as a YWCA retreat. Morgan also designed the stone pillar entrance gate. This California State park welcomes visitors to enjoy the architecture, beaches and trails. Free Visitor's Guide and Dunes

Walking Tour booklet in the gift shop which is open daily 7am-9pm. You may eat in the dining hall: breakfast, 7:30-9am, lunch 12-1pm, and dinner 6-7pm. Latte, espresso and cappuccino are available in the lobby. Free campfire programs are held several Saturdays a month at dusk, with hot chocolate, hot cider and snacks. Lodging: 372-8016. Call the park office for other information, 372-4076. www.asilomarcenter.com.

Pacific Grove Municipal Golf Links
77 Asilomar Avenue, 648-3175.

GOOD PLACES TO SEE WHALES FROM SHORE

Point Piños

Cypress Point

Pt. Lobos State Reserve

Garrapata State Park

Point Sur

Julia Pfeiffer Burns State Park

Coastal Cleanup Day is September 18

If you'd like to join the drive to save the coast from pollution, call 1-800-COAST-4U. You can purchase a Coastal Protection License Plate for your auto, or volunteer to help on California Coastal Cleanup Day. Sept. 18, 1999.

Inner City Parks & Playgrounds

All city parks have free admission; some permits may be required for special uses;
obtainable from the Recreation Dept., 515 Junipero St. 648-3130.

▲ **Jewell Park.** Lawn, big trees and native flowers, Victorian gazebo to sit or play in, benches with a bay view. Site of city concerts and events. A good place to sit under the trees and relax while the kids play. One block up from the bay, at Central and Grand avenues, bordered by the Chamber of Commerce, the museum and the library.

▲ **Elmarie Dyke Open Space** is located adjacent to Chautauqua Hall on Central Ave. Flowering plants, benches, tables and gazebo.

▲ **Caledonia Park** has lots of open space, slides, swings, jungle gym, picnic tables, tot's playing area, baseball field and basketball court. Restrooms. Open dawn to dusk. Caledonia St. and Central Ave., behind the post office.

▲ **George Washington Park**, a natural habitat with Monarch butterflies (Danaus plexippus), squirrels, deer and many species of birds. 20 acres, trails, play area, restrooms. $10 fee to use ballfield, barbecue/picnic area. Open dawn to dusk. Enter from corner of Spruce and Alder Streets.

▲ **Monarch Grove Sanctuary**, enter from Ridge Road just off Lighthouse. Mar-Oct, butterflies overwinter in the pine, cypress and eucalyptus trees.

▲ **Platt Park**, a triangle of grass and a few benches bounded by Morse and McFarland Streets and Platt Court, off David. Quiet. Elaborately decorated in December as part of a Candy Cane Lane Christmas tradition.

▲ **Earl "Topper" Arnett Park**, 3 acres with playground equipment. At Piedmont and Moreland Avenue, off David Avenue.

▲ **Higgins Park**, Highway 68 and David Avenue. Triangle park with benches, big trees and bay views.

The Eco-Corps of Pacific Grove

• Celebrates Arbor Day with a work party to replant or repair a local park.
• Ongoing Washington Park restoration "Weed and Water" Party.
• Volunteers welcome to all outings, meetings and events. Call 375-2026.

Lynn "Rip" Van Winkle Open Space

Lynn "Rip" Van Winkle Open Space is but a remnant of a once dense Monterey pine forest that stretched for unbroken miles and may have totaled over 18,000 acres on the peninsula. The forest was inhabited by the Ohlone who found game, acorns, shelter, and water necessary for their survival. Today it is preserved in its natural condition as open space on the west side of Congress Ave. between Sunset and Forest Lodge Rd. The trees are protected and no buildings or improvements of any kind shall be erected. This park is dedicated in honor of Lynn Van Winkle. Open dawn to dusk, <u>no fee</u>. 659-4488.

Rocky Shores Open Space

The Ohlone people once gathered here to visit and harvest the finfish and shellfish, when great pines grew right down on the water's edge. Today, Rocky Shores is a part of Asilomar State Beach and has a new pedestrian trail and restored native habitat. What were once threatened with extinction but have been preserved for posterity are the incomparable sunsets, the solitude

of dawn walks, and the unobstructed public access. Dunes restoration in progress. Monterey Peninsula Regional Park District, 659-4488.

➤ **Open Space**s throughout Monterey County are dedicated to remain natural habitats without manmade structures. Call the Monterey Regional Park District to find out where the locations are for other Open Spaces. 659-4488.

Monarch Butterfly Habitats

From **The Friends of the Monarchs:** We recommend you visit the Museum of Natural History to view the short close-up video on the life cycle of the Monarch and to see the exhibits. You will then be able to appreciate what you see at the habitats. Butterflies begin clustering in the groves in early October, and reach their peak of thousands about the end of November, staying until March. Monarch Butterfly Docents begin service on the day of the Butterfly Parade and will help you at the Sanctuary between 9am and sunset, Sat-Sun, and between 12-3pm on weekdays. October through February, Friends of the Monarchs provides docents every weekend afternoon with no advance notice

necessary. Special tours, call 375-0982 or 888/PG MONARCH.

The Friends of the Monarchs work to promote and protect the butterflies and their habitats, with meetings every 2nd Tuesday at 7pm at the P.G. Museum of Natural History. "Just imagine," says Ro Vaccaro, president of Friends of the Monarchs, "if someone promised you three hours a week when you could be away from all phones, breathe deeply the eucalyptus-scented P.G. air and stand quietly on ground so special it is called a sanctuary. Imagine sharing the glorious story of the monarchs' migration with gentle visitors who travel here to see the splendor of our trees draped with butterflies. We can promise you just that!" To volunteer as a butterfly docent, call Steve Bailey at the P.G. Museum of Natural History, 648-3118.

➤ Visit the **Butterfly Souvenir Shop**, to benefit Friends of the Monarchs, located in the beautiful **Wilkie's Inn**, 1038 Lighthouse Ave., 372-0982.

Butterfly Kids

Dedication of the Butterfly Kids statue in bronze at the post office in 1997. At left, sculptor, Christopher Bell, the founder of the annual parade, Millie Gehringer, at the podium is Les Reed of the Pacific Grove Arts Commission, attended by local children in butterfly costumes.

Education & Recreation Centers

■ **Pacific Grove Adult Education Department** offers a variety of educational, physical and cultural activities for all ages and abilities, some free. 1025 Lighthouse Ave., Pacific Grove, 646-6580, www.pgusd.org. 1998/9 Spring and Winter sessions: Jan 4 to Feb 20, Feb 22 to April 17, April 19 to June 12. Call Maria Nunez, Principal, at 646-6580, for more information.

▲ **Pacific Grove Recreation Department** offers many and varied free programs to visitors and residents. Quarterly Activity Guides are available at the P.G. Library. Picnic kits include softball bats, softballs, bases, volleyball net, frisbee, soccer ball, football, volleyball and horseshoes, available for a non-refundable fee of $20. Open 8-4:45 weekdays. 515 Junipero Ave., 648-3130.

■ **Sally Griffin Senior Center**, and **Meals on Wheels**, 700 Jewell Ave. Informational forums on various topics of interest to seniors, exercise workshops, parties, volunteer opportunities, AARP meetings and artist receptions are just some of the free events. Free blood pressure checks every Tues 10-11am; free exercise classes include hatha yoga at 9am and aerobics at 10am, Mon-Wed-Fri; flexibility and low-impact aerobics at 9am Tues/Thurs; movement group at 10am Tues, and Wed 4-5pm. Volunteers always welcome by Meals on Wheels to help deliver warm food to homebound persons on the peninsula. Call 375-4454 for more information on activities, and how you can help.

▲ **Pacific Grove Youth Center,** The Nodilo Building. Open, no admission fee, to P.G. students in grades 6 through 12, Mon-Thurs 2:30-6:30pm, Fri 2:30-10pm, Sat 1-5pm and 7-11pm. Special events include dances, concerts, karaoke, movie matinees, coffeehouse/Open Mic nights, tournaments and more. Job Teen Fair, March 25, 4-6pm. Refreshments. Street Dance, April 9, 7-9pm, Bank of America parking lot. Voice your opinions, concerns and ideas at the **Youth Advisory Committee** meetings every 2nd Wed at 7pm. Obtain a complete calendar of events at the Youth Center, 302 16th St., or the Recreation Center at 515 Junipero. 648-3134 or 648-3130.

Free & Fun in
Pebble Beach

The Lone Cypress

Golf Courses

The Restless Sea

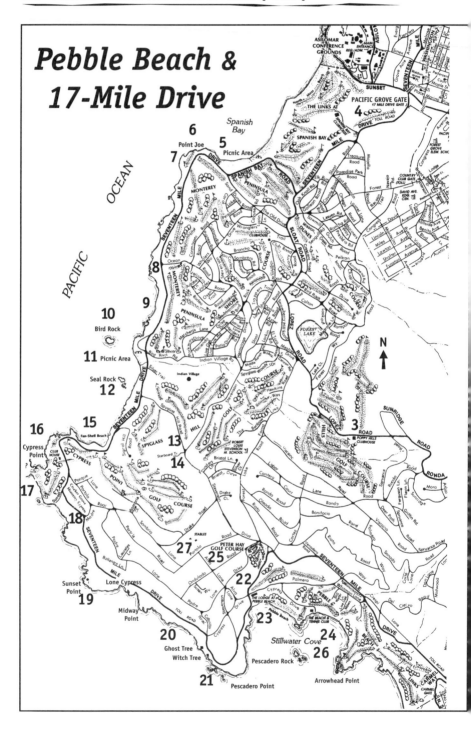

Pebble Beach & 17-Mile Drive

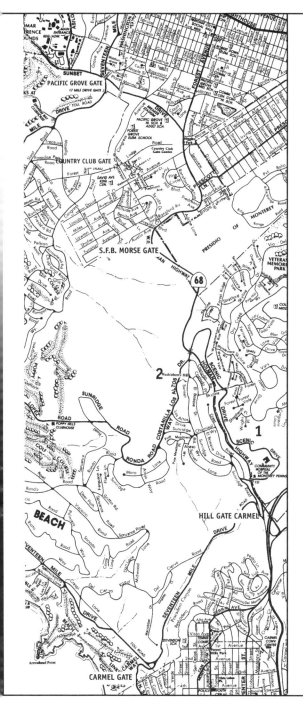

Pebble Beach, an upscale paradise for coastal living, offers many recreational, scenic, shopping and sightseeing opportunities ~ from surfing at Spanish Bay, bicycling one of the best courses in the world, picnicking next to the ocean, wildlife viewing, hiking trails, world-class shops and art galleries, events and entertainment.

The Scenic 17-Mile Drive

Originally called the "Circle of Enchantment," this scenic drive originated at the elegant Hotel Del Monte in Monterey, home to the Naval Post Graduate School, and was used to entice would-be investors to the area. Begin tour at any of the five gates, and although there is an entrance fee of $7 per car, it is reimbursed to resort guests. Dining at any of the restaurants will get the fee waived, as will shopping. The world-famous drive winds along the coastline, through scenic Del Monte Forest and past stately mansions and world-class golf courses. Open to the public daily during daylight hours. Bicyclists, walkers and hikers enter free. Information, 624-3881, 625-8553, 800/654-9300.

Here are 27 scenic points of interest, presented here in the order in which they appear once you've passed through the Highway 1 gate. Bicyclists must sign a waiver at the P.G. gate; no bicycle entry at Carmel gate.

1 Shepherd's Knoll Vista Point. There is a turnout here to view Monterey Bay and the San Gabilan Mountains.

2 Huckleberry Hill. Huckleberry Hill, one of the highest points in Del Monte Forest, is experiencing a regrowth of the native bushes after a 1989 fire.

©Pebble Beach Company, reproduced by permission

3 Poppy Hills Golf Course, home of the Northern California Golf Association, with a clubhouse, pro shop, restaurant, and bar; open to visitors.

4 The Inn and Links at Spanish Bay. Site of Gaspar de Portolá's landing in 1769, it is now home to a 270-room luxury hotel and 18-hole golf course, restaurants, pro shop, and several fine shops. The Clubhouse Bar & Grill, an informal bar and grill featuring spectacular sunsets, also presents Scottish bagpipers playing each day at sunset for your enjoyment. This is an excellent place for breakfast and lunch. With al fresco dining on the ocean-view patio, and sea birds to accompany you, you can watch groups of golfers tee off with the beautiful Pacific behind them.

5 Spanish Bay. Have your picnic here and enjoy the fabulous ocean vista. Hikers can take a dirt path from the Pacific Grove gate, through the pines, past the golf course, to The Inn, then to a boardwalk to the beach. You can reach Sunset Drive on a path behind the parking lot.

6 The Restless Sea, just south of Moss Beach, accessible by boardwalk, bike or car. Underwater topography is responsible for the exciting colliding currents off this point. Stop and watch the waves smash from different directions.

7 Point Joe. Site of numerous shipwrecks of mariners looking for Monterey Bay, in the 1890s there was a small Chinese fishing village here. The point is supposedly named after a Chinese man named Joe who was the lone inhabitant at the turn of the century. Surfing for the experienced only.

©Pebble Beach Company, reproduced by permission

8 Coastal Bluff Walking Trail. Take a pleasant walk along the scenic trail on the coastal bluffs overlooking the rich tidepools.

9 Coastal Bluff Restoration. Please stay on the boardwalks and designated trails as extensive programs are in progress to reestablish the area's natural balance and encourage native plants and wildlife.

10 Bird Rock - Hunter Steeplechase Course. Prior to World War II, the 11th Cavalry used these grounds for riding and saber practice.

11 Seal and Bird Rocks Picnic Area. A good place to picnic and watch the waves. Restrooms.

12 Seal and Bird Rocks. These landmarks are home to countless shoreline birds as well as offshore herds of sea lions and harbor seals. A one-mile, self-guided nature walk leads away from the beach here, through the dunes and into the forest, looping through Indian Village.

13 Spyglass Hill Golf Course and Pro Shop. Open to the public, Spyglass Hill is ranked one of the top 40 courses in the U.S. Legend has it that while writing *Treasure Island*, Robert Louis Stevenson was inspired by the view from his favorite hill. In honor of this literary heritage, the course and each of its 18 holes were named from Stevenson's classic.

14 The Spyglass Grill. The Grill is a great spot for a snack or lunch while claiming a bird's-eye view of the 9th green of Spyglass Hill Golf Course.

15 Fanshell Beach. Fanshell Beach boasts pure white sand. Harbor seals return here to bear their young every spring.

16 Cypress Point Club. Opened for play in 1928, Cypress Point Club is ranked among the top 10 golf courses in the U.S. A private club, it is reserved for members' use only.

17 Cypress Point Lookout. This lookout offers the finest view of the Pacific coastline on the drive. Excellent whale-watching, Dec-Mar.

18 Crocker Grove. 13 acres of native pines and cypress in a protected reserve. Crocker Grove and Pt. Lobos are the only places where the Monterey Cypress grows wild, and the oldest and largest Monterey Cypress is here.

19 The Lone Cypress. One of California's most familiar landmarks, access is restricted to protect the roots of this famous tree, which is also the symbol of the Pebble Beach Company.

©Pebble Beach Company, reproduced by permission

20 Ghost Tree. With a trunk bleached white by wind and sea spray, the Ghost Tree is one of the more fanciful examples of the Monterey Cypress.

21 Pescadero Point. Pescadero Point marks the northern tip of Carmel Bay and Stillwater Cove. The film *Rebecca* was made here.

22 The Pebble Beach Shops. Only a few steps from The Lodge at Pebble Beach, the Pebble Beach shops offer the finest in goods and services.

23 The Lodge at Pebble Beach. The Lodge is one of the world's best known resorts. Built in 1919, it offers travelers superb accommodations, with 161 guest rooms and suites presenting sweeping views of the ocean and the famed 18th green of Pebble Beach Golf Links. Enjoy a variety of dining options: The Tap Room - Casual pub with a collection of golf memorabilia. Club XIX - Fine dining offering award-winning French cuisine.The Gallery - Breakfast and lunch in an informal atmosphere. The Pebble Beach Market - Gourmet deli and market featuring fine wines, cheeses, meats, and fruits, with picnic tables conveniently close on a nearby lawn.

24 Considered by many to be the world's premier golf course, **Pebble Beach Golf Links** entices golfers and spectators alike with emerald fairways buttressed by the rugged Pacific coast. Opened in 1919, Pebble Beach has been a favored site of the U.S. Open and PGA Championship.

25 Peter Hay Golf Course. A 9-hole, par-3 course, Peter Hay is open to the public. Greens fees, $10. Inquire at the Pebble Beach pro shop for golf club rentals. 625-8518.

26 Stillwater Cove is recognized for its rich and undisturbed marine life, and is a haven for visitors and diving enthusiasts. Enter through the Beach & Tennis Club parking lot. Call ahead to reserve parking space: 625-8507. No parking between 11am-2pm. Restrooms.

27 The Pebble Beach Equestrian Center and Collins Polo Field are the sites of many major West Coast equestrian events, free to spectators.

17-Mile Drive by Bicycle

The 17-Mile Drive in Pebble Beach, through the Del Monte Forest, may be considered one of the top one hundred places to ride a bike in America. Enter at the Pacific Grove gate on Sunset Drive near Spanish Bay and Asilomar. Fill out the Rules and Regulations form on the sidewalk, receive a free map of bike trails, and enter the Del Monte Forest free. The bicycle path follows the 17-Mile Drive and begins with .9 miles of unimproved bike route, followed by a coastal loop of 4.4 miles, turning around at Bird Rock for the return to Spanish Bay. Further on, the Spyglass Hill Loop of 1.7 miles is very steep; turn around at Stevenson Drive or it's .8 miles to the Forest Lake Road just past the Lodge. After that, there is no bike lane on the 17-Mile Drive into Carmel. It's a 1.8 mile narrow road with heavy traffic to the Carmel exit which has no bike entry.

Hiking in the Del Monte Forest

Pick up a free pamphlet with bridle trail directions at the Equestrian Center or in the Del Monte Lodge. There are color-coded bridle trails from 3 to 9 miles in length; the Fire-break Trail (coded yellow) leads through the **Morse Botanical Reserve**. Another pleasant and easy one-mile walk begins 1.1 miles south on Congress from the intersection of Congress and Forest Lodge Rd., where you may park off the road. Follow the trail to a fire road, turn left and then left again onto fire road #2. Walk down to

©Pebble Beach Company, reproduced by permission

Congress Ave., about .2 miles from where you started. You will see Monterey pines, oaks, ferns and wildflowers.

Pebble Beach Golf Courses

▲ **Peter Hay Golf Course**, 17-Mile Dr. at Stevenson Dr. $10 per adult, with children under 12 free. A beautiful nine-hole, par 3, 819 yard course. Call 625-1555 for information about free lessons for resident children ages 7-17. Free golf at Peter Hay during the P.B. Equestrian Classics. 625-8518.

▲ **Poppy Hills**, home of the Northern California Golf Association, 3200 Lopez Road, 625-1513.

▲ **The Links at Spanish Bay**, 2700 17-Mile Drive, 624-3811, 647-7495.

▲ **Spyglass Hill**, Spyglass Hill & Stevenson Dr., 622-1300, 800-654-9300.

▲ **Pebble Beach Golf Links**, 17-Mile Drive, 625-8518, 800-654-9300.

1999 Calendar of Events

Information subject to change. Please call in advance to verify.

February 1-7   AT&T PEBBLE BEACH NATIONAL PRO-AM $$
Spyglass Hill, Pebble Beach and Poppy Hill golf Courses. 800/541-9091, 649-1533. 72-hole PGA Tour Championship Tournament with a $2.8 million purse. Tickets range from daily tickets ($20-$30), Season badge and grandstand badge ($95-$110). <u>Under 12 free with paid adult</u>. Teen ticket for entire week is $10. There's a long waiting list for volunteers, but the Pebble Beach Company is always looking for temporary help and invite you to the AT&T Employee Selection, Jan. 8, 11am-6pm, Jan. 9, 8am-6pm, at The Lodge at Pebble Beach Conference Center. Pebble Beach Company Employment Office, 2790 17 Mile Drive (next to Pacific Grove gate). Job Hotline 649-7694, fax 649-7696. www.attpbgolf.com.

March 31-April 4   SPRING HORSE SHOW   Free
Pebble Beach Equestrian Center, Alva Rd. and Portola Ln. Free horse-jumping competition. Pony rides (book ahead $20, under 6 free), food and horse items for sale. Gate fee only. 8am-5pm. 624-2756.

April 1   HARBOR SEAL PANELS   Free
Local schoolchildren paint large murals which are put in place at Cypress Point to protect pupping harbor seals from curious onlookers. Sponsored by The SPCA and the Pebble Beach Company. 625-8402.

May 29-30   MEMORIAL DAY REGATTA $$
Contact The Beach & Tennis Club, 625-8507.

June 21-26   CA STATE AMATEUR GOLF CHAMPIONSHIP $$
Pebble Beach Golf Links and The Links at Spanish Bay. Roger Val, 625-4653.

July tba   YOUTH CONCERTS   Free
Young musicians ages 12-23 at California Summer Music workshops through July at Robert Louis Stevenson School. Concerts, master classes open to the public free of charge. For dates, call 626-5300.

July 27-Aug 1, Aug 3-8   EQUESTRIAN CLASSICS   Free
Pebble Beach Equestrian Center, corner of Alva Road and Portola Lane. 624-2756. 8am-5pm each day. Hunter and jumper events, a petting zoo and food booths, free ice cream sundaes on Thursday afternoons both weeks at ringside. Pebble Beach gate fee only. Special events include: The $10,000 Pebble Beach Jumper Derby Brunch, benefiting the YWCA of Monterey. Tickets 649-0834. SPCA of Monterey County Auxiliary Cocktail Party and Benefit Luncheon. Tickets 373-2631 ext. 224. Family Fun Day benefitting Chartwell School. "Annual Horse Show Dog Show" with prizes. Peter Hay Welcome Golf, free for kids.

August 23-27   NCGA AMATEUR GOLF CHAMPIONSHIP $$
Spyglass Hill Golf Course. Contact Roger Val, 625-4653.

August 25-29   BLACKHAWK COLLECTION OF CLASSIC CARS   Free
Traveling showcase of rare, vintage, classic and one-of-a-kind automobiles featuring over 60 of the world's premier examples for sale. Pebble Beach gate fee only applies. Wed-Sun, 10am-8pm. Peter Hay Golf Course. 925/736-3444.

August 26-29   CONCOURS D'ELEGANCE   Free+$$
Prestigious event to view more than 100 classic automobiles at The Lodge. Tickets: United Way 372-8026, fax 372-4945. Information, 659-0663, 375-1747. www.pebble-beach-concours.com. On August 26, a 50-mile tour of the antique

cars drives from Pebble Beach through Pacific Grove and Monterey, then out on Highway 68 to Laureles Grade, and to the Holman Ranch for lunch before returning via Carmel Valley Road and downtown Carmel. The tour provides a great chance for many more people to see the magnificent cars for free. 624-3811.

September 4-5   LABOR DAY REGATTA   Free to spectators
Contact The Beach & Tennis Club, 625-8507.

September 15-19   STRIDES & TIDES HORSE SHOW   Free
Contact Tim Postel, 624-2756.

November 10-14   EQUESTRIAN CHAMPIONSHIPS   Free
Contact Tim Postel, 624-2756.

November 18-21   CALLAWAY GOLF, PRO-AM $$
Del Monte Golf Course, Pebble Beach Golf Links and Spyglass Hill. Call 625-8443.

Entertainment

◆ **Lobby Lounge**, next to Roy's Restaurant at the Inn at Spanish Bay. Happy Hour, Mon-Fri, 4-7pm. No cover, free valet parking. 647-7423.

◆ **Tap Room**, dance, Fri-Sat, 10pm-1am, no cover, The Lodge. 625-8535.

◆ **Terrace Lounge**, live music, 6-10pm, at The Lodge, no cover. 625-8535.

◆ **Spanish Bay Clubhouse**, from the patio, bagpipers play at sunset.

Art Galleries

● **Richard MacDonald Galleries**, 17-Mile Drive, at the Lodge. Sculpture by MacDonald; also the only ongoing show of MacDonald's original drawings and paintings, lithographs, and hand drawn serigraphs. Sun-Thurs 10-6, Fri-Sat 10-9. 648-7356.

● **Coast Gallery**, 17-Mile Drive, at the Lodge. Unique collection featuring wildlife bronze sculptures of Loet Vanderveen, paintings by Van Megert, prints of Henry Miller, eagle sculpture of Dennis Lee. Daily 10-6. 624-2002.

● **Ansel Adams Gallery**, 2700 17-Mile Drive, at the Inn at Spanish Bay. Daily 10-6. Works by Ansel Adams and other fine art photographers, crafts, creative gifts, and Native American crafts and jewelry. Free Camera Walks depart from the Gallery Fri-Sat,10am-noon. 375-7215.

Work for the Concours d'Elegance

➤ **The Lodge at Pebble Beach** invites you to be a part of the Concours d'Elegance and apply for several positions: food servers, buspersons, roomservice runners, housepersons, van drivers. Apply in person to the Human Resources Office, 8-4:30pm, across from the P.G. gate entrance.

Classy Transportation for Rent

➤ If you get the urge to drive or own a classic automobile yourself, call **Auto Gallery**, 624-3438, fax 624-3033, for rent to drive, chauffeured tours, special events and sales.

PEBBLE BEACH™

We Welcome All Riders to the Most
Beautiful Setting in the World

TRAIL RIDES

1999 Equestrian Center Events

March 31-April 4   SPRING HORSE SHOW   Free
Pebble Beach Equestrian Center, Alva Rd. and Portola Ln. Free horse-jumping competition. Pony rides (book ahead $20, under 6 free), food and horse items for sale. Gate fee only applies. 8am-5pm. 624-2756.

July 27-Aug 1, Aug 3-8   EQUESTRIAN CLASSICS   Free
Hunter and jumper events, a petting zoo and food booths, free ice cream sundaes on Thursday afternoons both weeks at ringside. Special events include: The $10,000 Pebble Beach Jumper Derby Brunch, benefiting the YWCA of Monterey. Tickets 649-0834. SPCA of Monterey County Auxiliary Cocktail Party and Benefit Luncheon. Tickets 373-2631 ext 224. Family Fun Day benefitting Chartwell School. "Annual Horse Show Dog Show" with prizes. Peter Hay Welcome Golf, free for kids.

November 10-14   EQUESTRIAN CHAMPIONSHIPS   Free
For more information, contact Tim Postel, 624-2756.

Explore the beauty of the Monterey Peninsula with the Pebble Beach™ Equestrian Center. Experienced instructors take riders to some of the most breathtaking spots on earth. Riding times are at 10am, 12pm, 2pm and 3:30pm. Guided Beach trail rides are available for $45. Private $60-$90. For more information or reservations, please call 831-624-2756.

Free & Fun in
Salinas

Mariachi Events

Creekbridge Park

Salinas Farm Show

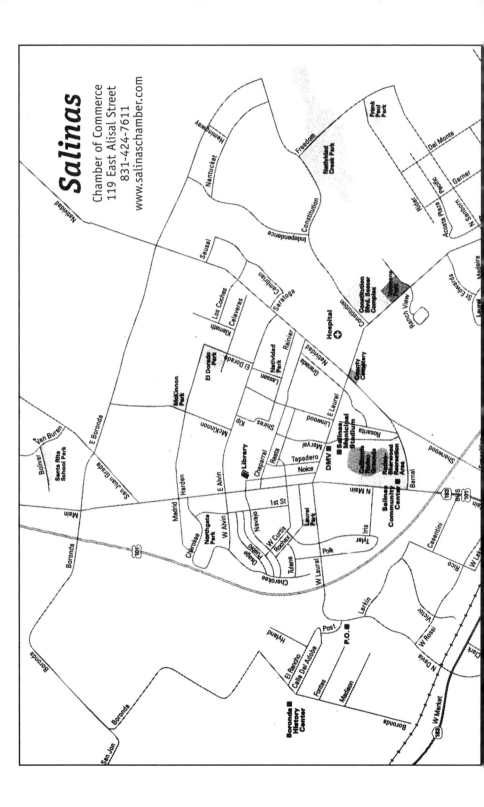

Salinas

Chamber of Commerce
119 East Alisal Street
831-424-7611
www.salinaschamber.com

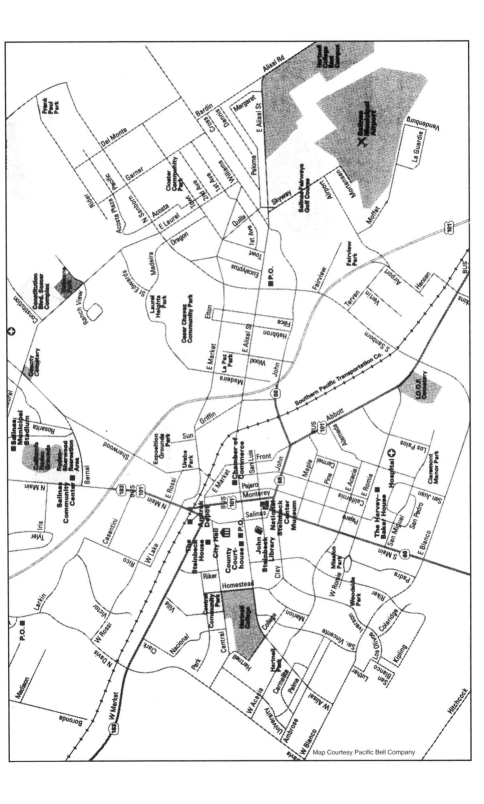

Map Courtesy Pacific Bell Company

Salinas Landmarks

■ **National Steinbeck Center**, One Main Street, near Market Street. Tele 796-3833, fax 796,3828, www.steinbeck.org. A new, multimedia experience of literature, history and art. Located in the heart of historic Oldtown Salinas, 20 miles from Monterey. 10am-5pm daily. Occasional free days - March 27, June 26, 1999, Watch the newspapers for other free days. Adults $7, Seniors (over 62) and students with ID $6, Children 11-17 $4, free to members and children 10 and under. Closed Thanksgiving, Christmas and

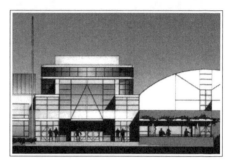

New Years Day. Museum and archives celebrate the life and work of author John Steinbeck with seven themed galleries and changing art and cultural exhibits. A variety of special programs,classes and children's events are scheduled throughout the year. The museum includes a gift shop and a cafe. (Illustration: Kasavan Architects & Thompson Vairoda Assoc.)

■ **Annual John Steinbeck Birthday Celebration** last weekend in February may include these free events: Complimentary birthday cake at the Cannery Row Visitors Center in the green Heritage Railcar on the Recreation Trail, between Hoffman and Prescott in front of the Edgewater Packing Company. Birthday Fete at the Aquarium Auditorium with music and entertainers. Free symposium at the Monterey Bay Aquarium Auditorium about Cannery Row and Steinbeck. Fee events may include: Luncheon in Salinas; bus tour of Monterey and box lunch. Guided tours of Cannery Row, "Doc" Ricketts lab and Hopkins Marine Station. For more birthday information, call 372-8512, fax 375-4982, e-mail info@canneryrow.org.

■ **The Steinbeck House**, John Steinbeck's birthplace and boyhood home, 132 Central Ave. This Victorian is now a restaurant featuring local produce, wines and beers. Photos and memorabilia of the Steinbeck family are on display. Dining 11:30-2pm,Mon-Sat. Gift shop is open Mon-Fri, 11am-3pm, Sat 11am-2:30pm. Profits to local charities. 424-2735.

■ **Harvey-Baker House**, 238 E. Romie Lane, near Main St. 1868 home of the first mayor, Isaac Harvey, now a museum with period furniture and decor. Free admission, Sun 1-4pm. 424-7155.

■ **Boronda History Center**, 333 Boronda Road at Calle Del Adobe. Open weekdays 9am-3pm. Tours 10-2 by appointment; Robert B. Johnston Archival Vault by appointment only. The José Eusebio Boronda Adobe, built in 1844, and the Lagunita schoolhouse, built in 1848, are the highlights of this history center. 757-8085.

■ **Center for Medieval Studies**, Fritz Auto Clinic, 276 E. Market. Call Tom for a free tour of the Armory, a coal forge using anvils to make helmets and armor, 8am-5pm, Mon-Fri. Join the Center for $35 a year and receive a newsletter, access to the forge equipment, and an open invitation to spend weekends brushing up on your jousting. 443-6451.

Farmers Markets

● **Northridge Mall Certified Farmers Market**, 8am-noon on Sundays, N. Main St. at Boronda Road. Under colored umbrellas on Main St. 728-5060.

● **Oldtown Salinas Farmers Market**, 3-7pm, Wed, weather permitting, 200 block Main Street. Live entertainment, produce, fish, flowers, baked goods, crafts, weekly "Market Basket" giveaway (entry forms at bread cart). "Healthy Living Day," 4th Wed, free screenings (anemia, blood pressure, glucose) by Natividad Medical Center. Free parking. 758-0725.

Art Galleries

● **Artistic Hangups**, 257 John St. Mon-Fri, 10am-5:30, Sat 10-5. Local art, Western and local event posters, fine art reproductions, gifts. Free coffee, seating area. www.artistichangups.com. 757-4703.

● **Theodore's Art Gallery**, 210 Main St. Tues-Fri, 10am-4pm. Limited & open editions, seriographs, originals, gifts, custom embroidery. 422-6861.

Valley Art Gallery

A gallery owned & staffed by local artists
Two & three dimensional art, unique gifts & wearables

● **Salinas Valley Art Gallery**, 218 Main St. Tues-Sun, 10am-5pm, Mon 11am-3pm. Co-op of 37 local artists since 1969; all media. 422-4162.

● **Peninsula Arts & Crafts**, 225 Main St. Mon-Fri, 9am-5:30pm. Lithographs, Eng Tay, fine art, fine art supplies. 758-2741.

● **Hartnell College Seminar Gallery**, 155 Homestead Ave. Mon-Fri, 10am-1pm and 6pm-8pm. Student art. 758-9126.

Public Art

➤ **"Hat in Three Stages of Landing,"** mural behind the Salinas Fairgrounds Auditorium at 900 Main St.

Personal Tour Guide

➤ Historic downtown walking and step-on bus tours by **Carol Robles**. Learn past and present importance of Monterey's county seat. Also Steinbeck and Valley tours. Fees vary, call 751-3666.

1999 Calendar of Events

Information subject to change. Please call in advance to verify.

Ongoing   UNITY CELEBRATION PRAISE CONCERT   Free
Every two or three months. Free food and clothing. 7pm at Washington Middle School, 560 Iverson St., with Christian music by local singers and musicians. Admission is free, but guests are asked to bring a canned food donation for the needy. Art Garcia, 449-8758.

February 21-27 STEINBECK BIRTHDAY CELEBRATION $$
Free tours of Steinbeck House, www.infopoint.com/mry/orgs/steinbeck, 424-2735. The National Steinbeck Center speakers and luncheon highlight this annual celebration. Call 796-3833 for more information.

March-Sept   "GRAFFITI NIGHTS AT ROY'S DRIVE-IN"   Free
Bi-weekly meets at Roy's Drive-In. All makes and models cars, raffles, '50s & '60s music. Presented by the Salinas Valley Street Rodder's Assn. 305 N. Main Street, 449-2525.

April 17   EARTH DAY/ARBOR DAY '99   Free
Natividad Creek Park. Call for more information, 754-1705.

June 5,6   KENNEL CLUB AGILITY TRIAL   Free
Del Monte Kennel Club presents an opportunity for the public to see many different breeds of dogs perform over very complex and entertaining obstacle course. A great spectator sport! 8am-5pm. Toro Park. Parking, $6 per car. 333-9032.

June 12-13   SALINAS VALLEY SALAD DAYS $$
From the "Salad Bowl of the World," a two day food, music, arts and wine festival at Sherwood Park in the Salinas Sports Complex. 5Krun Sat, Hispanic dancers, 75 arts and crafts. Greek, Oriental, Mediterranean, Mexican and American salads. 3 entertainment stages and the "Salinas Salad Sprint." Salinas Sports Complex/Sherwood Park. 10am-6pm. $8 adults. 751-6000.

July 4   LIBERTYFEST CELEBRATIONS   Free
Begins with a Main Street parade from 10am to noon. Sherwood Park on North Main Street will then host a "Picnic in the Park" from 12:30 to 5pm Food, contests, games, music and dancing. Fireworks at 9:15pm Call 484-6522 for tickets to other entertainment.

July 15-18   CALIFORNIA RODEO   Free+$$
Wed, 7pm, free Kiddie Kapers parade in Oldtown Salinas, featuring children in Western togs, with their pets, decorated bicycles and neighborhood floats. Free horse parades to the Rodeo grounds proceed down Main Street beginning at 12:15pm Saturday and Sunday. Other rodeo-related events include a barbecue at the Yellow Hat Area, Cowboy Poetry at the Rodeo Arena, dances at the Salinas Community Center, and Big Week Carnival at Expo Park at 101 Market St. Tickets $10-$17. 757-2951, 800/771-8807, 775-3100.

July 25   SALINAS OBON FESTIVAL   Free
Buddhist Temple of Salinas, 14 California Street. Noon-9pm Sunday. Sponsored by the Buddhist Temple of Salinas, featuring Japanese food and drink, martial arts and flower-arranging demonstrations, tea ceremony, taiko drumming, Japanese dancing, children's games, raffle. Culminates with the Obon dance at 7pm; continuous free shuttle service from Salinas City Parking Lot No. 4 on Monterey Street, between Gabilan and Market. 424-4105.

August tba   SALINAS AIRPORT OPEN HOUSE   Free
The Salinas Owners and Pilots Association, the Women's Monterey Bay 99's and the Salinas Chapter of Experimental Aircraft Association invite you to experience the thrill of flying and small aircraft. Older and home built aircraft. Cars of the same vintage. Tour air traffic control tower and maintenance shops. 30 Mortensen Avenue.

August 5-8   STEINBECK FESTIVAL XIX   Free+$$
The Steinbeck Center presents Steinbeck Festival XIX. Walking and bus tours, speakers, films, panels, theater. Call for more info, 775-4720.

August 22   TORTILLA FESTIVAL   Free
Variety of foods to roll in tortillas, beverage booths. Music, games, contests for all ages. Sponsored by Salinas Valley League of United Latin American Citizens, Mrs. Maya 758-6947, Juan 754-2849. 11am-7pm at Monterey County Sheriff's Posse Grounds, Old Natividad Road, Salinas. Free admission, parking $3.

Sept tba   MARIACHI FESTIVAL & CONFERENCE   Free+$$
Free mariachi mass Sunday at Sherwood Hall, followed by free Fiesta del Mariachi until 2pm with local and regional mariachi and folklorico groups at Sherwood Park. To volunteer, call 373-6767, ext. 213, ask for Sylvia Salazar. Salinas Community Center, 940 No. Main St. 800-307-3378, 758-7477, 758-7396, 758-7387.

September 13   ANNUAL "EL GRITO FIESTA"   Free
Two stages for entertainment, booths. Noon-6pm, East Alisal Street between Wood and Filice streets. Sponsored by the Hispanic Chamber of Commerce of Monterey. Vendor opportunities: Jessika Juarez or Denise Estigoy at 757-1251.

Sept 17-19 STREET RODDERS NOSTALGIA RUN TO OLDTOWN   Free
Four block street rod display, daily motorcade through Oldtown, over 50 awards each day at 3pm; additional four blocks with swap-meet booths, kiddie carnival, food booths, entertainment stage with music of the 1950s, '60s and '70s. Car registration begins at 8am Sat-Sun, activities until 4pm. 200-300 blocks South Main St., 449-9334, 758-0725.

September 18   COMMUNITY CARE DAY   Free
United Way of Salinas Valley hosts an annual Community Care Day of painting projects, small construction, clean-ups, landscaping, office work. Have breakfast, get a free t-shirt and win one of 150 raffle prizes. Call the United Way at 424-7644.

September 18-19   FOX 35 KIDFEST   Free
Free admission & live entertainment, fun zone karaoke, fun jump, face painting, clowns, song & dance. Sat 10-4, Sun 11-4. Northridge Mall. 422-3500.

September 22   SALINAS FARM SHOW   Free
An all-day demonstration of the latest farming and ag techniques and equip-

ment. Seminars, barbecue lunch, rodeo contest and more. Proceeds benefit the Gonzales Young Farmers Ag Scholarship Fund. Approximately 1000 growers and 150 exhibitors. Wednesday, 8:30am-4pm, Salinas Sports Complex/California Rodeo grounds. Show information: Kevin Hall, 209/248-0924.

October tba **BIKE RODEO AND SAFETY FAIR** **Free**
Bring bike and helmet. Prizes, free bicycle, registration and some helmets. Emergency vehicles on display. Face painting, refreshments, door prizes. Call for more information, 758-7906.

October tba **AUTUMN FESTIVAL** **Free**
Quilt show, art show, bake sale. Student works on show and for sale. At Salinas Adult School, 20 Sherwood Place. End of month. 753-4268.

October tba **PUMPKIN CARVING CONTEST** **Free**
Free, preregistration required, one adult with one child, bring carving kit. Prizes, refreshments. Sponsored by Salinas Recreation Dept. and California Culinary Academy. 1-3pm at Hebbron Heights, 683 Fremont St., Salinas. 758-7900.

October 1-3 **CALIFORNIA INTERNATIONAL AIRSHOW** **Free+$$**
Friday will be Fireworks and Pyrotechnic Extravaganza featuring air acts, ground acts, breathtaking fireworks and the Wall of Fire. Sat-Sun will feature air acts, ground acts, military fly-bys and demos, warbirds plus military and civilian displays. U.S. Navy Blue Angels, Robosaurus, Wayne Handley, Gene Soucy, Team E-Z, U.S. Navy Leapfrogs Parachute Team, Northern Lights Aerobatic Team and more!! Watch the airplanes and jets land and take off from Monterey Airport the day before and the day after the Airshow. Show also includes monster trucks, pyrotechnic extravaganza. At the Salinas Airport. Children under 6 free. Tickets $6-$16; private boxes available, $160-$400. 754-1983. Ticket information: 888/845-SHOW. www.ca-airshow.com.

October 2 **FALL FEST** **Free**
Church of the Good Shepherd, 301 Corral de Tierra Road, Salinas, will hold its Fall Fest beginning at 10am. Games, pony rides, music, crafts fair with children's activities. 10K run, 5K family walk and barbecue. Kim, 484-2153.

October 31 **A HALLOWEEN SPOOKTACULAR** **Free+$$**
The weekend before Halloween at the Firehouse Recreation Center, 1330 E. Alisal Street. $4 per person includes 1 visit to each carnival game, a treat bag, a tour through the haunted hallway and entry in the costume contest. Sponsored by the City of Salinas Recreation Dept. 758-7948, 758-7223. Drop by during the month for the October Fun Program which features a Pumpkin Face Contest, Pumpkins Krispies and Pumpkin People. 758-7900.

October 31 **CHILDREN'S HALLOWEEN PARTY** **Free**
Live puppet performances, booths and crafts, tricks and treats. Goodie bags for all. Must pre-register. Sherwood Hall, 940 N. Main St. 758-7223.

October 31 **TRICK OR TREAT** **Free**
For costumed youngsters at stores and businesses in Oldtown. 758-0725.

November 1 **HALLOWEEN CANDY TRADE** **Free**
Drop by the Children's Miracle Network Dental Center at 631 E Alvin Dr., Suite E1, so your kids can trade Halloween candy for bags of fun items and healthy treats from 9am-1pm. Call 443-5801.

November 1 **EL DIA DE LOS MUERTOS** **Free**
Celebrated by the Steinbeck Center with a children's procession from the 200 block of Main Street to the Steinbeck Museum, where admission will be free to county residents, 10am-5pm. 796-3833. www.steinbeck.org

Nov/Dec   **CENTRAL COAST FILM FESTIVAL**   **Free**
Third annual Central Coast Christian Film Festival at the Northridge Cinema, 350 Northridge Shopping Center. Admission is free to the festival, which will include a dozen films, children's matinees and animated features. Shows begin at 11am each day for a two week period. Information: 424-7020.

November 25   **THANKSGIVING DINNERS**   **Free**
11am-3pm at the American Legion, 14 W. Laurel Drive. Open to all. Volunteers and donations also are welcome. Call 449-1690. Dinner will be served 11am-4pm at Dorothy's Kitchen, 30 Soledad St. Volunteers and donations welcome. 757-3838. Dinner will be served by the Salvation Army from 10am-1pm at El Sausal Middle School, 1155 E. Alisal St. 424-0588.

December tba   **LAS POSADAS**   **Free**
Nativity procession. Midmonth. Alisal merchants. Call Micky Ito or Carlos Ramos, 373-6767.

Entertainment

Music, Dancing, Open Mike

◆ **Rodeo Inn**, 808 N. Main St. No cover unless noted. Thurs, Ladies Night, 8-12:30, dance to DJ, Fri-Sat, 9-1; Sun, pool tournament, cash prizes; Monday Night Football with beer specials, hot dogs; Tues at 6:30 Karaoke Night, Happy Hour prices all night; Wed, Cuervo Night with Dj. 424-8661.

◆ **King's Den**, 22 W. Alisal. Karaoke Thursdays, no cover. 422-1116.

◆ **The Penny Farthing Tavern.** Live music every Fri-Sat. No cover. 9 E. San Luis St., Oldtown Salinas. 424-5652.

◆ **Book Worm Cabaret**, 342 Main St. Live music at 6pm. 753-2099.

◆ **Spados**, 66 W. Alisal. Fridays, Happy Hour 5:30-7:30pm, vocal jazz, pop-jazz and R&B. No cover. 424-4139.

◆ **Chapala Restaurant**, 438 Salinas St. Open Mic Thursdays 7-10pm, Happy Hour 4-8pm daily. No cover. 757-4959.

◆ **Introduction to Vocal & Guitar** Accompaniment with Caminos del Arte sessions at Bread Box Recreation Center, 745 N. Sanborn Road. Call for times. Free, everyone welcome. Preregistration: 758-7908, 594-9407.

◆ **Ballroom Dancing**, Active Senior Center, Pajaro & Harvest. Music by the Joe Ingram Group. $5 includes refreshments. Every Tues 7-10pm. 424-5066.

◆ **All-City Band** now forming. No charge to play but must have own instrument. Call Jeannie Echenique, 753-5740 days, 476-1322 evenings.

◆ **Hartnell College Community Band** gives free concerts. Call for dates and times, 755-6905, 755-6906.

Movies and Theater

◆ **Gay Movie Night** 7-9pm, second/fourth Tuesday at Monterey County AIDS project office, 12 E. Gabilan; open to all ages in the gay, lesbian, bi and transgendered community. Free, refreshments. 772-8202.

◆ **Century Park Cinema**, 10 E. Market at Simas, 753-1055. Fox California, 243 N. Main at Boronda Road, 449-9101.

◆ Free concerts at Main Stage of the Performing Arts Center at Hartnell College, West Alisal St. and Homestead Ave. Call for dates and times. **Salinas Concert Assn.** 754-6829.

◆ **ARIEL Theatrical**, 182 San Benancio Road. 484-2228. 759-1530.

◆ **The Western Stage**, 156 Homestead Avenue. 755-6818 or 375-2111.

Libraries and Learning

● **Cesar Chavez Library**, 615 Williams Road. 758-7345. Hours Mon-Wed, 10am-9pm, Thurs-Sat, 10am-6pm. Homework Center Mon-Thurs, 2-5pm. Volunteers needed. Reading garden, ages 6-11, Tues 10am; Adventure Seekers, ages 6-11, Tues 4pm; Preschool storytime, Thurs 10am; Cuentos Para la Familia, all ages, Thurs 4pm.

● **El Gabilan Library**, 1400 North Main. 758-7302. Hours Mon-Wed, 10am-9pm, Thu-Sat, 10am-6pm. Call for program information: Thumbkin stories for kids ages $2^1/2$-4, 10:15am, Rookie Readers $3^1/2$-6, Thurs 10am.

● **John Steinbeck Library**, 350 Lincoln Avenue, 758-7311. Mon-Wed, 10am-9pm, Thu-Sat, 10am-6pm. Preschool stories ages $3^1/2$-6, Tues 10am; Slither's Night (meet 'library snake'), first Tuesday, all ages; Thumbkins, ages $2^1/2$-4, Wed 10am; Grandparents and Books, kids of all ages practice listening and reading skills with a library grandparent, Mon & Wed 3-5pm.

● **Toy Lending Library**, 344 Salinas Street, Ste.. 201, across from the John Steinbeck Library. To May 5 from 1-5pm. Call Margaret Sirtak, 753-4977.

● **Salinas Slams**, free every second Saturday, 7pm at the Cherry Bean Coffeehouse, 332 Main St. Poets should sign up at 6:45pm. The events are co-hosted by "Slam Granny" Parmalee Paula Cover and Frank Sanchez, president of Baktun-12, a group of seven youths from East Salinas mentored by El Teatro Campesino founder Luis Valdez. Poetry slams have gained popularity across the United States and Europe in the past decade. Each participant gives a three-minute performance of their material, and is then scored on an Olympics-style scale. Audience participation is encouraged. For information call 758-4955 or 768-1880. For more information on National Poetry Slam, Inc., which hosts national slams, check out www.slampapi.com

● **Hartnell College** hosts free events, lectures, concerts. Call 755-6700. Seniors learn free at Hartnell College. For more information or a complete schedule of classes, contact program coordinator Glenna Teti in the college's office of instruction, 755-6721.

Parks and Recreation

▲ **Central Community Park**, corner of Homestead and Central avenues, behind Hartnell College. 8 acres. Large park with big trees, exercise course, tennis courts, playground with a full-size locomotive, small recreation center with games and crafts, barbecues and picnic tables. Parks Dept. 758-7945.

▲ **Claremont Manor Park**, San Fernando Dr. and San Miguel Ave. 5 acres. Ballfield, picnic area, playground, tennis, restrooms.

▲ **Closter Community Park**, Towt St. and Dewey Ave. 7 acres. Ballfield, basketball, horseshoes, picnics, playground, tennis, restrooms.

▲ **El Dorado Park**, El Dorado Dr. near Alvin. 20 acres. Ballfield, basketball, community building, picnic area, playground, restrooms.

▲ **Hartnell Park**, West Acacia and Alisal streets. Grassy areas, trees, basketball court, playground, restrooms and water fountains.

▲ **Rodeo-Sherwood Recreation Area**, 940 N. Main St. near Bernal Dr. 100 acres. Ballfield, community building, horseshoe pits, picnic area, playground, swimming, tennis, volleyball, restrooms.

▲ **Toro County Park**, three miles west of Salinas, 11.7 miles east of Monterey, 27742 Portola Drive off Highway 68. 4882 acres. Mon-Fri, $3/car, Sat-Sun, $5/car. Hiking and equestrian trails, views, mountain biking trails, grasslands and wooded hillsides, ballfields, volleyball courts, horseshoe pits, picnic facilities and playgrounds. 8am-5pm. Camp for youth groups is available; call 755-4899.

▲ **Skateboard Park**, on Las Casitas Drive in the Natividad Creek Park near Creekbridge. New skateboard course of 1500 square feet and a BMX track.

Activities

▲ **Card Collecting Star Cards & Collectibles**, 1241 South Main St. Hosts Free Pack Wars one Saturday a month. Everybody's a winner. Free food and drink. Call Johnny, 757-8234, for more information.

▲ **Toys Galore, Inc.**, 921 So. Main Street, 424-3488, has free play days on 2nd Saturdays, reservations recommended. Always take something home FREE! Paper Stick Horse, Pipe Cleaner Bug, Color A Picture Frame.

▲ **Drop in and Play.** Free Parent/Child Activity class for children 5 and under, Tues-Wed 3-5pm. The Parent Center, Salinas Adult School, 20 Sherwood Pl. Call Karen Estes or Carole Singley at 753-4273. Parent must stay.

▲ **Kid's Cafe** operated by the Salvation Army for ages 7-16 at 180 Williams Road. Karate lessons, swimming, computers, reading, library, athletic programs, Cub Scouts, Sunbeams, Girlguards, art and other classes. Recreation room with board games, ping-pong, pool, video games, homework help; hot nutritious dinner at 5pm. Everything is free, volunteers and donations needed, call Chuck Rowe, 424-0568.

Recreation Centers

Salinas Parks and Recreation Centers. Administration: 758-7945.

▲ Sherwood Center, 758-7218, teen lounge, Mon-Thurs, 6:30-8:45pm; Tues and Thurs 3-4:45pm, ages 12-18. Pool tournaments every Tues 6:30-8:45pm, 12-18. Ping-pong tournaments Thurs 6:30-8:45pm, ages 12-18, paddles provided.

▲ Firehouse Recreation, 758-7900, 758-7354, 758-7220, drop in program, Mon-Fri 3-5pm. Holiday, vacation hours, 12-4pm Evening hours, 5:30-9pm. 1330 E. Alisal St. Trips, brown bag program, social times, walking, square dancing, and more. Free Chair & Dance Movement classes, 10-11am, Tues. Gentle program designed with seniors in mind.

▲ El Dorado Community Park, 758-7223, 758-7305, 758-6220. Volleyball Tues-Thurs 3:30-4:30pm, 12 and up.

▲ Central Community Park, 758-7305, 758-7223, 758-7220.

▲ Breadbox Recreation Center, 758-7905, 758-7304, 758-7220.

▲ Hebbron Heights Service Center, 758-7905, 758-7304, 758-7220, Kids Bingo every Thurs 3:30-4:30pm, 6 yrs and up, small prizes will be awarded.

Creekbridge Community Park
1793 Declaration Street

Friday movies 3-5:30, free with popcorn and punch.

▲ Lincoln Street Recreation Center, 320 Lincoln. Many free activities and programs. Pick up a free guide. 758-7326 or 758-7413.

▲ Closter Community Park, 758-7905, 758-7304, 758-7220, variety of free programs. After school Mon-Fri, 3-5:30pm during school year, Holiday/ vacation hours noon to 4pm. Ping-pong tournaments every 1st Thursday, 3:30-5:20, ages 8 and up. Teen lounge, Tues & Thurs, 3-4:45pm, vacation hours Mon-Thurs, 1-4:45pm, evening hours 6:30-8:45pm. 758-7352.

Walking at Toro Park

➤ **Fifty-Plus Fitness Association** walks at Toro Park. Call Gloria for details. 422-9937. **Walk and Run** meets on first Saturdays at 7:45am at the Toro Park entrance near Salinas off Hwy. 68. Leaves at 8am. For more information call Gloria Drake at 422-9937 or (650) 323-6160.

You Can Adopt-a-Park

➤ **Salinas Adopt-a-Park** is a program by which businesses, civic organizations, groups and individuals can aid in supplementing park maintenance by working 2-3 hours, once a month, pulling weeds, cleaning, and planting. Call 758-7382 to adopt a park.

Free & Fun in the
Salinas Valley & South County

Historic Churches

The Hearst Hacienda

Rural Life Museum

Spreckels

March 13-14   **MINERAL SOCIETY ROCK SHOW**   **Free**
Gems and rock displays. Children's activities, rock bags, rock wheel of fortune, food booths. 10-6 Sat, 10-5 Sun at Spreckels Memorial Bldg., corner of 5th and Llano. "Rainbow Rock Show" features exhibits, hands-on demonstrations, games, jewelry, gems, minerals, fossils, equipment. Free hourly door prizes. Snack bar. 422-0530, 679-2896.

July 4   **SPRECKELS FOURTH OF JULY**   **Free+$$**
Begins with 10K Run ($18) and Special Olympics 10K run ($12) and One-Mile Run for children (free), registration 7:30-8:50am at Spreckels Park, Third and Llano. 455-2211, 455-8548. Children's Parade registration at 10:30am at Spreckels Memorial Building. Music, entertainment, crafts, children's games at 1pm in park, free admission. Firemen's Muster on Llano Avenue, 1-4pm Benefit for Spreckels Volunteer Fire Co. 455-8548.

● **Buena Vista Free Public Library**, Buena Vista Middle School, 18520 Tara Drive, off River Road. Preschool storytime; call for hours. 455-9699.

Gonzales

Chamber of Commerce, 147 Fourth St., 831-675-9019.

● **Gonzales Library**, 851 Fifth St. Family night, 1st and 3rd Thurs 6:30pm, Toddler storytime, last Wednesdays 10-noon. Storytime (all ages) Saturdays, 12:30pm. Homework Center (grades 1-12), Tues and Thurs 2:30-6:30pm, Wed 2:30-6pm. 675-2209.

■ **Gonzales Community Presbyterian Church**, built in 1883, has been placed on the National Register of Historic Places. 301 4th Street.

▲ **Gonzales Senior Center**, 675-9057.

▲ **Central Park**, 5th and Center Streets, 3 acres. Basketball, picnic area, playground, sand volleyball court, restrooms. 659-2809.

Soledad

City Hall, 248 Main, 831-678-3963. Chamber of Commerce, 678-2278.

June 28   **MISSION CHICKEN BBQ FIESTA**   **Free+$$**
Mass at 10:30am, barbecue at 12:00. Call Grace 678-3197.

July 4   **OLD-FASHIONED FOURTH OF JULY**   **Free**
Celebration & fireworks begins at 9am in Gallardo and Little League parks, Metz Road and Andalucia Drive. Games, old-timers' softball, music, food. Fireworks at 8:45pm. Call Raquel, 678-3963 ext. 116.

October 3   **MISSION GRAPE STOMP**   **Free**
Help stomp the grapes to make wine! Call Grace 678-3197.

December 4   **CHRISTMAS PARADE**   **Free**
Down Front Street, starts at 5pm after the merchants light up the stores. Food and craft booths will open at noon and entertainment will begin at 1:30.

● **Soledad Library**, 179 Main St. Homework Center (grades 1-12) Tues and Thurs, 2:30-5:30pm. Volunteers needed. 678-2430.

■ **Soledad Correctional Training Facility**. Hobby Store with leather goods, jewelry, etc.; reasonable prices. Open to public Sun-Mon, 8am-3pm, Thurs-Fri, 11am-5pm. Off Hwy 101 between Soledad and Gonzales. 678-3951.

■ **Mission Nuestra Senora de la Soledad**, originally built in 1791, the 13th of 21 California missions. The current building is a smaller chapel built in 1828 and restored in 1954. Free and open to the public. Gift shop, museum and gardens are open daily except Tuesday. The original adobe ruins can be seen in the rear of the quadrangle. Continued restoration and maintenance of Soledad Mission is made possible by donations and money earned at two major fund-raisers, the June Barbecue and the Fall Fiesta. Your donations are appreciated: Mission Soledad Restoration Committee, 36641 Fort Romie Road, Soledad 93960. 678-2586.

▲ **Pinnacles National Monument**, the east side of the park is south of Hollister, 5 miles off Calif. 25. The west side can be reached from Soledad off U.S. 101 via Hwy 146. There is NO direct road connection between the east and west sides. Distinctive geological features with caves to explore and an abundance of wildflowers in the spring. Fabulous scenic hiking trails: Bench trail, 1.3 miles, easy; Old Pinnacles, 2.3 miles, easy; Moses Spring/Bear Gulch Caves, 1 mile, moderate; Bear Gulch, 1.6 miles, moderate, Balconies Trail, 1.4 miles, moderate; Tunnel Trail, 1.2 miles, moderate; High Peaks, 5.3 miles , strenuous; Condor Gulch, 1.7 miles, strenuous, Juniper Canyon, 1.8 miles, strenuous; Chalone Peak, 3.3 miles, strenuous, North Wilderness, 7.6 miles, very strenuous. Rock climbing formations provide nesting habitat for several hawk and falcon species and should not be attempted during the nesting season, January 15 to July 1. Trailhead climber information boards give specific guidelines on climbing. Base camp with restrooms and picnic tables is free; there is a fee to enter the hiking area. Very hot in the summer. Call 389-4485.

▲ **Paraiso Hot Springs Resort**. Paraiso Springs Road. Fee. A private resort with small rental cottages, camp, trailer and picnic sites. Indoor and outdoor hot pools with temperatures from 70° to 100°. Snack bar, recreation room with ping-pong, books, magazines. Originally used by the padres at the mission to heal the sick or afflicted. From an elevation of 1400 feet, the Salinas Valley, the Pinnacles and the Gabilan Mountain Range views are superb. 678-2882.

Greenfield

Chamber of Commerce, 831-674-3222.

September 4-5   **BROCCOLI FESTIVAL**   **Free+$$**
An opportunity to showcase one of the Valley's top cash crops. Non-stop entertainment, food and refreshments, youth-oriented entertainment and activities for the younger generation, arts and crafts (many revolving around the broccoli theme), a parade, barbecue and many other fun activities. Held within the shady environs of Oak Park. For more information, call 674-5240.

● **Monterey County Free Library**, Ninth Street and Palm Avenue, 674-2614. Family storytime Sat 11am. Preschool storytime 2nd and 4th Wed 1:15pm.
▲ **Jay Hicks Park** is adjacent to the library, offering a place to sit outside and enjoy the sunshine.

Downtown Greenfield

▲ **Oak Park**, located three miles east of town on Elm Avenue, named for its impressive stand of oak trees. Picnic tables, barbecue area, tennis courts, horseshoe pits, community swimming pool open in summer months.

▲ **Patriot Park**, on 13th Street, between Oak and Elm avenues. Two baseball/ softball fields, soccer field, skateboard ramp, amphitheater and Children's Services Center.

▲ **Arroyo Seco Recreation Area**, take the Greenfield turnoff from King City, turn left on Elm Street, follow Elm until it ends at Arroyo Seco Road. Turn left on Arroyo Seco Road - 15 miles to the Recreation Area. Camping, fishing, swimming, canoeing, access to the Ventana Wilderness. 674-5726.

■ **Elm Avenue Bridge**, built in 1915-16 and designated by Monterey County Supervisors as having historical significance; reflects distinctive characteristics of the era; construction methods are significant in engineering history. Spans the Arroyo Seco River and connects Arroyo Seco Road and Greenfield. 268 feet long.

▲ **Ventana Wilderness**, also known as "A Window to the Wild." Contains 167,323 acres straddling the Santa Lucia Mountains and located entirely within Monterey County and the Los Padres National Forest. There are approximately 197 miles of trails. Pine Ridge trail is the most popular and most heavily traversed. Other trailheads include: Carmel River, China Camp, Arroyo Seco, Memorial Park, Bottcher's Gap, Cone Peak, Kirk Creek and Partington Ridge. Topographical Ventana Wilderness Maps and Los Padres National Forest recreation maps are available for $3 each at the Forest Service Office at 406 S. Mildred Street in King City.

King City

Chamber of Commerce, 203 Broadway, 831-385-3814.

April 18-19   **JUNIOR RODEO** $$
King City Riding Club at the Fairgrounds. 385-1484.

May 13-16   **SALINIS VALLEY FAIR**   Free+$$
Call for more information, 385-3814.

September 24-26   **SALSA FEST** $$
Call for more information, 386-1812.

▲ **San Lorenzo County Park**, 1160 Broadway off Hwy 101, 384-8020. Fee. 380 acres. **Monterey County Agricultural and Rural Life Museum**: Antique farm equipment and mining, farming and local history displays. A working blacksmith shop, a century-old farmhouse and a one-room schoolhouse. Exhibits: tack shop, country store and antique printing press, cook wagon, railroad caboose and the old King City train depot. The main exhibit barn and the outdoor displays are open daily, 10am-4pm, year-round. The other buildings are open weekends, April-October, call for hours. Park has horseshoe pits, picnic and barbecue areas, playgrounds, walking trails, campground, water activities in the Salinas River. Spreading oak trees and eucalyptus groves. 385-5964. Celebrates the 4th of July with a Valley Heritage Day - a 4-day camping rally; call 800/588-2267.

■ **Crinklaw Farms** offices, 333 E. San Antonio St. The Southwestern Holiday Chile Wreath was specifically designed for the 1998 postage stamp by Chris Crinklaw and her team. The stamps will be sold only in 1998, but you may purchase the wreaths any time. 385-3261.

GREETINGS
32 USA

▲ **Leo Meyer Senior Center**, 385-4562. **Recreation Center**, 212 S. Vanderhurst Ave., 385-3575. **Library**, 402 Broadway, 385-3677.

▲ **City of King Park**, Division and San Lorenzo Ave. 17 acres. Ballfield, community building, horseshoe pits, multi-use field, playground, swimming, tennis, racquetball courts, lap and wading pools, dive tank, water slide, restrooms. 385-3575.

San Lucas

● **Library**, 54692 Teresa, 831-382-4382.

■ **San Lucas Bridge**, built in 1915 and designated by Monterey County Supervisors as having historical significance; reflects distinctive characteristics of the era; the construction methods are significant in engineering history. Spans the Salinas River and connects the community of San Lucas with Jolon Road. 870 feet long.

Bradley

■ **Nacimiento Lake Drive Bridge,** built in 1921 and designated by Monterey County Supervisors as having historical significance; reflects distinctive characteristics of the era; the construction methods are significant in engineering history. Spans the San Antonio River and connects the Bradley-Jolon Road and the town of Bradley to the Lake San Antonio area. 292 feet long. To be demolished in 2000.

▲ **Lake San Antonio Recreation Area,** 85 miles south of Salinas on Highway 101. Turn on Jolon Road. Picnic areas, fishing, swimming, boat launches, convenience store. 755-4899. Eagle Watch tours, Jan-Mar, 888/588-2267.

▲ **Lake Nacimiento Resort,** Highway 101 south of Salinas to Lake Nacimiento Drive. Campsites, general store, marina, boat ramps, hiking trails, fishing. 805/238-3256.

Parkfield

▲ **Cholame Road Bridge,** built in 1932 and designated by Monterey County Supervisors as having historical significance and reflects distinctive characteristics of the era and construction methods significant in engineering history. Spans Little Cholame Creek on the county road that connects Parkfield with State Hwy. 46 east of Paso Robles in San Luis Obispo County. 135 feet long.

■ **Parkfield-Coalinga Road Bridge,** built in 1932 and designated by Monterey County Supervisors as having historical significance; reflects distinctive characteristics of the era; the construction methods are significant in engineering history. Spans Little Cholame Creek and connects Parkfield with Coalinga in Fresno County. 118 feet long.

Jolon/Ft. Hunter Liggett

■ **The Hacienda** was the Ranch House for William Randolph Hearst. Now open to the public as a lodge, restaurant and lounge. Live music and dancing during the summer, Fri-Sat, 9pm-1am. Line dancing lessons on occasion. Near to Mission San Antonio. From Hwy 101 just north of King City, take Jolon Rd. Southwest 17.5 miles to Mission Rd., go west 5 miles into Hunter Liggett and Del Ventura Rd. 386-2446, fax 386-2262.

■ **Mission San Antonio,** founded by Fr. Junipero Serra in 1771, the third of the California Missions and still active as a parish church. Annual Fiesta is June 13, 1999. $1 donation to see the grounds and museum. Picnic grounds with tables under the shade trees to relax and enjoy the peace and quiet of the secluded area and the many varieties of roses in the garden. Mass Schedules: Daily at 7:30am, Sunday at 10am. Museum hours, 9am-6pm daily. Gift Shop hours: Sun 11:15-4:30pm, Mon-Sat 10am-4:30pm. 385-4478.

Monterey Wine Country

Monterey County Area Code is 831

Monterey County Vintners & Growers Association, 375-9400,
fax 375-1116, www.wines.com/monterey.
Wine Institute, www.wineinstitute.org, 415/512-0151.
Monterey County Wine Country Magazine, call 373-3720 for a free copy.
AgVenture Tours, custom winery tours, 643-WINE, fax 645-WINE.

Important Wine Events

February 23-28   MASTERS OF FOOD & WINE $$
At the Highlands Inn, various times. Exceptional gastronomic event with internationally famous chefs and winemakers. Lunches, dinners, winery tours, wine tastings. Free cooking demonstrations. Call info, 624-3801.

April 15-17   MONTEREY WINE FESTIVAL   Free+$$
Monterey Bay Aquarium & various locations. Tastings, lectures, dinners, seminars, wine display, parties, tours. Open house and complimentary tastings at participating wineries. Call for dates, places and times. www.Montereywine.com. 656-WINE.

April 29   A VINTNERS GARDEN GALA $$
A preview party at the Carmel Garden Show at Quail Lodge Resort featuring 20 Monterey County wineries. 375-9400.

August 14-15   WINEMAKERS' CELEBRATION $$
Custom House Plaza, Monterey. Ticketed event with outdoor festival, wine tasting, various exhibits and food fair. Open house events at winery tasting rooms. Monterey County Vintner's & Growers Assn., 375-9400.

August to November   WINE HARVESTING   Free+$$
Observe grape harvest activities at these wineries: Chateau Julien, Monterey Vineyards, Chalone, Smith & Hook/Hahn Estates, Paraiso Springs and Cloniger. September & October most active time; call for dates and times.

October 3   MISSION GRAPE STOMP   Free
Mass at 10:30am, Chicken barbecue at 11:45 ($6), participants invited to stomp grapes to make wine at 1:30pm; wine auction after the stomp. At the Soledad Mission. Grace, 678-3197.

November 6   ANNUAL WINE TASTING EVENT   Free
Cornucopia Community Market, 11am-3pm. Outdoor courtyard music, entertainment, wines and food from local vendors. 26135 Carmel Rancho Blvd, just east of Highway 1 at CV Road. 625-0230.

November 12-15   GREAT WINE ESCAPE WEEKEND $$
Various locations. Feast of Eden, winery open houses, gourmet foods, live music, vineyard tours. Benefit Kinship Center Foster Care and Adoption. Monterey County Vintner's & Growers Assn, 375-9400.

Mostly Free Wine Tasting

1. **Bargetto Winery** – <u>Free wine tasting</u>. Daily 10:30am-6pm. 700 Cannery Row, Monterey. Oldest Monterey tasting room, over 30 selections. 373-4053.

2. **A Taste Of Monterey** – $5 for 6 tastes, rebate with purchase. Daily 11am-6pm. 700 Cannery Row. Exhibits: corks, barrel-making, viticulture. 646-5446.

3. **Bottles N' Bins** – Retail store, deli. Sun-Thurs 10am-12am, Fri-Sat 10am-1am. 898 Lighthouse Ave., New Monterey. 375-5488.

4. **Ventana Vineyards** – <u>Free wine tasting</u>. Daily 11am-5pm. 2999 Monterey-Salinas Highway, Monterey. 372-7415.

5. **Mediterranean Market** – Retail store, specialty food market since 1959. Daily 9am-6pm. Ocean Ave. and Mission, Carmel. 624-2022.

6. **Bountiful Basket** – <u>Free wine tasting</u>. Mon-Sat 10am-6pm, Sun 12-5pm. 153 Crossroads Blvd., Carmel. 625-4457.

7. **Rancho Cellars** – Wine tasting $10-$40. Mon-Sat 11am-7pm. Sun 12-5pm. Carmel Rancho Center in Carmel Rancho. 625-5646.

8. **Chateau Julien** – <u>Free wine tasting</u> Mon-Fri 8:30am-5pm. Sat-Sun 11am-5pm. 8940 Carmel Valley Road, Carmel Valley. www.chateaujulien.com. 624-2600.

9. **Durney Vineyards** – $3 tasting charge. Mon-Fri 11am-5pm, Sat-Sun 10am-5pm. 69 West Carmel Valley Road, Carmel Valley Village. 659-6220.

10. **Talbott Vineyards** – Free glass with tasting price. Sun-Thurs, 11am-5pm. Carmel Valley Village. Karen, 675-3000.

11. **Georis Winery** – Minimum half bottle purchase. Thurs-Sun 12-4pm. Call for information about special events. 4 Pilot Road, CV Village. 659-1050.

12. **Bernardus** – <u>Free white wine tasting</u>, red $3. Daily 11am-5pm. 5 W. Carmel Valley Road, Carmel Valley Village. 659-1900.

13. **Galante Vineyards** – <u>Free wine tasting</u> by appointment, <u>free tours</u>, Sun-Fri 11am-3pm. 18181 Cachagua Rd., Carmel Valley. 415/331-1247.

14. **Joullian Vineyard** – Tasting by appointment, Mon-Fri 11am-4pm. 20300 Cachagua Rd., Carmel Valley. 659-2800.

15. **Cloninger Cellars** – <u>Free wine tasting</u>. Mon-Thurs 11am-4pm, Fri-Sun 11am-5pm. 1645 River Road, Salinas. 675-9463.

16. **J. Hahn Estates/Smith & Hook** – <u>Free wine tasting, free tours</u>. Daily 11am-4pm. 37700 Foothill Road, Soledad. Highway 101 exit Arroyo Seco, right on Fort Romie road, left on Colony, right on Foothill. 678-2622.

17. **Paraiso Springs Vineyards** – <u>Free wine tasting, tours</u>. Mon-Fri 12-4pm, Sat-Sun 11am-5pm. Special events. 38060 Paraiso Spgs Rd, Soledad. 678-0300.

18. **Chalone Vineyard** – <u>Free wine tasting, tours</u>. Picnic area. Sat-Sun 11:30am-4pm. Highway 146 at Stonewall Canyon Road, Soledad. 678-1717.

19. **Jekel Vineyards** – <u>Free wine tasting</u>. Daily 11am-4pm. 40155 Walnut Ave., Greenfield. 674-5522. Highway 101 to Greenfield exit, then west on Walnut.

20. **Scheid Vineyards** – <u>Free wine tasting</u>. Daily 11am-5pm. 1972 Hobson Ave. exit off Highway 101, 5 miles south of Greenfield. 386-0316.

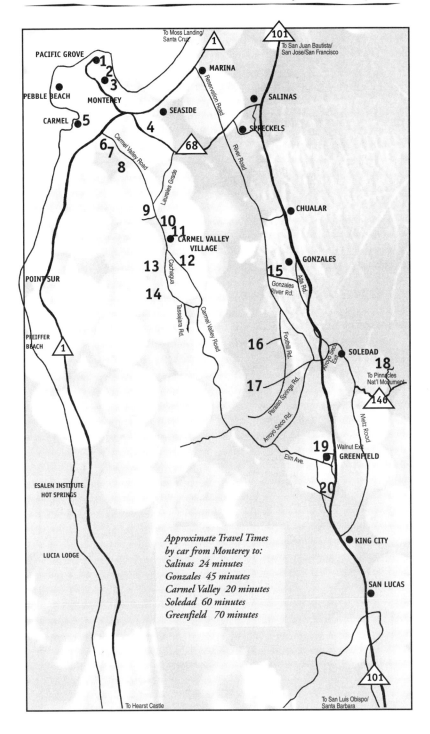

Approximate Travel Times
by car from Monterey to:
Salinas 24 minutes
Gonzales 45 minutes
Carmel Valley 20 minutes
Soledad 60 minutes
Greenfield 70 minutes

#17

Paraiso Springs Vineyards

Spend the day in wine country! Paraiso Springs Vineyards tasting room is open year round for complimentary wine tasting. Bring a picnic lunch and come enjoy our panoramic view of the Salinas Valley with the Pinnacles Monument beyond. Five other tasting rooms are within a ten mile radius.

Vineyard Tasting Room – 1999 Calendar of Events

Saturday, April 10, 1999
"Steinbeck Wine Country Spring Open House"
From 11am to 4pm. Paraiso Springs Vineyards will welcome the public to enjoy tastes of their unreleased spring wines with one-day special discounts. Each of the six Salinas Valley Tasting Rooms will participate. Lawn seating and live music provided at Paraiso Springs Vineyards Tasting Room.
Call 831/678-0300 for a map.

Saturday, May 15, 1999
"Paraiso Springs Vineyards Sixth Anniversary Open House"
From 11am-4pm. The public is welcome to celebrate with the Smith Family the sixth year of opening their tasting room in the vineyard. Hors d'oeuvres, live music, barrel tastings and complimentary tasting of selected varieties.
Call 831/678-0300 for a map or information.

Sunday, August 15, 1999
"Monterey County Winemakers' Celebration - 2nd Day Celebration"
From 11am-4pm. Paraiso Springs Vineyards will host complimentary tasting of selected wines with live music at the tasting room. Gourmet Barbecue tickets may be purchased for $25.00 per person. Tours of the estate and two glasses of your favorite Paraiso Springs Vineyards wine in a souvenir logo wine glass are included with barbecue only.
Call 831/678-0300 for barbecue tickets and map.

Free & Fun in
Seaside & Sand City

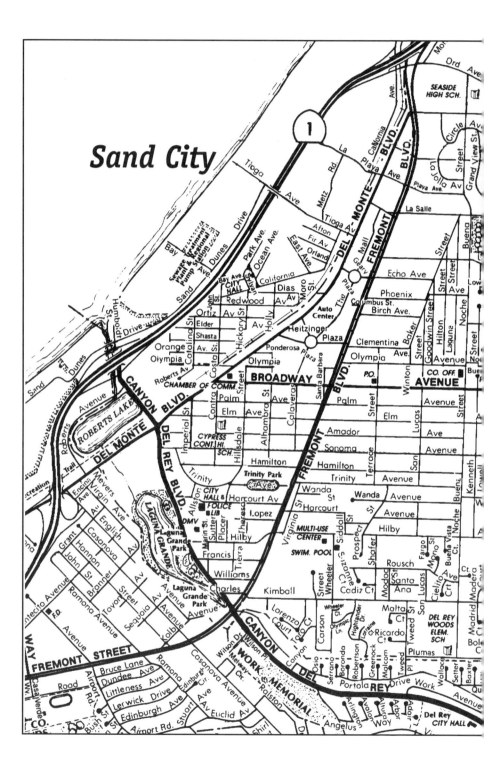

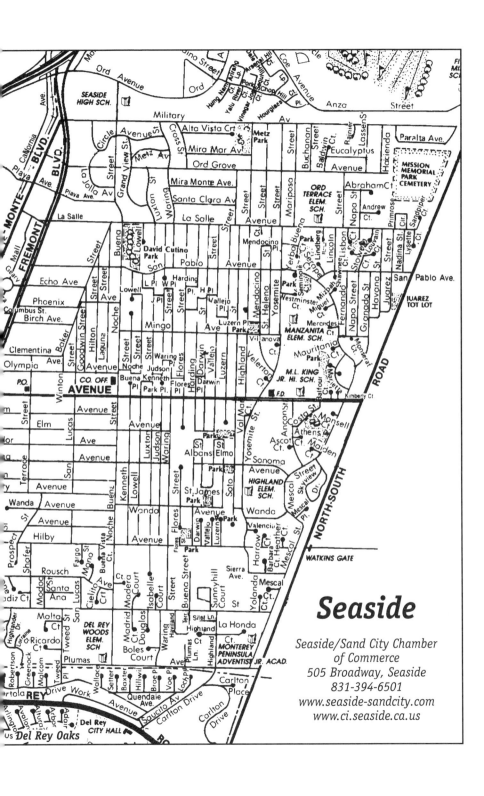

Seaside

Seaside/Sand City Chamber
of Commerce
505 Broadway, Seaside
831-394-6501
www.seaside-sandcity.com
www.ci.seaside.ca.us

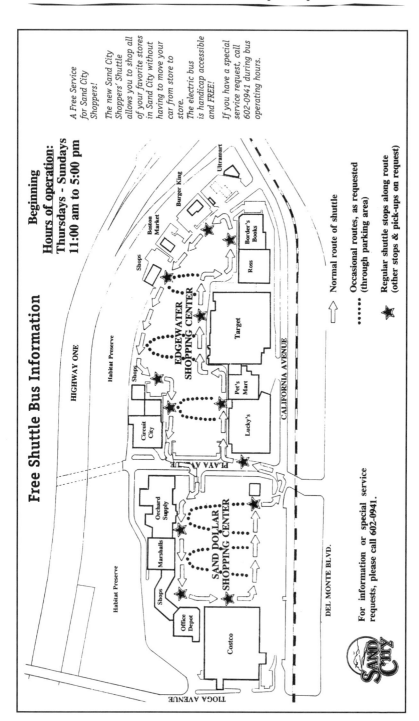

Free Shuttle Bus Information

**Beginning
Hours of operation:
Thursdays - Sundays
11:00 am to 5:00 pm**

*A Free Service
for Sand City
Shoppers!*

*The new Sand City
Shoppers' Shuttle
allows you to shop all
of your favorite stores
in Sand City without
having to move your
car from store to
store.*

*The electric bus
is handicap accessible
and FREE!*

*If you have a special
service request, call
602-0941 during bus
operating hours.*

HIGHWAY ONE

Habitat Preserve

Habitat Preserve

Ultramart

Burger King

Boston Market

Shops

Border's Books

Ross

EDGEWATER SHOPPING CENTER

Target

Shops

Circuit City

Pet's Mart

Lucky's

PLAZA AV TR

CALIFORNIA AVENUE

Orchard Supply

Marshalls

Shops

Office Depot

SAND DOLLAR SHOPPING CENTER

Costco

DEL MONTE BLVD.

TIOGA AVENUE

→ Normal route of shuttle

•••• Occasional routes, as requested (through parking area)

★ Regular shuttle stops along route (other stops & pick-ups on request)

For information or special service requests, please call 602-0941.

SAND CITY

Browsing the Shops

● **Sand Dollar and Edgewater Shopping Centers**, see map at left for free shoppers' shuttle bus service. Sand City, Highway 1 and Fremont Blvd.

● **Big K-Mart Plaza**, on Canyon Del Rey and Highway 1, Seaside. K-Mart, Smart & Final, Staples, McDonald's Playplace.

● **Laguna Plaza Shopping Center**, Fremont Blvd., near Kimball, Seaside. The Breakfast Club, Radio Shack, Mail Boxes Etc., Hollywood Video.

● **University Plaza**, Fremont Blvd. and Echo Ave., Seaside. Olympia Beauty Supply, Gold's Gym, Seaside Furniture, Beverly Fabric Store, Annie's Bookstop.

● **Motor City**, billed as the 2nd largest auto mall in the country, between Del Monte Ave. and Fremont Blvd., enter at Plaza or Echo Ave., Seaside.

Free Wooden Cat

Show your *Free & Fun Guide* at Mary's Angels, 425 Elder Avenue, Sand City, and receive a free handcarved 50-year-old wooden cat with a purchase of $50 or more. Handcarved wood & cast stone for home & garden. Winter hours: Wed-Sat, noon-4pm. Spring hours: daily with extended hours. 393-0345.

Art Galleries

● **Three Spirits Arts Center**, 361 Orange Ave., Sand City, 393-2787.

● **Sand Dollar Art & Framing Center**, 824 Playa Ave., Seaside, 394-1618.

● **Merigraphics**, 1760 Fremont, Seaside. Tues-Fri, 12:30-5:30, 392-0926.

● **Gray's Art Gallery**, 1104 Broadway Ave. #K, Seaside, 899-1069.

● **Seaside City Hall**, Seaside Arts Commission, changing exhibits of local artists. 440 Harcourt. 8am-5pm. 899-6336.

● **Borders Book Store**, 2080 California, Sand City. Local art in Café Espresso. 899-6643.

● **Family Center for the Arts**, 530 Elm, Seaside. Affiliated with the Salvation Army. Low cost classes in painting, piano keyboard, computers and martial arts. Anita Amos, 899-0525, 899-1335.

Free Chocolate Samples & Tour

The Chocolate Factory, 1291 Fremont, gives free tours and chocolate samples. Store hours: Mon-Fri, 9:30am-8:30pm, Sat 10am-8:30pm, Sun 12:30-5:30pm. 899-7963.

1999 Calendar of Events

Information subject to change. Please call in advance to verify.

January 18   MARTIN LUTHER KING JR. PARADE   Free
11am march starts on Broadway and concludes at Oldemeyer Center, 966 Hilby St. Seaside. 1pm speakers. Elias Oxendine IV, chairman, 333-9106.

February all month   BLACK HISTORY MONTH   Free
Art exhibition, cultural program and reception at City Hall, 440 Harcourt Ave. Art Gallery hours are 8am-5pm, Mon-Fri. 899-6270.

June 6   MONTEREY BONSAI CLUB EXHIBITION   Free
Numerous trees on display and for sale. Demonstrations of bonsai techniques, door prizes. Buddhist Temple, 1155 Noche Buena. Joe Byrd, 649-5934.

June/October   HOT CARS/COOL NIGHTS   Free
Every Friday. Rod and Classic Car Show, 5-8pm, West Broadway at Fremont. Hosted by Gold Coast Rods, pre-'73 cars, awards, raffles, 50-50 raffle, music. After the show, cruise with the winners to downtown Monterey and Cannery Row. No registration fee. 394-4254.

July 4   SEASIDE PARADE OF CHAMPIONS   Free
At noon on Fremont Blvd. at Harcourt Ave., with main reviewing stand on West Broadway at Alhambra. Participants include Central California marching units, drill teams, bands, floats, horses, antique cars with numerous dignitaries. 899-6270.

July/August   BLUES AND ART IN THE PARK   Free
First Sundays, 1-4:30pm. Six free concerts of blues and art in the park on Sundays. Laguna Grande Park, Canyon Del Rey near Highway 1, across from Seaside Police Dept., 899-6270.

July 15-18   COWBOY CRAZY DAYS   Free
For senior citizens, at Oldemeyer Center, 986 Hilby Ave. Salinas Rodeo Week event. Police horses, line dancing, cowboy art exhibit, country-style dancing. Call for times. Seaside Cultural and Leisure Services, 899-6270.

July 31   WALK FOR THE GOLD   Spectators free
Gather at Sand City beach, 10am-2pm, with a team of 10 or more people; pledge $100 or more per person, for 5K walk followed by barbecue and live music. To benefit Special Olympics Monterey Bay Region. 373-1972

August 26   MONTEREY BAY RIB COOKOFF   Free+$$
Noon-6pm on the lawn at Seaside City Hall, across from Laguna Grande Park. Part of the nationally recognized California Cookoff Series attracts amateur barbecue enthusiasts from around the state. Live music, games, rides, arts & crafts, foods, beverages and the best ribs you ever wrapped your lips around! Seaside Chamber of Commerce, 394-6501, 899-6270.

August 28, 29   FALL FUN FEST   Free
Carnival, crafts, food, music, fireman's relay, pie eating contest, cake cutting for city's birthday. **Annual Diaper Derby**: Parents of children from crawling age to age 4 are encouraged to bring them to participate in the race on Canyon Del Rey in front of Seaside City Hall. Entry is free and prizes awarded

to the fastest babies. Preregister: 899-6270 or on-site. **Annual Bed Races**: Teams push double beds that have been modified with wheels and extra-long push bars for the races. One person climbs aboard a thin mattress and the other four push as fast as they can down Canyon Del Rey from Harcourt to Hilby avenues. 899-6270.

October tba   BIKE RODEO & SAFETY FAIR   Free

10am-2pm at Boys & Girls Club of the Monterey Peninsula, 1332 LaSalle Ave. Bring bicycle and helmet to participate. Police motorcycle and canine demonstrations, free bicycle inspections and licensing, free child fingerprinting and photos. Emergency services vehicles on display. Prizes. Appearance by McGruff the Crime Dog, Vince & Larry the Crash Test dummies, Buckle Bear, Spanky the Fire Dog. 759-6678.

October 31   HALLOWEEN FESTIVITIES   Free

Holiday specific art exhibit at Gray's Art Gallery, 1104 Broadway Ave., Suite K. Day of the Dead celebration, November 1, 6-8 pm. 899-1069. Halloween Pumpkin Patch Party at 6pm, Seaside Assembly of God Church, 1184 Hilby Ave. Free food, games and videos. 899-4124.

November tba   TURKEY TROT   Spectators free

4.8 mile cross-country loop begins on asphalt at the CSUMB campus and goes on to grass, dirt and sand. Benefit athletics. Call 582-3015 to sign up.

November 25   THANKSGIVING DINNERS   Free

Sand City Police Department will deliver Thanksgiving meals to anyone on the Monterey Peninsula who is homebound and cannot make it to the Community Thanksgiving Dinner at the Monterey County Fairgrounds. Sponsored by the Kiwanis Club. Call Sand City Police Chief Michael Klein at 394-1451 to arrange for a delivery or to volunteer. **Thanksgiving Dinner** open to the public at American Legion Post 591, 1000 Playa Ave. $6 per person, turkey or ham with all the fixin's. Call 394-6604 for reservations.

December tba   DOLLS' TEA PARTY   Free

Tea party and refreshments by the Salvation Army. Holiday items for sale to benefit needy children and local programs. 1491 Contra Costa. 899-4911.

December 11   SEASIDE HAPPY HOLIDAY PARADE   Free

Parade of floats, cars, bands, drill teams, clowns and Santa Claus down Fremont Blvd. at Broadway to City Hall where the city tree is lighted at 6:30pm in the Stephen E. Ross Park. Santa treats for the children, who are invited to bring handmade decorations for the community tree. 899-6270.

December tba   LA POSADA   Free

Bring candles or flashlights for the children, dress warmly. Celebration begins at 6pm at City Hall, 440 Harcourt Ave. 899-6270.

December 21-31   HOLIDAY PLAYLAND   Free

Holiday break activities for children ages 5-11, from 1-5:30pm. Call Oldemeyer Center for details, 899-6270.

December 25   CHRISTMAS DINNER   Free

Noon to 4pm at Seaside Assembly of God Church, 1184 Hilby Ave. The church youth group and other volunteers will deliver dinners to shut-ins as well as public servants who have to work. Volunteers call 899-4198.

Entertainment

Movies

◆ **Seaside MCAP** sponsors Gay Movie Night, 7-9pm, first and third Wednesdays at 780 Hamilton Ave. Free and open to all ages in the gay, lesbian, bi and transgendered community. Refreshments. 772-8202.

Music

◆ **Cuppers Coffee House**, Sunday jazz jam, 1-4pm. Musicians and vocalists sign up before 1 pm. No cover. 1130 Fremont Blvd., Seaside, 393-2216

◆ **Jem's Philippine Cuisine**, 1257 Fremont Blvd., 393-9665. Karaoke, Fri-Sun, 9pm-1am. No cover.

Books, Poetry, Open Mic

◆ **Seaside Library**, 550 Harcourt Ave. 899-2055. Preschool Storytimes, ages 3-5, Thurs 10:30am. Homework Center, Tues-Thurs 3-6pm, for students in grades 1-12.

◆ **Borders' Bookstore**, 2080 California Avenue, in the Sand Dollar Center. On-going venue for local musicians, speakers, poets, writers. Call for information or drop by for free monthly newsletter. **Book Group** meets 1st Mondays in the cafe at 6:30pm. **Mystery Book Group** meets 2nd Tuesdays at 6:30pm. New members are always welcome. In the Café Espresso. Mon-Sat, 9am-11pm. Sun 9am-9pm. 899-6643.

◆ **Cupper's Coffee Cafe.** Poetry readings, 3rd Mondays, 7pm, followed by Open Mic. Seaside Cultural & Leisure Dept., 1130 Fremont Blvd., 899-6270

Monterey Bay Dunes Open Space

The Monterey Bay dunes extend inland under most of Marina, Sand City, and Seaside. These ancient inland dunes exist as consolidated sandhills while the dunes on the shoreline are the progeny of a once receding ocean that is now reclaiming them as sea-level rises. The first Europeans found little use for the dunes and settled in the sheltered forested areas and uplands where the ground was suitable for building. Later, after WWII, sand mining became the most prevalent use for the dunes and several operations established themselves along the 12-mile stretch of dunes from Sand

City to Marina. Landfill dumping and off-road use was another activity in the dunes. In the near future almost half of Sand City's dunes will be restored and added to the Monterey Bay State Seashore as open space and endangered species habitat. Monterey Peninsula Regional Park District, 659-4488.

Parks and Recreation

▲ **Seaside State Beach**, Canyon Del Rey at Highway 1. Long, walkable stretches of sand and beautiful dunes. Fly a kite, walk the dog, take a sunset stroll, check out the native plant dune restoration project currently underway. Volunteer to assist by calling 659-4488.

▲ **Cutino Park**, Noche Buena St. and La Salle Ave. 10^1/$_2$ acres. Ballfield, basketball, picnic area, playground, tennis, restrooms. 899-6270.

▲ **Laguna Grande Regional Park**, Canyon Del Rey Blvd. and Del Monte Ave. 34 acres of grass and trees with freshwater marsh and lake, two picnic areas, bicycling, paths and playground. Russian Orthodox Church near picnic areas. Site of several city celebrations. 659-4488.

▲ **Roberts Lake**, across Del Monte Blvd. from Laguna Grande Park, is a nesting place for a variety of sea birds: Canadian geese, mallards, American coot, seagulls, cormorants, and others. Model boat racing Sat-Sun afternoons. Named for the "Father of Seaside," Dr. John L. Roberts. 659-4488.

▲ **Frog Pond Natural Area**, Canyon Del Rey at the Via Verde intersection, Del Rey Oaks. 17 acre habitat for the rare Pacific Tree frog. Park and pick up guided walk brochure across the street at City Hall. The entrance is along the northbound shoulder of Highway 218. Dawn to dusk. 659-4488.

▲ **Monterey Bay Dunes Open Space** includes nearly half of Sand City's dunes to be restored and added to the Monterey Bay State Seashore as open space and endangered species habitat. Open dawn to dusk. Off Highway 1, north of Seaside State Beach. 659-4488.

Laguna Grande Community Park

Once a source of tules for Ohlone structures, boats and other uses, Laguna Grande was later a regular watering spot for Spanish military horses and civilian use. The lake is now two district lakes with the northern and smaller lake named after Dr. John Roberts, the "Father of Seaside." With generous Federal, State and Joint Powers Agency funding, the park now offers trails, children's play areas, picnic facilities, restrooms, lake restoration, and landscaping. Seaside Cultural & Leisure Services, 899-6270.

Recreation Centers

▲ **Seaside Recreation Department**. The City of Seaside sponsors games, sports activities, swimming, excursions and special events free for children ages 5-11. Register at Oldemeyer Center, 986 Hilby Ave. or Del Rey Woods School, 1281 Plumas Ave., 899-6270.

▲ **Oldemeyer Senior Center**. Activities for seniors. 986 Hilby Ave., 899-6270. Sage Stompers Square Dance Club welcomes all square dancers Tuesdays at 7:30pm. For info call Bill Herrold at 647-9392. Scrabble players meet every Wed 6-9pm. No dues, all levels welcome; for info call 633-4649.

▲ **B.J. Dolan Youth and Education Center**, 1136 Wheeler St., Seaside. Open Mon-Thurs 3-8pm, Fri 3-9pm, Sun 1-9pm. Center offers educational, social and recreational opportunities to Seaside students in middle and high schools. Among the opportunities available are job hunting assistance, volunteer opportunities, pool, air hockey, Nintendo, television and recording studio facilities. 899-6270, 899-6375.

▲ **Boys & Girls Club**, 1332 LaSalle Ave., Seaside. Programs for Youths ages 7-18. Annual fee is $3. Support for their activities is welcomed. 394-5171.

Rock Climbing • Martial Arts • Mini Golf

➤ **Sanctuary Rock Gym**. Indoor rock climbing with over 5600 square feet of molded and sculpted "RADWALL"™, art gallery and proshop. Free indoor rock climbing orientation and tour. Mon-Fri 12-10pm, Sat 10am-10pm, Sun 10am-6pm. 1855a East Avenue, Sand City, 899-2595, fax 899-2597, www.rockgym.com/.

➤ **BodyWorx, Kickboxing and Martial Arts**. First class is free! Kickboxing, Tang Soo Do karate, and kempo karate private lessons. 20'x20' ring. Day and evening classes, childcare, open 6 days a week, family rates and military discounts. Hours: 10:30am-9pm Mon-Fri, 11am-3pm Sat. Closed Sun. 1173 Broadway Ave., 899-WORX.

➤ **Mini Golf Course**, a challenging nine holes, is open to the public Sat-Sun, 1-5pm. $1 for resident youth, $1.25 for non-resident youth, $2 for resident adults and $2.50 for non-resident adults. 1136 Wheeler Street, next to Pattulo Swim Center at 1148 Wheeler. 899-6272.

California State University (CSUMB)

Ft. Ord, which lies between Seaside and Marina, is now home to California State University at Monterey Bay (CSUMB), which schedules many free events. For dates and times, call 582-3330. Music hall, call 582-4085.

◆ **Black Box Cabaret.** Spin Cycle techno show, Tues 8:30-11:30pm; Hip-Hop night, Weds 8-11pm; Open Mic, Thurs 8-11; no cover. Live bands, Fri 8-11pm, $3. Bldg #81, off 3rd St., near North-South Road. 582-3597.

■ **Monterey Institute for Research in Astronomy.** Weaver Student Observatory is the only one in the county dedicated to free public access. www.mira.org shows a virtual "Field Trip to the Stars." Hosts December Annual Friends of MIRA potluck, first Sunday 5-8pm. Food and music, tours, stargazing. Free. 200 8th St. 883-1000 ext. 58. Laura Cohan, Director.

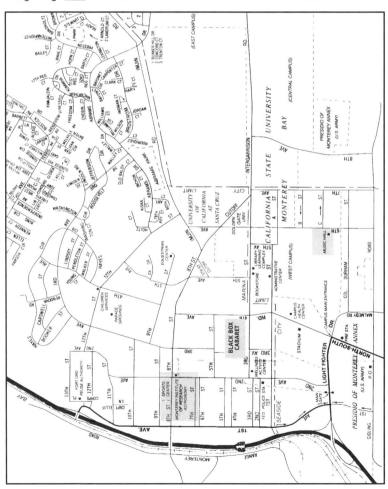

Fort Ord Public Lands

Fort Ord Public Lands, on the site of the former Army base, <u>with free entry</u>, are managed by the Bureau of Land Management (BLM) to protect 35 species of rare plants and animals and their native coastal habitats. More than 50 miles of roads and trails for hiking, bicycling and horseback riding. For information, or to participate in BLM Volunteer Programs, call 394-8314.

➤ **California Native Plant Society** wildland restoration volunteers needed. Call Bruce Delgado at 394-8314.

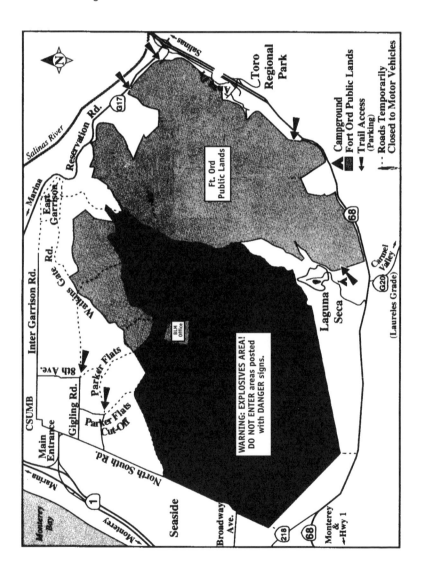

Free & Fun
Clubs & Organizations

Meet with like-minded individuals to enrich your life and have fun.
Some charge annual dues, some are free. Call for all the details.

Animals

Animal Lovers' Hour at 7:30 pm, 3rd Wednesday at Borders Bookstore, 2080 California Ave., Sand City. Monthly gathering with veterinarian JoAnn Donahoe. Bring questions about your pets. 899-6643.

Cage Bird Club, Monterey Bay. 3rd Sunday 1-3pm. For information and place, call Diane Grindol at 642-0514.

Society for the Prevention of Cruelty to Animals, SPCA, P.O. Box 3058, Monterey, CA 93942. 373-2631.

The Arts

Oriental Art Society of the Monterey Peninsula. Public welcome; refreshments. 624-7126.

Creative Edge: The Way of the Arts, 1st Saturdays with Donald Mathews at 8 Stratford Place, Monterey. 373-7809.

Friends of the Arts, Pacific Grove, meets 1st Tuesdays. This is the fund-raising organization for the P.G. Arts Commission. 373-7342/372-8221.

Civic Organizations

Jaycees, Monterey Peninsula, 641-9358.

Junior League of Monterey County, 375-5356.

Kiwanis Club of Pacific Grove, 645-4717.

Lions Club of the Monterey Peninsula, 646-4535.

Monterey Civic Club, 540 Calle Principal, 643-0604.

Monterey Peninsula Masonic Lodges, 375-1263. **Eastern Star**: Monterey, 372-4685. Carmel, 394-5273.

Optimist Club of Monterey, 883-1062 or 384-5304.

Rotary Club, meeting information, 394-0100.

Soroptimist International of Carmel Bay. Shari Hastey, 394-4279.

Collectors

Antique Glass Bottles and Glass Milk Bottles Collectors Club. Luncheon meeting every second Tuesday. 394-3257 after 7 pm.

Carmel Doll and Toy Study Group meets 3rd Mondays at The Crossroads community room at 7pm. Visitors are welcome. 373-6983.

Mission Trail Historical Bottle Club, Mission Trail promotes history and collections of historical bottles. Meets 2nd Tuesday for 11:30am. Luncheon at various eateries. Call Bruce Kendall, 394-3257.

Computer

ClubMac of Monterey meets 2nd Fridays in the computer lab at PG Adult School at 1025 Lighthouse Ave., P.G. bcbelknap*redshift.com. Call 373-5717 for time.

Monterey Bay User's Group - Personal Computer Club meets 1st Fridays at 7:30pm at PG Adult Education Center, 1025 Lighthouse Ave. Novice and experienced users of IBM PCs or compatibles invited. Family membership $25; meeting open to all. 373-6245.

Conservation

Eco-Corps, Pacific Grove, meets 2nd Wednesdays, 7:30pm, at the Pacific Grove Museum of Natural History, Central and Forest avenues, P.G. Dan Koffman, 375-2026.

Friends of the Monarchs, 375-0982.

Friends of the Sea Otter, 373-2747. Gift shop/education center, 642-9037.

Monterey Dunes Natural History Association. Meetings 1st Thursdays, 7-9pm. Call Walter Gourlay or Dave Dixon at 626-2632.

Save the Whales, 899-9957.

Ventana Wilderness Sanctuary, 624-1202.

Crafts

Carmel Crafts Guild meets 3rd Thursdays at 10 am, Monterey Senior Center, Lighthouse and Dickman avenues, New Monterey. 646-0559.

Embroiderers' Guild of America, Monterey Peninsula Chapter, meets at 9:30am, 2nd Mondays in the Community Room in The Crossroads. 375-3878.

Dance

Monterey Peninsula Dance Assn., 71 Soledad Drive, Monterey, has a Dance Party every Fri-Sat, fun and easy lessons. 648-8725.

Over Thirties Ballet Club meets Thursday evenings at Classical Ballet School, American Legion Hall, Carmel, and in Pebble Beach. Includes outings, lectures, free video shows. 655-5598.

SageStompers Square Dance Club meets 2nd Tuesdays at 7:30pm at Oldemeyer Center, Seaside. Refreshments, beginner and brush-up classes available. Visitors welcome. 899-0752, 375-2354.

Scottish Country Dancers of Monterey, 373-8324.

Ethnic

American-Scandinavians of California holds monthly or quarterly meetings concerning the culture and heritage of Scandinavians. Open to all interested persons. 659-3363 or 422-1759.

Filipino American Community of Monterey Peninsula, 384-5383.

Filipino Community of Salinas Valley, 422-0830.

Korean & American Communities of Monterey County, 384-2400.

Sons of Italy, Monterey Lodge No. 2003, meets 3rd Mondays at San Carlos Parish Hall, 6pm. Dinner and meeting $5. Newcomers welcome. 626-0424.

Sons of Norway, Aagaarden Lodge No.112-6. 372-3749, 424-9944.

Historical

Big Sur Historical Society, 667-0549.

Carmel Valley Historical Society, meets 1st Wednesdays. Call Jauna Gregory, 624-9611.

Central Coast Chapter of the American Historical Society of Germans from Russia. Quarterly meetings. 373-4603.

Corral of the Westerners, Monterey County, an international organization, meets 6:30pm 2nd Mondays, St. John's Chapel Parish Hall, Monterey. Potluck dinner followed by talk relating to the West and its history. Annual dues: $15 single, $25 couple. First visit free; lectures free and open to the public. Details 626-8156, 624-0435.

Daughters of the American Revolution, Commodore Sloat Chapter, invites visitors and new members. Call 624-0571.

Genealogy Society, Monterey County. Membership open to any interested person. Meets 7pm 1st Thursdays at the Family History Center, corner Noche Buena & Plumas streets, Seaside. 759-1727. Rick Bergman, 443-8156.

Los Amigos de la Historia y del Arte, an auxiliary of Monterey History & Art Assn., 372-2608.

Monterey County Historical Society, 333 Boronda Road, Salinas, 757-8085. www.dedot.com/mchs

Monterey History & Art Assn., 372-2608.

Sons of the American Revolution, Monterey Bay chapter. 625-1640, 372-5812.

Horticultural

Begonia Club meets 7:30pm, 4th Thursdays, at the Senior Center on Dickman in New Monterey. Don Englund, 373-3548.

Cactus & Succulent Society, Monterey Bay, 449-2002.

California Native Plant Society, Monterey Bay Chapter, meets at P.G. Museum of Natural History, Forest and Central, 659-2528, 659-4252.

Carmel Orchid Society meets 7:30pm, 1st Mondays at 1st Presbyterian Church, 501 El Dorado. President Sheila Bowman, 622-0292.

Fern Study Group, Monterey Bay, meets 7pm one Thursday each month at CSU Monterey Bay, Instructional Center East Building #15, Room 163, First Street and Fifth Avenue, Seaside. 659-4104.

Gardeners of America, 375-2300.

Ikebana International of Monterey Bay. Club president Carol Marchette, 373-4691.

Monterey Bay Orchid Society, meets 6:30pm, Bank of Salinas (sixth floor), Main at Alisal, Oldtown Salinas, 484-1052, 424-4972. Public welcome.

Sacred Garden Guild, headed by artist Elizabeth Murray, meets 4th Saturdays at the Thunderbird Bookshop Cafe in The Barnyard, Carmel. Visitors welcome. Free. Guest speakers. 624-1803.

Literary

Calligraphy Guild: The Sea Scribes meet 1st Thursday at 7 pm, The Park Place, 200 Glenwood Circle, Monterey.

British Mystery Book Roundtable meets 3rd Fridays, 4pm, at Bookworks, Pacific Grove. 15% off selected book.

Dickens Fellowship, Monterey Peninsula, meets monthly in members' homes. Call 372-7625 for details.

Great Books Club meets every Friday at 2:30pm at Carmel Valley Library. Judy Benjamin, 659-9344.

International Language and Cultural Foundation, 642-2224.

Jung Friends meet 2nd Fridays at 7pm, 284 Foam Street, New Monterey. Donation. Reservations: 649-4018.

Marina Arts Council Writers Group, all genres, meetings. 883-8750.

Mystery Book Group meets 2nd Tuesdays at 6:30pm at Borders Bookstore, 2080 California Ave., San City. New members welcome. 899-6643.

Robert L. Stevenson Club, 375-0195 ext. 00.

Scrabble players meet every Wednesday from 6-9pm at the Oldemeyer Center, 986 Hilby Ave., in Seaside. All levels of play welcome. No dues. 633-4649.

Spirit of Speech Club. International training in communications; a small supportive group which teaches all forms of communication skills. Meets 1st Wednesdays at 7pm 649-8751. Call Betty Powell for place, 646-9873.

TaleSpinners, Monterey Bay, meets at 7pm on 1st Mondays at the Monterey Public Library Community Room, 625 Pacific Street, Monterey. Storytellers and would-be storytellers welcome. 384-3227.

Thunderbird Book Club meets 10am-1:30pm 2nd Tuesdays at Thunderbird Bookshop Cafe in The Barnyard, Carmel, 624-1803.

Marine

American Cetacean Society, Lecture Hall at Hopkins Marine Station, 130 Ocean View Blvd., PG. (across from American Tin Cannery). Free talks on marine mammals and fisheries. Meet 7:30pm last Thursdays of the month except Nov-Dec, meet the 1st Thurs. of Dec. Allan Baldridge, 663-9488.

Military

Fleet Reserve Association, Monterey Peninsula branch 178, meets 2nd Tuesdays at 7:30pm at Marina American Legion Post, 694 Legion Way. Membership is open to all enlisted personnel - active duty, reserve and retired - in the U.S. Navy, Marine Corps and Coast Guard, with at least one day of enlisted service. Call Shipmate Secretary Wade Willingham at 648-1058.

Ladies Auxiliary to Veterans of Foreign Wars, Post 811, offers Surf 'n Turf dinners at reasonable prices Friday evenings at the post, 3131 Crescent Ave., Marina. Public welcome. 384-6743, 384-7668.

Naval Order of the United States, open to U.S. citizens who have served as commissioned officers in the maritime services. Meets 7 Dec, 17 Feb and on call. 372-5812.

Navy League of the U.S., Monterey Peninsula Chapter, Jane Lembing, 372-5812.

Retired Enlisted Assn., 422-4964.

Retired Officers Assn., Monterey County Chapter. Call Capt. Harry Nicholson at 646-0822.

Special Forces Assn. Chapter XIV meets 2nd Thursdays at 7pm in the Marina VFW, 3131 Crescent Ave. Interested and qualified veterans are invited to attend. Call 633-4137.

Veterans of Foreign Wars Post 7895, 242 Williams Rd., Salinas, 758-5505.

Mineral Societies

Carmel Valley Gem and Mineral Society, David Dimitriou, 384-8815. Meets 2nd Fridays, 7:30pm, Crossroads Community Room.

Monterey Bay Mineral Society of Salinas. Meets 3rd Tuesdays, 7:30pm, Sherwood Hall, Salinas. Cindy L. Davenport, 449-6820.

Miscellaneous

Alano Club of Monterey Peninsula, 519 Hartnell, 373-0830.

Astronomical Society of the Central Coast. Meets last Tuesday, 7:30pm at MIRA, 200 Eighth St. at Second Ave., Marina. 883-1000.

Casa Abrego Club, 592 Abrego, 375-0626.

Central Coast Chapter for Disney Enthusiasts. Call 449-9672 or 449-3408 for meeting location. Info: P.O. Box 10315, Salinas 93912-7315.

Flying Doctors, the volunteer organization that treats children in Latin American countries, often presents public educational meetings. 646-8740.

Friends of Kinship invites anyone interested in attending or joining the group to call Dolores Johnson at 624-7179.

Monarca Club, 679-2787.

Monterey County Vegetarians meet 7pm, 1st Tuesdays in The Crossroads Community Room, Highway 1 at Rio Road. (Park behind Mailboxes Etc.) Bring a vegetarian dish to share without animal ingredients, a list of ingredients, a place setting, a candle for the table and a beverage. Monthly meetings include speakers and demonstrations of vegetarian food preparation. Members share recipes, pamphlets and exchange vegetarian magazines. 622-7427.

Old Capital Club, 516 Polk, Monterey, 372-8173.

Pacheco Club, 602 Abrego, 373-3011.

Padre Trails Camera Club meets 1st and 3rd Wednesdays, 7pm, Monterey Public Library. Refreshments. 649-1521.

Political

African-American Democratic Club, 394-4445.

Democrats, Monterey County. 655-3121 or 783-1980.

League of Women Voters of the Salinas Valley, 636-6759.

NAACP, Monterey Peninsula Branch, 1104 Broadway Ave., Seaside. 394-3727.

Republican Women, Monterey County. Connie Perry, 647-9225.

Republicans, Campaign Headquarters, 298 Pearl Street, Monterey. 646-5120.

United Nations Association, Monterey Bay Chapter, 659-3758.

World Affairs Council presentations by experts on international issues. Call 643-1855 for current programs.

Recreation

99's, Monterey Bay Chapter of the International Organization of Women Pilots. Gabrielle Adelman, 728-0692 or 722-4580; Donna Crane-Bailey, 688-9616.

Audubon Society, Monterey Peninsula. Field trips, hikes, 648-3116, Jim Booker, 624-1202.

Camber Ski Club. Salinas, 633-6828. www.ski-camber.org.

Carmel Ski Club, 648-4140.

Faultline Shootish Society, affiliate of Single Action Shooting Society. Emphasis on safety. 615-9007.

Fly Casters, Monterey Peninsula, meet 7:30pm every 3rd Wednesday, Monterey Senior Center, Lighthouse at Dickman avenues, Monterey.

Hash House Harriers, Monterey Bay: Noncompetitive 4 to 5 mile cross-country hare-and-hounds adult fun run at various locations in the Monterey Bay area every other Sunday at 1pm. Information: Tim Thomas, 728-2117 or 24-hour hot line at 267-1504.

Monterey Chess and Dart Center, 430 Alvarado, 646-8730.

Mountain Bike Assn., Monterey, 7pm 3rd Wednesdays at Allegro Pizza, 1184 Forest Ave., P.G. 373-5656, 626-2705, 422-2380.

Sea Otters DIVE Club, Monterey Bay, meets last Wednesdays, April through October, at Marina Village Restaurant, 215 Reservation Road. No host dinner 6:30, meeting at 7pm. Guest speakers. Visitors welcome. 372-9235.

Sierra Club, meets last Thursdays. Call 624-8032 for place and time.

Ski & Social Club, Monterey. We ski in the winter and do activities year round! Meet 2nd and 4th Wednesdays. New members welcome. Call 582-9303 or gregrobi@ix.netcom.com. We participate in volunteer activities at the AT&T, Concours de Elegance and at Laguna Seca.

Social Bridge, meets Mondays at 12:30pm at Meals on Wheels, 700 Jewell Ave., P.G. $1. 657-5351.

Trail Runners of the Monterey Peninsula. All ages and levels welcome. 384-0353.

Underwater Photographers, Monterey Peninsula, meets 1st Fridays 6:30-9:30pm. Monterey Bay Aquarium Education Center. Guests welcome, membership open to all. Includes divers, nondivers, biologists, authors, photographers, videographers, friends and families. Educational outreach program. 649-5299, 626-9136, 455-2000.

Velo Club Monterey, Monterey County Bicycle Club. Regular rides. Call Jim Gilman 649-1506. jimg@gwjcpa.com.

Seniors

Active Seniors, Inc., 100 Harvest St., Salinas. A nonprofit organization. 424-5066.

Alliance on Aging meets every Friday at 11:30am at the P.G. Community Center, 515 Junipero Ave. Lunch 12:30. 646-4636. Salinas, call Alcida Boissonnault, information & referral specialist, 758-2811.

Singles

Primetime Singles, 644-TIME.

Parents Without Partners meets monthly, 6:30pm at the Monterey Public Library Community Room; educational-social, adult family events. 644-2773. Salinas meets 7:30-8:30pm at John Steinbeck Library, San Luis and Lincoln, Salinas. Paul Connes 275-9057 or toll-free 888-828-6555, ext. 9602.

Single Friends International for Seniors, men and women 60 and older, for social outings. 659-9144.

Singles Off and Running (SOAR) discussion Wednesdays, 7:30-9pm at First Presbyterian Church, 501 El Dorado, Monterey. 373-3031.

Thunderbird Singles: A social club for men and women 55 and older. Meets Sundays at 6:30pm on the patio at the Thunderbird Bookshop Cafe, The Barnyard, Carmel, 646-5191.

What's Next Singles: outdoor, cultural, social activities, personal growth. 648-4698. Call for calendar of events.

Widowed Persons Assn. of California, Monterey chapter, 3rd Wednesdays 4-5:30pm in The Crossroads Community Room, Carmel. Make friends, overcome grief, social/recreational activities. For questions about the group or upcoming activities, call Betty Johnson at 373-7069, 373-6221.

Toastmasters

Bayview Toastmasters meets 6pm, 1st and 3rd Wednesdays, Monterey Beach Hotel, 622-9507.

Forest Toastmasters meets from 5:10-6:10pm every 1st and 3rd Tuesdays at the Pebble Beach Training Center, 2130 Sunset Ave., P.G. Open to beginners, guests and all levels of expertise. 649-6538/655-3233.

Monterey Peninsula Toastmasters 934 meets at 6:45am each Thursday at Holiday Inn Resort, 1000 Aguajito Road, Monterey, 373-4155.

Naval Postgraduate School's Toastmasters Club meets Fridays at noon, EEO Room, Herrman Hall, Naval Postgraduate School, 663-5606.

Pebble Beach meets at The Lodge 5pm every other Tuesday; new members welcome. 649-6538/625-8563.

Peninsula Pros Toastmasters meets last Wednesdays at 6pm at the Monterey Beach Hotel. Membership is free and open to the public. Call Steve Dellaporta at 384-5481.

Realtor's Toastmasters Club meets Fridays, noon-1pm. Visitors from all professions and walks of life welcome. For meeting place in downtown Monterey call Sandra Collingwood, 648-9673.

Salinas Sunrisers meets 6:30am every Tuesdays at 1205 S. Main St. 424-0771.

Speakeasy Toastmaster Club meets noon-1pm on Wednesdays at DPIC, 2959 Monterey-Salinas Highway, Monterey, 646-1540.

TGIF meets every Friday in the conference room at Dennis the Menace Park, Monterey, 373-5352.

Women

Altrusa International of the Monterey Peninsula. Diane Johnson, 647-8295.

American Association of University Women, 624-6672.

American Business Women's Assn., Central Coast Charter Chapter, Connie Golden Rodriques, 883-2124, Frances Berry, 384-4568.

Business and Professional Women, Seaside, 394-3746.

Business Women's Network, Salinas Valley, 757-4311, 757-6201.

Carmel Women's Club. Clubhouse at San Carlos and Ninth, 624-2866.

Panhellenic, National Alumnae, Monterey Bay Area, encourage alumnae members of national sororities who are new to the community to attend. Call Ann Marshall at 649-5449 or Lisa Hollo at 373-0542.

Professional Women's Network of the Monterey Peninsula. Meets 1st Wednesday, 6:45pm in the Community Room of the Crossroads Shopping Center, Carmel. Guests are welcome; meetings are free. For more information, call 464-0796.

Women "In the Company of My Sisters," a multi-cultural women's network and support group meets 2nd Saturdays, 1-3pm at the Old Chapel, First St. Ave., PM Annex (Old Ft. Ord). For more information or copy of newsletter, call Loretta Sultzer at 394-2421.

Women in Science Association, Monterey Bay Chapter, 633-2224.

Women's Community Center meets 7-8:30pm 2nd Mondays, at the Unitarian-Universalist Church, 490 Aguajito Road, Carmel. Enrichment, education and empowerment of women. 647-2307.

Women's League for Peace and Freedom, Monterey Branch, 372-6001.

Women's Spiritual Studies Institute, 647-1454.

Women's Works Book Club, 2nd Tuesday, 12 noon, 150 Mar Vista. Read and discuss books women have written. Free to members of YWCA of Monterey County. Call Tina Wilkensen 649-0834.

YWCA, 150 Mar Vista Drive, Monterey, 649-0834.

Youth

Boys & Girls Club of the Monterey Peninsula, 1332 La Salle Ave., Seaside. Ages 7-18, noon-8pm weekdays, 2-6 pm Sat. Teen room, computer instruction, educational assistance, weight training, sports. 394-5196.

Boys & Girls Club, Carmel Valley Branch. 24 Ford Road. Jeff Magallanes, 659-2308.

YOUTH Boys & Girls Clubs, Salinas Valley, Sherwood Unit. Activities for youth 7-17, 2:30-6:00 pm., 110 South Wood Street, Salinas, 422-2442.

Camp Fire Boys & Girls Clubs, weekly Thursday meetings of kids in Kindergarten thru 7th grades. Crafts, service projects, and other fun activities. 6:15-7:45pm. For info call Cheryl Jencks, 620-8613.

Gay Teen Alliance, Monterey, meets the 2nd and 4th Fridays at 7pm. The Salinas GTA meets every 3rd Saturday from 1-3pm. www.gtamonterey.org 393-3457, 772-8202.

YMCA, 600 El Camino Estero, Monterey, 373-4167.

Hobbyists Web Site

If you've got a hobby and have a question about it, you may want to try the Hobby Industry Association's new Web Site at http://www.chib.com/

At the site you'll find a mixture of how-to projects, tips, product samples and statistical data.   *The Monterey County Herald*

THE STOWITTS MUSEUM & LIBRARY

Best small Museum on the California coast!
Travel West Magazine

Changing Exhibitions
Paintings, Sculpture, Photographs & Drawings
The Jazz Age through The Atomic Age

•

Wednesday – Saturday 1 to 5 P.M.
Free Admission

591 Lighthouse Avenue
Pacific Grove, California 93950
(831) 655-4488 Fax (831) 649-5396
www.stowitts.org

Free & Fun on the
World Wide Web

Access on the Internet

http://www.infobuy.com/freefax/ - Free fax from your e-mail account

http://www.juno.com/getjuno.html - You don't need to buy Internet access to use free Internet e-mail. Get completely free e-mail from Juno at their website, or call Juno at (800) 654-JUNO [654-5866].

www.hotmail.com - get free e-mail, then configure it to check your regular e-mail account by clicking the Options link and then the External Mail link. You'll need to know the name of your POP server (for example, pop.earthlink.com), your e-mail ID (usually the first part of your e-mail address), and your e-mail password. To set up Hotmail to check up to four POP accounts, click the Options link and then the POP Mail link. (Lon Poole, *www.macworld.com*, Dec, 1998)

www.switchboard.com - Free telephone listings. You can find a person or a business, or search for an occupation. Phone numbers, addresses and maps to a specific location are accessible.

www.homestead.com - Free personal web site

www.magicradio.com - Free personal radio web site

www.mobie.com/mobie.html - Monterey Bay Internet Enthusiasts

Access Providers

www.dra.com - DRA Business Internet

www.dedot.com - Dedot Com

www.fullsteam.com - Stoked Media

www.garlic.com - South Valley Internet

www.mbay.net - Monterey Bay Internet

www.mbayweb.com - Monterey Bay Online

www.montereybay.com - Guardian Information Services

www.monterey-netcenter.net - Monterey Network Center

www.netmarc.com - Netmarc Internet Services

www.onm.com - Online Marketing Partners

www.pacificwebcreations.com - Pacific Web Creations

www.redshift.com - Red Shift Internet Services

www.rknrobin.com - User Friedly Systems

www.ultimanet.com - Ultima Networks

www.universal-net.com - Universal Internet

www.webgeek.com - Webgeek Communications

www.webhomepages.com - Web Home Pages

Accommodations

www.andrilcottages.com - Pacific Grove

www.asilomarcenter.com - Asilomar Conference Center, Pacific Grove

www.bigsurlodge.com - Big Sur Lodge

www.carmeliving.com - List of Carmel's dog-friendly lodging and dining

www.carmelvillageinn.com - Carmel Village Inn

www.casamunras-hotel.com - Casa Munras, Monterey

www.devi-inc.com/ramada - Ramada Limited - Fremont St.

www.devi-inc.com/ramadach - Ramada Limited - Carmel Hill

www.doubletreemonterey.com - DoubleTree, Monterey

www.ernestallen.com:80//tr/CA/Munraslodge

www.ernestallen.com:80//tr/CA/BestWesternParkCrest - Park Crest Motel

www.highlands-inn.com - Highlands Inn, Carmel

www.hotelpacific.com - Hotel Pacific, Monterey

www.hrs-avanti.com - Hospitality resource service

www.innaccess.com/OMI/ - Old Monterey Inn

www.innsbythesea.com - Pacific Grove

Super 8 Monterey
Free Continental
Breakfast, local phone
calls, coffee in lobby.
2050 No. Fremont St.
Monterey 831/373-3081

www.lhls.com - Lighthouse Lodge & Suites, Pacific Grove

www.loneoakmotel.com - Lone Oak Motel, Carmel Valley

www.marriotthotels.com/MRYCA/ - Marriott, Monterey

www.merritthouseinn.com - Merritt House Inn, Monterey

www.monterey.org/mcc - Monterey Conference Center

www.monterey-reservations.com - Monterey Peninsula Reservations, no fee

www.montereybayinn.com - Monterey Bay Inn

www.montereybeachhotel.com - Monterey Beach Hotel

www.montereycoast.com - Kendall and Potter Property Management

www.montereyinns.com - Pacific Grove

www.montereyrentals.com - Vacation rentals, free lists, fax 831/655-7845

www.pacificgardensinn.com - Pacific Grove

www.peninsula.com - Quail Lodge Resort, Carmel Valley

www.pine-inn.com - Pine Cone Inn, Carmel

www.resortdetectives.com - Resort Detectives

www.sandpiper-inn.com - Sandpiper Inn, Carmel

www.spindriftinn.com - Spindrift Inn, Pacific Grove

www.ticklepink.com - Ticklepink Inn, Carmel

www.timetocoast.com - Lodging finder

www.travelweb.com - Hotel search

www.valleylodge.com - Valley Lodge, Carmel Valley

www.ventanainn.com - Ventana Inn, Big Sur

www.victorianinn.com - Victorian Inn, Pacific Grove

www.woodsidehotels.com - Monterey Plaza Hotel

The Arts

www.amsterdamfineart.com - Amsterdam Fine Art

www.bleich4art.com - Bleich Art

www.cdesigns.com - Cromartie designs: apparel, ceramics and furniture

www.classicartgallery.com - Classic Art Gallery

www.crystalfoxgallery.com - Crystal Fox Gallery

www.danielsgallery.com - Daniel's Gallery

www.loranspeck.com - Loran Speck

www.marytitusart.com - Mary Titus

www.mastersgallery.com - Masters Gallery

www.montereyart.org - Monterey Museum of Art

www.montereyart.com - Artists co-op available August 1999

www.mbay.net/~bluedog/ - George Rodrique

www.ricmasten.com - nationally known poet/artist/philosopher Ric Masten

www.stowitts.org - Hubert J. Stowitts Museum & Library

www.thomaskinkade.com - Thomas Kinkade

www.zantmangalleries.com - Zantman Galleries

Attractions & Activities

www.canneryrow.com - Cannery Row

www.carmelfun.com - Carmel

www.cinemacal.com - Movies

www.critics-choice.com - Peninsula activities, lodging, restaurants

www.mbay.net/~mshp/ - Monterey Historic Parks

www.monterey.com- Visitors and Convention Bureau

www.montereybayaquarium.com - Monterey Bay Aquarium

www.movie-tickets.com - Dream Theater, New Monterey

www.planetgemini.com - Comedy club, Cannery Row

www.redshift.com/~donald - Monterey County Fair

www.rent-a-roadster.com - Rent-a-Roadster, Cannery Row

www.steinbeck.org - Steinbeck Center, Salinas

www.themorganhouse.com - Coffeehouse with entertainment

www.torhouse.org - Robinson Jeffers' Tor House, Carmel

www.toursontape.com - Audio tour tape

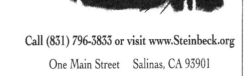

City Sites

www.bestofcal - Pacific Grove and other local city information

www.bigsurcalifornia.org - Big Sur

www.carmel-by-the-sea.com - Carmel

www.ci.marina.ca.us - Marina

www.fora.org - Ft. Ord Reuse Authority

www.mpcc.com - Monterey Chamber of Commerce

www.monterey.org - Information about the community and links to employment opportunities, the library, city parks and other departments.

www.ci.seaside.ca.us - Seaside City

www.salinaschamber.com - Salinas

www.sandcity.com - Sand City, available in the year 2000

www.seaside-sandcity.com - Seaside and Sand City Chamber of Commerce

Conservation/Ecology

www.bonita.mbnms.nos.noaa.gov/ - Monterey Bay Marine Sanctuary

color.mlml.calstate.edu/www/ - Moss Landing Marine Laboratories

www.spcamc.org - Society for the Prevention of Cruelty to Animals

Education

www.csumb.edu - California State University at Monterey Bay

www.monterey.org/lib/lib.html - Monterey Public Library

www.mpc.edu - Monterey Peninsula College

www.pgusd.org - Pacific Grove Unified School District

www.themint.org - Northwestern Mutual Life site to increase the economic and financial literacy of middle and high school students.

www.ucsc-extension.edu - University of California at Santa Cruz

Employment

www.caljobs.ca.gov - the State Employment Development Department job-search system

www.callmarshall.com - The Marshall Group Personnel Service

www.interim.com - Interim Personnel

www.manpowersj.com - Manpower Staffing Services

www.norrell.com - Norrell Staffing Services

www.universalstaffing.com - Universal Staffing Inc.

Events & Festivals

http://Montereyscotgames.com - Scottish/Irish Festival and Games

www.attpbgolf.com - AT&T Pebble Beach

www.bachfestival.org - Carmel Bach Festival

www.ca-airshow.com - California International Airshow

www.carmelfest.org - Carmel Performing Arts Festival

www.carodeo.com - California Rodeo Salinas

www.dixiejazz.com/monterey.html - Dixieland Monterey

www.firstnightmonterey.org - First Night®Monterey

www.montereyjazzfestival.org - Monterey Jazz Festival

www.laguna-seca.com - Laguna Seca Raceway

www.montereycountyfair.com - Monterey County Fair

www.montereyworldmusic.org - World Music Festival

www.pebble-beach-concours.com - Concours d'Elegance

www.ridepebblebeach.com - Pebble Beach Spring Horse Show

www.seaotter.org - Sea Otter Classic at Laguna Seca

www.tricalifornia.com - Wildflower Triathlon Festival, Lake San Antonio

www.turkiye.net - Turkish Arts & Culture Festival

Free & Fun

www.freeandfun.com - free stuff galore

www.freemania.net/ - cosmetics, t-shirts and more

www.PersonalGuidetoFreeFun.com - *Text of this Guide*

www.rebateco.com - Products with sometimes 100% rebates

www.thefreesite.com/ - products - More products

www.4freestuff.com/ - Product samples, magazines

Health

www.chomp.org - Community Hospital of the Monterey Peninsula

www.drgrant.com - J. Gary Grant, MD.

www.gestaltcenter.net - Gestalt Growth Center

www.hffcc.rog - Hospice Foundation

www.montereycpc.com - Compassion Pregnancy Center

www.natividad.com - Natividad Medical Center

www.ovvh.com - Ocean View Veterinary Hospital

www.vetdoc.com - Jo-Ann Van Arsdale, Veterinarian

www.wellnessmd.com - Abraham Kryger, MD

History

http://caviews.com - California Views Historical Photos - Pat Hathaway

www.carmelnet.com/heritage - Carmel Heritage Society

www.dedot.com/mchs - Monterey County Historical Society Inc.

www.Monterey.edu/history/historicevents.html. This educational site describes the development of the Monterey area, and provides links to other local history sites.

Information

www.abooksearch.com - A Book Search Bookstore, New Monterey

www.carmelpinecone.com - Carmel Pine Cone, newspaper

www.coastweekly.com - Coast Weekly, newspaper

www.hm-lib.org - Harrison Memorial Library, Carmel

www.internet-books.com - Thunderbird Book Store, Carmel

www.kcba.com - KCBA television station

www.monterey-herald.com - The Monterey County Herald, newspaper

www.miis.edu - Monterey Institute of International Studies

www.newschannel46.com - KION News Channel 46

www.pilgrimsway.com - Pilgrim's Way Bookstore, Carmel

www.sunweekly.com - Sun Weekly, Carmel Valley newspaper

Music & Dancing

http://members.aol.com/kaplandisc - Ron Kaplan: jazz, swing, blues.

http://members.xoom.com/xoros/ - Greek Folk Dancing

www.abstractvision.com - Patt Spears-Casion: Original jazz.

www.beinworld.com - Amagon Mollies: original alternative rock.

www.best.com/~wulf - Visitor 42: alternative punk.

www.billboardtalentnet.com/ron_wright - Ron Wright: new age, world, pop, reggae, classical.

www.geocities.com/sunsetstrip/venue/6461/ - Moromix: alternative, electronic, rap, hip-hop, R&B, funk.

www.globalmusic.com/artists/mchrislock/mchrislock_v1.html - Melodie Chrislock: Original pop.

www.jps.net/bflat7/ - Stu Reynold Saxtet: jazz, latin, blues, funk. R&B, world beat.

www.jps.net/bflat7/outbound/ - Outbound: smooth jazz.

www.kellypro.com - Andrea Jones: Scottish/Celtic bagpiper.

www.kellypro.com - Bravo Ara: folk, classical, flamenco, international.

www.kellypro.com - Charles DeWeese: folk, rock, blues, jazz, country, world Latin, classical guitars.

www.kellypro.com - Daryl Lowery: disc jockey.

www.kellypro.com - Joe Indence: piano & keyboard: blues, jazz, Latin, big band, classical.

www.kellypro.com - Michael Culver: Pop, jazz and classical harp and vibes.

www.kellypro.com - Monterey String Quartet: jazz, classical, pop.

www.kellypro.com - Original Substitutes - 50s rock, 60s variety.

www.kellypro.com - Peter Burkhard: disc jockey

www.kellypro.com - Sound Bytes: rock, clues, jazz, country.

www.kellypro.com -Alan Berman: swing, blues, jazz, Latin, Big Band keyboard and vocals.

www.lorylynn.com - Lory Lynn: country rock, ballads.

www.mbay.net/~lascott/ferret51.htm - Ferrit 51: original rock.

www.mbay.net/~rlugo - Misshapen: Original metal.

www.messaround.com - The Broadway Band: blues.

www.nuthouse.com/contra/ - YMCA contra dancing

www.redbeans.com - Red Beans & Rice: blues.

www.redshift.com/~bhpstudios/website - B H Piano Studios

www.redshift.com/~bgibson: Bill Gibson: acoustic guitar

www.redshift.com/~jlm - Jonathon Lee

www.redshift.com/~singring/ - Piper Manu band

www.smoothjazz.com - Sandy Shore Productions 649-1223.

www.ultramarineblue.com - Maureen Evans-Hansen: original fusion

www.unknownjeromes.com - Unknown Jeromes: Funk, rock.

Real Estate

www.agdavi.com - AG Davi Real Estate

www.apr-carmel.com - Alain Pinell Realtors

www.apr.com (home video tours)

www.beachproperty.com - Connie Perry Realtor

www.benheinrich.com - Ben Heinrich Real Estate

www.burchellhouse.com - Burchell House Properties

www.carmel-realty.com - Carmel Realty Company

www.c21scenicbayproperties.com - Century 21

www.gregshankle.com - Greg Shankle Real Estate

www.laspalmas.com - Las Palmas Ranch New Home Communities

www.montereybay.com/calandra - Calandra Real Estate

www.pacificbaycorp.com - Pacific Bay Real Estate

www.pineconerentals.com - PineCone Property Management

www.redshift.com/~harborr - Harbor Realty

www.segalrealestate.com - Segal Real Estate

Restaurants

www.allegropizza.com - Allegro Gourmet Pizzeria

www.bluefin-billiards.com - Blue Fin Billiards and Cafe

www.cibo.com - Cibo Restaurant

www.critics-choice.com - Pocket guide to dining

www.eatfree.com - Free Monterey dining offers and other information

www.gilsgourmet.com - Gil's Gourmet

www.go-dining.com - Adventures in Dining guide to the Central Coast

www.grapesofwrath.com - Grapes of Wrath, caterer

www.jardinesrestaurant.com - Jardine's Restaurant, San Juan Bautista

www.laboheme.com - LaBoheme, Carmel

www.lecoqdor.com - Le Coq'dor, Carmel

www.monterey.infohut.com/laplayahotel - La Playa Hotel, Carmel

www.pollorey.com - Pollo Rey, Monterey

www.rocky-point.com - Rocky Point Restaurant, Carmel

www.sanjuanoaks.com - San Juan Oaks, San Juan Bautista

www.sardinefactory.com - Sardine Factory, Cannery Row

Shopping

www.antiqnet.com/canneryrow - Cannery Row Antique Mall

www.basquetique.com - Basket store

www.candlesandclay.com - Candle store

www.carmelcrossroads.com - Carmel Crossroads Shopping Center

www.carmoco.com - Carmel motoring company store and gallery

www.chatelco.com - Fine wristwatches and jewelry

www.chelseagca.com - women's clothing

www.citysearch.com/sfo/charmsbybay - Fine jewelry & charms

www.clairemurray.com – Hand-hooked rugs, woven throws, wearable art

www.delmontecenter.com - Del Monte Shopping Center

www.dovecote.com - Women's clothing

www.firstnoel.com - Christmas items

www.goodsforsale.com/dudley - Dudley Doolittle's Travel Shoppe

www.holidayhutch.com - Gifts

www.impostors.com - Jewelry

www.ladyfingersjewelry.com - Jewelry

www.letitbead.com - Let it Bead store

www.marysboutique.com - Ladies wear

www.OnLineFlowers.com - Swenson & Silacci Flowers and Gifts.

www.otterlimits.com - Otters, dolphins, whales and more.

www.papersite-carmel.com - Paper goods

www.phillipsmuseumshop.com - Phillips Museum Shop

www.romancebydesign.com - Romance by Design

www.rosamond.com - Rosamond

www.succulentgardens.com - Succulent Gardens

www.thebackshop.com - The Backshop

www.thebarnyard.com - The Barnyard Shopping Center

www.thewhiterabbit.com - Clothing

www.treadmill.com - Sport clothes

www.twgs.com - The Wharf General Store

www.villageprovence.com - Gift shop

www.wbucarmel.com - Wild Birds Unlimited

Sports & Recreation

http://ventana.org - Sierra Club, Ventana Chapter

www.adventuresbythesea.com - Kayaks, skate, bicycle rentals

www.athand.com - Freewheeling Cycles

www.bsim.org - Big Sur International Marathon

www.carmelfly.com - Fly fishing

www.carmel-golf.com - Rancho Cañada Golf Club

www.carmelwalks.com - Guided tours of Carmel

www.chamisal.com - Chamisal Tennis & Fitness Club

www.crusio.com/~bilswhls - Bill's Wheels

www.cruzio.com/~kayakcon - Kayak rentals

www.flymac.com - Monterey Airplane Company

www.golf-monterey.com - Laguna Seca Golf Club

www.inline-retrofit.com - Skate sales and rentals

www.laguna-seca.com - Laguna Seca, World Class racing

www.monterey-bay.net/elkhornslough - Elkhorn Slough Safari

www.montereybaywatch.com - Benji Shake cruises

www.montereybaywhalewatch.com

www.montereyexpress.com - Monterey Express Charters

www.montereykayaks.com - Kayak rentals

www.monterey.org/rec/rec.html - Monterey Dept. of Recreation

www.montereysportfishing.com - Sport fishing

www.nativeguides.com - Ventana Wilderness outfitters and guides

www.ridepebblebeach.com - Pebble Beach Equestrian Center

www.randysfishingtrips.com - Fishing and whale watching

www.rileygolf.com - Riley Golf

www.rockgym.com - Rockclimbing gym

www.sealifetours.com - Glass bottom boat tours

www.seaotter.org -Classic Cycling Festival at Laguna Seca

www.skydivemontereybay.com - Skydiving

www.soarhollister.com - Hot air ballooning

www.sportscenterbicycles.com - Sports Center Bicycles

www.usafishing.com/kahuna.html - Tom's Sportfishing

Volunteer

www.communitylinks.net - Community Links©

www.monterey.org/vol/vol.html - Monterey City Volunteers

www.yesillhelp.org - Volunteer Center of Monterey County

Weather

www.accuweather.com - Accu Weather

www.cnn.com/WEATHER - CNN weather

www.earthwatch.com - EarthWatch - Weather On Demand

www.intellicast.com- Intellicast

www.marineweather.com - Marine Weather.Com

www.ndbc.noaa.gov - National Data Buoy Center

www.noaa.gov/ - National Oceanic Administration

www.weather.com - The Weather Channel

www.wunderground.com - The Weather Underground

www.usatoday.com/weather/wfront.htm - USA Today Weather

http://cirrus.sprl.umich.edu/wxnet - WeatherNet

Wineries

www.chateaujulien.com - Chateau Julien

www.montereywine.com - Monterey Wine Festival

www.ranchocellars.com - Rancho Cellars

www.secretcellars.com - Wine club

www.usawines.com/paraiso - Paraiso Springs Vineyards

www.tastemonterey.com - Taste of Monterey, Cannery Row

www.wineinstitute.org - Wine Institute

www.wines.com/monterey - Monterey County Vintners & Growers Assn.

Weddings

www.baysidewedding.com - Wedding services

www.critics-choice.com - Complete wedding information

www.floresque.com - Floresque flowers

www.mbay.net/~weddings - Wedding services

www.montereyweddings.com - Wedding services

www.onlineflowers.com - Swenson & Silacci Flowers

www.woodsidehotels.com - Bridal suite

www.800send.com - Salinas florist

Resources & References

A Guide to Eccentric California, P.O. Box 8744, Monterey, CA.

Adventures in Dining, 1998. Mail Mart, Carmel, CA.

Big Sur, A Complete History & Guide, Tomi Kay Lussier, 1993. Big Sur Publications

Big Sur, The Way it Was, Robert K. Blaisdell, 1995. Big Sur Country Film Co. CA.

Buying the Best, 1998. Carmel Publishing Company, Carmel, CA.

California Grassroots Tours, Eric J. Adams. 1993. Renaissance House, Frederick, CO.

California With Kids, Carey Simon and Charlene Marmer Solomon, 1989. Simon & Schuster Inc. NY.

Carmel at Work and Play, Daisy F. Bostick and Dorothea Castelhum, 1925. The Seven Arts, Carmel, CA

Carmel Pine Cone, 1998. Carmel Communications, Inc., Carmel, CA.

Central Coast Magazine, 1998. Local Videomagazine on TCI Cable Channel 2.

Coast Weekly, 1998. Milestone Communication Inc., Seaside, CA.

Complete Monterey Peninsula and Santa Cruz Guidebook, Editor B. Sangwan, 1998. Indian Chief Publishing House, Davis, CA.

Critics Choice Dining Guide, 1998. P.O. Box 221881, Carmel, CA.

Europe for Free, Brian Butler, 1987. Mustang Publishing, CT.

Ft. Ord, A Place in History, U.S. Army Corps of Engineering, Sacramento, CA.

Glorious Gardens, Priscilla Dunhill and Sue Freedman, 1993. Clarkson Potter, NY.

Guestlife Monterey Bay, 1998. Desert Publications Inc., Carmel, CA.

Guidemap to California Highway One, Map Easy, Inc., Armagansett, NY.

Key Magazine, 1998. Tri-County Publishers, Carmel, CA.

Light on Monterey, 1998. Carmel, CA.

Lover's Guide to America, Ian Keown, 1974. MacMillan Publishing Co, NY.

Monterey Bay and Beyond, Lucinda Jaconette, 1994. Chronicle Books, CA.

Monterey Bay Marine Diver's Map, E. Cooper, 1994. Pacific Grove, CA.

Monterey County Family, 1998. Salinas, CA.

Monterey County Post, 1998. Diogenes Communications, Inc., Carmel, CA.

Monterey Peninsula Exploring, Nancy M. and Neil A. Evans, 1994. Worldview Assoc. Inc., El Granada, CA.

Monterey Peninsula Guide, Somerset Publications Inc, Monterey, CA.

Peninsula Family Connection, 1998. Creative Connection, Pacific Grove, CA.

The Fairy Tale Houses of Carmel, 1974. Joanne Mathewson, Carmel, CA.

The Insiders Guide to the Monterey Peninsula, Judy Andréson and Tom Owens, 1998. Insider's Publishing, Helena, MT.

The Monterey County Herald, 1998. Knight-Ridder, Monterey, CA.

The Sun, 1998. Elizabeth Cowley, Carmel Valley, CA.

Touring California's Central Coast, 1998. Bay Publishing Company, Monterey, CA.

Trips on Tape, The Monterey Peninsula and Big Sur, 1993. The Rider's Guide, 484 Lake Park Ave., Oakland, CA.

Walk This Way Please, Irene Montagna, 1993. Afterwords, Pacific Grove, CA.

Index

Travel Notes

As you travel through this life...
Stand not a beggar at the gate
For thought is form and soon or late
What you believe you will create.
– Whatever you can do or dream you can, begin it. –
Boldness has genius, power and magic in it.
~ Goethe

Order Form

Telephone orders: Call 1-888-702-4500 toll free.
Have your credit card ready.
E-mail orders: info@PersonalGuidetoFreeFun.com
Postal orders: Park Place Publications, PO Box 829,
Pacific Grove, CA 93950-0829. USA. Telephone: 831-649-6640.

Please send _____ copies of *Your Personal Guide to Free & Fun Things to Do and See in Monterey County*. Price: $14.95 each.

Name: _____

Address: _____

City: _____State:_____Zip:_____

Telephone: _____

E-mail address: _____

Sales tax: Please add 7.25% for books shipped to California addresses.
Shipping: US: $4 for the first book and $2 for each additional book.
International: $9 for first book: $5 for each additional book.

Payment: ❐ Check ❐ Credit Card:
❐ Visa ❐ MasterCard ❐ AMEX ❐ Discover
Card number:_____

Name on card:_____Exp. date:____/_____

Signature: _____

Entry Form

Here is my entry(s) of a free and fun thing to see or do in Monterey County. I will receive an autographed book if it is chosen for publication!

Free Item: _____

Available at: _____

_____

My Name: _____

Address: _____

City: _____State:_____Zip:_____

Telephone: _____

(Entries for year 2000 must be postmarked by Sept. 1, 1999. Earliest postmark wins.)